# Taliban, Militant Islam and Afghanistan

# TALIBAN, MILITANT ISLAM AND AFGHANISTAN

V. Sahay. Comdt. (Retd.)

NEHA PUBLISHERS & DISTRIBUTORS
DELHI

*Publisher*
**NEHA PUBLISHERS & DISTRIBUTORS**
4832/24,Prahlad Lane,S-207 Ansari
Road, Daryaganj, Delhi-110002
Ph.: 43570976, 23278261
Email: nehapubdistributors@gmail.com

**Edition:** 2015



**ISBN:** 978-93-80318-71-4

Laser Typesetting
**JEE-VEE Graphics,** Delhi

**Price:** 1195/-

*Printed*
Vikas Computers, Delhi

# Preface

The Taliban and its rule arose from the chaos of post-Soviet Afghanistan. It began as an Islamic fundamentalist politico-religious movement composed of students in the Helmand and Kandaharregion of Afghanistan. Overwhelmingly local ethnic Pashtuns, the Taliban blended Pashtunwalitribal code with elements of Deobandi Islamic teaching to form an anti-Western, anti-modern, and highly restrictive Islamic fundamentalist ideology with which it ruled.

The Taliban association emerging from the refugee settlements provided a natural political vehicle for this Pakistani strategy. It depended on the cooperation of the Islamist political parties that sponsored the Taliban in the camps. The task merely involved lightly arming and training Taliban cadres, and negotiating their entry through Quetta to join those Pushtun militia leaders inside Afghanistan who deplored the country's internal disintegration and aspired, however crudely, to pacify, reunify and rebuild Afghanistan.

The Taliban is a predominantly Pashtun, Islamic fundamentalist group that ruled Afghanistan from 1996 until 2001, when a U.S.-led invasion toppled the regime for providing refuge to al-Qaeda and Osama bin Laden. The Taliban regrouped across the border in Pakistan, where its central leadership, headed by Mullah Mohammed Omar, leads an insurgency against the Western-backed government in Kabul. Both the United States and Afghanistan have pursued a negotiated settlement with the Taliban, but talks have little momentum as international forces prepare to conclude combat operations in December 2014 and withdraw by the end of 2016.

This work is essentially useful for scholars researchers social activists academics government functionaries and the general reader alike.

*—Editor*

# Contents

# 1

# Afghanistan: Reconstruction and Development

The objective of current development and reconstruction efforts in Afghanistan is to help build a stable, democratic and prosperous country that contributes to regional and global security. Guided by the Afghanistan Millennium Development Goals, the Afghanistan Interim National Development Strategy and the Afghanistan Compact, the Afghan government is working with international partners to address the country's immediate and long-term needs in areas as diverse as health, education, governance, policing, agriculture and infrastructure rehabilitation. This chapter provides an overview of these activities and situates Canada's commitments – amounting to $1.2 billion from 2001 to 2011 – within the larger context of international assistance.

It also reviews the primary obstacles to reconstruction and development, the most significant of which is the fragile security environment in the country.

## ISLAMIC EMIRATE OF AFGHANISTAN

The Islamic Emirate of Afghanistan, was founded in 1996 when the Taliban began their rule of Afghanistan and ended with their fall from power in 2001. Even at the peak of their influence, the Taliban never controlled the entire area of Afghanistan, as about 10% of the country in the northeast was held by the United Islamic Front for the Salvation of Afghanistan.

## History

The Taliban and its rule arose from the chaos of post-Soviet Afghanistan. It began as an Islamic fundamentalist politico-religious movement composed of students in the Helmand and Kandaharregion of Afghanistan. Overwhelmingly local ethnic Pashtuns, the Taliban blended Pashtunwalitribal code with elements of Deobandi Islamic teaching to form an anti-Western, anti-modern, and highly restrictive Islamic fundamentalist ideology with which it ruled. Spreading from Kandahar, the Taliban eventually seized Kabul in 1996. By the end of 2000, the Taliban were able to capture 90% of the country, aside from the opposition (Afghan Northern Alliance) strongholds primarily found in the northeast corner of Badakhshan Province. The Taliban sought to impose a strict interpretation of Islamic *Sharia law* and were later implicated as supporters of mujahideen, most notably by harbouring Osama bin Laden's Al-Qaeda network.

During the five-year history of the Islamic Emirate, much of the population experienced restrictions on their freedom and violations of their human rights. Women were banned from jobs, girls forbidden to attend schools or universities. Those who resisted were punished instantly. Communists were systematically eradicated and thieves were punished by amputating one of their hands or feet. Meanwhile, the Taliban managed to nearly eradicate the majority of the opium production by 2001.

Following the Taliban's harsh treatment of Afghanistan's Shia minority, Iran stepped up assistance to the Northern Alliance. Relations with the Taliban deteriorated further in 1998 after Taliban forces seized the Iranian consulate in Mazari Sharif and executed Iranian diplomats. Following this incident, Iran almost went to war with the Taliban regions of Afghanistan but intervention by the United Nations Security Council and the United States prevented an imminent Iranian invasion.

## International Relations

Only Pakistan, Saudi Arabia, and the United Arab Emirates recognized the Taliban government. The state was not recognised in the UN. Turkmenistan, however, was known to have held official meetings and agreements with Taliban government ministers. One reason for lack of international recognition was the Taliban's disregard for international law as demonstrated by their actions on taking power. For example, one of the first acts of the Islamic Emirate was the murder of the former President of Afghanistan, Mohammad Najibullah. Before the Taliban had even taken control of Afghanistan's capital they sent out a squad to arrest, torture, mutilate and murder Najibullah, leaving his body hanging from a street lamp outside the presidential palace for two days. As Najibullah was staying in the United Nations compound in Kabul, this was a violation of international law. As a further example, the Taliban regime was also heavily criticised for the murder of Iranian diplomats in Afghanistan in 1998. The Taliban supported the Islamic militants operating in Chechnya, Kashmir and Xinjiang, thus antagonizing Russia, India and the People's Republic of China simultaneously.

## *Sanctions*

In 1999, the UN Security Council established a sanctions regime to cover individuals and entities associated with Al-Qaida, Osama bin Laden and/or the Taliban. Since the US Invasion of Afghanistan in 2001, the sanctions were applied to individuals and organizations in all parts of the world, also targeting former members of the Taliban government.

On January 27, 2010, a United Nations sanctions committee removed five former senior Taliban officials from this list, in a move favoured by Afghan President Karzai. The decision means the five will no longer be subject to an international travel ban, assets freeze and arms embargo. The five men, all high-ranking members of the Taliban government:

- Wakil Ahmad Muttawakil, former foreign minister.
- Fazal Mohammad, former deputy minister of commerce.
- Shams-us-Safa Aminzai, former Taliban foreign affairs press officer.
- Mohammad Musa Hottak, former deputy minister of planning.
- Abdul Hakim, former deputy minister of frontier affairs.

All had been added to the list in January or February 2001. Mohammed Omar continues to speak in the name of this Emirate.

## FOREIGN INTERFERENCE AND WAR

After the fall of Najibullah's government in 1992, the Afghan political parties agreed on a peace and power-sharing agreement (the Peshawar Accords). The accords created the Islamic State of Afghanistan and appointed an interim government for a transitional period to be followed by general elections. According to Human Rights Watch:

The sovereignty of Afghanistan was vested formally in the Islamic State of Afghanistan, an entity created in April 1992, after the fall of the Soviet-backed Najibullah government. With the exception of Gulbuddin Hekmatyar's Hezb-e Islami, all of the parties were ostensibly unified under this government in April 1992.

Hekmatyar's Hezb-e Islami, for its part, refused to recognize the government for most of the period discussed in this report and launched attacks against government forces and Kabul generally. Shells and rockets fell everywhere.

Gulbuddin Hekmatyar received operational, financial and military support from Pakistan. Afghanistan expert Amin Saikal concludes in *Modern Afghanistan: A History of Struggle and Survival*:

Pakistan was keen to gear up for a breakthrough in Central Asia. Islamabad could not possibly expect the new Islamic government leaders to subordinate their own nationalist objectives in order to help Pakistan realize its regional ambitions. Had it not been for the ISI's logistic support and supply of a large number of rockets, Hekmatyar's forces would not have been able to target and destroy half of Kabul.

In addition, Saudi Arabia and Iran – as competitors for regional hegemony – supported Afghan militias hostile towards each other. According to Human Rights Watch, Iran was backing the Shia Hazara Hezb-i Wahdat forces of Abdul Ali Mazari to "maximize Wahdat's military power and influence". Saudi Arabia supported the Wahhabite Abdul Rasul Sayyaf and his Ittihad-i Islami faction. A publication by the George Washington University describes:

utside forces saw instability in Afghanistan as an opportunity to press their own security and political agendas.

Conflict between the two militias soon escalated into a full-scale war. Due to the sudden initiation of the war, working government departments, police units or a system of justice and accountability for the newly created Islamic State of Afghanistan did not have time to form. Atrocities were committed by individuals of the different armed factions while Kabul descended into lawlessness and chaos as described in reports by Human Rights Watch and the Afghanistan Justice Project. Because of the chaos, some leaders increasingly had only nominal control over their (sub-)commanders. For civilians there was little security from murder, rape and extortion. An estimated 25,000 people died during the most intense period of bombardment by Hekmatyar's Hezb-i Islami and the Junbish-i Milli forces of Abdul Rashid Dostum, who had created an alliance with Hekmatyar in 1994. Half a million people fled Afghanistan. Human Rights Watch writes:

Rare ceasefires, usually negotiated by representatives of Ahmad Shah Massoud, Sibghatullah Mojaddedi or Burhanuddin Rabbani [the interim government], or officials from the International Committee of the Red Cross (ICRC), commonly collapsed within days.

Southern and eastern Afghanistan was under the control of local commanders such as Gul Agha Sherzai and others. In 1994, theTaliban (a movement originating from Jamiat Ulema-e-Islam-run religious schools for Afghan refugees in Pakistan) also developed in Afghanistan as a politico-religious force. When the Taliban took control of the city in 1994, they forced the surrender of dozens of local Pashtun leaders. In 1994, the Taliban took power in several provinces in southern and central Afghanistan.

In late 1994, most of the militia factions (Hezb-i Islami, Junbish-i Milli and Hezb-i Wahdat) which had been fighting in the battle for control of Kabul were defeated militarily by forces of the Islamic State's Minister of Defense Ahmad Shah Massoud. Bombardment of the capital came to a halt. The Islamic State government took steps to restore law and order. Courts started to work again. Massoud tried to initiate a nationwide political process with the goal of national consolidation and democratic elections, also inviting the Taliban to join the process but they refused as they did not believe in a democratic system.

## KEY DOCUMENTS AND INSTITUTIONAL FRAMEWORKS

After 30 years of conflict, Afghanistan is now among the poorest and least developed countries in the world. In 2007 the country ranked 174th out of 178 on the United Nations Development Program (UNDP) human development index and had showed some deterioration in real terms in comparison with results for 2004. Such conditions entrench a cycle of underdevelopment, vulnerability and conflict, perpetuating Afghanistan's position as a source of concern for regional and international security. In an effort to break this cycle, the post-Taliban Afghan government has set a course for development and reconstruction. The frameworks that set out priorities and strategies for this effort are as follows.

### *Millennium Development Goals (MDGs)*

Afghanistan came late, in 2004, to these UN-sanctioned targets to enable more of the world's population to enjoy the minimum requirements of human dignity by the year 2015. Special MDGs were developed to reflect local realities in Afghanistan; the baseline was set with data from 2002-2005, and the deadline was extended from 2015 to 2020. The key issues reflected in Afghanistan's MDG targets are: poverty and hunger; universal primary education; gender equality; child mortality; maternal health; HIV/AIDS, malaria and other diseases; environmental sustainability; a global partnership for development; and security.

### *Interim Afghanistan National Development Strategy (I-ANDS)*

Informed by the Afghanistan MDGs, the 2006 I-ANDS lays out a five-year program of action in four areas: security; governance; rule of law and human rights; and economic and social development. Released by the Afghan government at the 2006 London Conference, it also addresses cross-cutting issues such as the narcotics trade, gender inequity and corruption. The I-ANDS will be replaced in mid-2008 by a more developed strategy that is expected to lead to a fully costed, prioritized and sequenced development strategy.

## THE AFGHANISTAN COMPACT

Intrinsically linked to both the Afghanistan MDGs and the I-ANDS and signed at the 2006 London Conference, the Afghanistan Compact is a political agreement by which Afghanistan is committed to make progress in the I-ANDS and the international community has agreed to provide resources to support this endeavour and to improve the effectiveness and accountability of such assistance.

### *Coordination and Oversight*

Adherence to the Afghanistan MDGs, the I-ANDs and the Afghanistan Compact is coordinated and overseen by three primary mechanisms:

- the Joint Coordination and Monitoring Board (JCMB), co-chaired by the Afghan government and the United Nations, which is primarily responsible for the implementation of the Afghanistan Compact;
- the Afghanistan Development Forum (ADF), which brings the Afghan government and the donor community together on an almost annual basis to review priorities and strategies; and
- the Agency Coordinating Body for Afghan Relief (ACBAR), which supplements the activities of the ADF by acting on behalf of the international and national NGOs active in Afghanistan and is concerned with the civil-society dimension of the ANDS.

### *Donor Conferences*

A prominent feature of Afghanistan's post-Taliban reconstruction and develop-ment is the international donor conference. The 2002 Tokyo International Conference on Reconstruction Assistance to Afghanistan resulted in pledges estimated at US$4-5 billion. The 2004 Berlin Conference on Afghanistan resulted in pledges of over US$8 billion, which were later surpassed by pledges from the 2006 London Conference of over US$10.5 billion.

Development and reconstruction funds are channelled primarily through two instruments: the Afghan budget, and the Afghanistan Reconstruction Trust Fund (ARTF). Established at the 2002 Tokyo conference, the ARTF is currently funded by pledged contributions from 27 countries amounting to US$2.27 billion, of which US$1.83 billion have been received and disbursed. It is administered by the World Bank, while decisions about the allocation of funds are carried out by the World Bank, the UNDP, the Asian Development Bank and the Islamic Development Bank, in cooperation with the government of Afghanistan and the Special Representative of the Secretary-General. Its primary function is to cover recurring costs from the Afghan budget, such as salaries for teachers, health care workers, and civilian staff in ministries and provinces.

### *Provincial Reconstruction Teams (PRTs)*

Operating in 25 provinces, PRTs are hosted and assembled by individual countries, including Germany, the United Kingdom and the Netherlands. They comprise military units, civilian political advisors and development advisors working in an integrated fashion to provide humanitarian assistance and to support development activities. The priorities and configuration of each PRT are set out by the host country to reflect the conditions and needs in the particular province, but the overriding objective is to contribute to the stability, security and outreach of the central government's authority and to support local and provincial administrations. The primary mechanisms for achieving these objectives are regular interaction with the local authorities and the population, visibility, information-gathering with regard to security and stability, and support for the Afghan National Police. It is also important to note that, despite the internal integration of PRTs, their military components are part of NATO's International Security Assistance Force (ISAF) efforts.

## KEY INTERNATIONAL AGENCIES AND DONORS

Although Afghanistan takes the lead in its own development and reconstruction, the international community assists it in reaching its development goals, including the Afghanistan MDGs and the objectives of the I-ANDS. International partnersare active in health, education, infrastructure, food aid, landmine clearance, governance and institutional capacity-building, and rural and agricultural development. The key players include the following:

- United Nations Assistance Mission to Afghanistan (UNAMA). The central international and UN presence in Afghanistan, UNAMA has a multi-faceted mandate that includes responsibility for development and reconstruction activities of all UN agencies in the country, including their direction.
- United Nations Development Program (UNDP). The UNDP is equally if not more prominent in the international community's development work in Afghanistan. It operates within the framework of the integrated UNAMA, regularly works with international and local NGOs, and counts among its top ten donors the United States, the European Commission, Japan, Canada, the United Kingdom, the Netherlands, Italy, Germany, Norway and the World Bank.
- United Nations High Commission for Refugees (UNHCR). With Afghanistan its largest repatriation operation worldwide for five consecutive years, the UNHCR in part targets support for the reintegration and livelihoods of returnees.

Other UN bodies that are making an impact on Afghanistan's development and reconstruction include the United Nations Development Fund for Women (UNIFEM)and UNICEF. The World Food Programme (WFP) is active in providing emergency assistance as well as rehabilitation and recovery with respect to food aid and food distribution. The World Bank has committed over US$1.4 billion for 33 projects and two budget support operations since 2002. The Asian Development Bank (ADB) has provided approximately US$892.28 million in loans, making Afghanistan the bank's 17th largest borrower.

Non-governmental organizations also have a significant place in development and reconstruction efforts. They are numerous, have tremendous scope in their reach and activities, and are also the means of channelling donor funding toward development and reconstruction goals. Moreover, they have been present in Afghanistan for a long period, going back to 1961 in some cases. These NGOs include CARE, the Aga Khan Foundation and the International Committee for the Red Cross (ICRC). Indeed, Afghanistan is currently the ICRC's largest operation.

Among bilateral development and reconstruction contributions, the United States ranks the highest, having spent US$4,394 million in 2002-2006, and is projected to spend US$2,484 million in 2007-2008. Ranked second, the United Kingdom has spent over £490 million on reconstruction and development in Afghanistan since 2001 and is planning to spend £107 million in 2007-2008.

### The Canadian Contribution

Canada ranks among Afghanistan's top five donors, and Afghanistan is Canada's largest single aid recipient. Canada's aid contribution will total C$1.2 billion in the period 2001-2011 (when the I-ANDS five-year period expires). Its commitments have been pledged at the various donor conferences and are channelled mainly through multilateral organizations and agencies, such as the UNDP, UNICEF, the WFP, CARE Canada, the Red Cross, and the Aga Kahn Foundation of Canada. Accordingly, its support has been felt at the national and provincial level and in a range of sectors, including democracy-building and governance, economic and rural development, infra-structure, education, health, landmine clearance, counter-narcotics activities, military and police training, security and disarmament, demobilization and reintegration. In this respect, its priorities and activities correspond with the I-ANDS.

Canada's contribution reflects the integration of human and financial resources from various government departments and agencies. These include Foreign Affairs and International Trade Canada (DFAIT), the Department of National Defence (DND), the

Royal Canadian Mounted Police (RCMP), Corrections Canada and the Canadian International Development Agency (CIDA). For instance, to support the Afghan government's strategic development capacity, members of Canada's Canadian Forces have been deployed to the Strategic Advisory Team in President Karzai's office. In addition, DFAIT's Global Peace and Security Fund will have provided more than C$8.5 million in capacity-building, supporting, for example, security sector reform (specifically, training and the rehabilitation of Afghan National Police substations), justice sector reform, political and tribal engagement, and landmine clearance. These activities involve personnel from other departments such as CIDA, the Canadian Forces and the RCMP.

Since 2001, CIDA's investment of close to C$600 million in Afghanistan has promoted national and provincial projects and programs such as the National Solidarity Program, the Counter-Narcotics Trust Fund, landmine clearance, agricultural development, the rule of law, road reconstruction, and health. Canada also claims to be the lead donor in education and in the national micro-financing program, which provides services and small loans to Afghans who would normally be denied such access. In addition, CIDA supports the Canada Fund for Local Initiatives. Amounting to C$750,000, this fund is administered by the Canadian embassy in Kabul to support small projects and community-based development initiatives.

Canada's provincial efforts have been concentrated in Kandahar. Its strategy in this southern Afghan province focuses on basic human needs and on strengthening livelihoods (especially in rural areas), building infrastructure, promoting democracy and effective governance, improving the status of women and girls, and increasing the capacity of local governments.

Since 2005, Canada's activities in Kandahar have been enhanced by the establishment of a PRT in the province, which currently comprises 330 people, including a civilian advisor or political director from DFAIT, four RCMP officers, an officer from the Charlottetown City police, development aid specialists from CIDA, and military personnel. Their objective is to enhance security in

Kandahar, enhance links between the provincial, district and central authorities, improve the lives of the residents and build confidence among them about the international presence. In this way, the PRT intends to diminish the population's vulnerability to insurgent activities, thereby improving stability in the region as well as the implementation of development and reconstruction efforts. Kandahar is a former stronghold of the Taliban and a primary target of insurgent activity; thus, the challenge before Canada is not small.

Canada's PRT activities in Kandahar are many. They include security sector reform by way of building the capacity of the Afghan National Police in Kandahar with training and mentoring programs, engaging with local authorities and the population of Kandahar, supporting health and education programs, including immunization and adult literacy programs, supporting Afghan-led work to strengthen governance structures, administering the Kandahar Local Initiatives Program and the Rapid Response Health Fund, leading landmine awareness programs, and carrying out patrols in remote regions to enhance the presence of a security force and build confidence and trust among the population. The PRT also includes a Quick Reaction Force by which it can respond to sensitive situations and incidents, or to requests for assistance from ISAF.

In carrying out these activities, Canada in general and the PRT in particular uphold the principle of local ownership. Thus, development and recon-struction are supported by Canada but are ultimately the responsibility of the Afghan people and government. Moreover, Canada and its PRT work in close cooperation with other donors and implementing partners to ensure effective coordination and to maximize efforts. Canada's presence is also intended to achieve long-, medium- and short-term effects, with an emphasis on sustainable progress for the Afghan population.

### Challenges

The development and reconstruction of post-Taliban Afghanistan are not abstract concepts but, rather, deliberately designed strategies of the Afghan government that are documented in international frameworks and are significantly supported by donor countries and other participants. However, the security landscape of post-Taliban Afghanistan, the changing nature of international development work, the lack of sufficient capacity among government partners, and issues relating to the donor community present significant challenges to the rehabilitation of Afghanistan.

## INCONSISTENT SECURITY SITUATION

The uneven security situation in Afghanistan is reflected in the two extremes of the deteriorating situation in the south, where insurgent activities are on the rise, and the relative calm in the north. Dangerous conditions on the ground impede development and reconstruction work and make access to its beneficiaries more difficult. For example, the fragile security situation in southern Afghanistan affected the vaccination of children against polio in 2005 and was later reflected in disease incidence: 7 out of the 9 polio cases reported in Afghanistan in 2006 were in the south.

When development and reconstruction activities are compromised by insecure conditions, the local population is vulnerable to choices that perpetuate instability. Thus, it is not uncommon for fighters to be recruited and armed against international forces in return for food and protection. These perceptions are reinforced when civilian casualties result from international forces engaging with insurgents, thereby undermining the dividends of confidence and trust otherwise gained from development and reconstruction activities.

Thus a vicious circle persists whereby insecurity undermines development, thus making it difficult to establish the conditions that would foster stability. One option that has been suggested is to hold back on development and reconstruction in areas where insurgent activities are on the rise and to concentrate on the northern or at least more stable areas where efforts are likely to be more productive. An alternative is to focus resources on the more insecure regions, where they are most needed to build up defences against destabilizing elements. A consequence of either approach could be to create regional distinctions based on the degree of stability and the level of development attention and financing; this in itself would not be conducive to building national solidarity in a country already beset by divisions and conflict.

## THE CHANGING NATURE OF INTERNATIONAL DEVELOPMENT WORK

A second and related complication is the changing nature of development work in war-torn countries. In the case of Afghanistan, development and reconstruction activities and gains, not to mention the workers themselves, have become targets of the insurgency. This presents development agencies and NGOs with a difficult choice. To withdraw from unstable areas would offer the best protection to the workers, and might be financially responsible given that development and reconstruction cannot viably take place under insecure conditions. However, the greater the instability, the greater the need for development aid and reconstruction as populations are displaced and infrastructure is destroyed. Therefore, some development groups have resorted to hiring armed guards to protect staff and resources. Others work intimately with military support already in the field. In other situations, military personnel carry out development and reconstruction work, as they are better able to defend their positions against attack. However, as some development groups argue, this close relationship with private armed guards or military personnel blurs the lines between humanitarian and military activities, militarizes development and reconstruction work, and seriously injures the reputation of neutrality so jealously guarded by NGOs.

### *Lack of Capacity*

The Afghan government's capacity to develop strategic plans and implement decisions appears to be uneven across the various departments. The results of this weakness include unreliable performance data for development programs, difficulty in meeting deadlines (e.g., release of the full ANDS has been delayed to mid-2008 from mid-2007) and in consolidating military gains achieved by international and national forces, as well as suboptimal working relationships with international donors and development agencies.

Ultimately, the role of the Afghan government in directing development and reconstruction is undermined, along with the strength of its leadership and public confidence. The longer this situation persists, the longer and more extensive becomes the involvement of the international community.

## The Donor Community

The international donor community, including national funding agencies, international organizations and NGOs, has also been portrayed by come commentators as contributing to the difficulties of reconstruction and development. For instance, funding has been inconsistent, whereas the proper planning and prioritization of projects and programs requires confirmed, long-term, multi-year funding. Moreover, a growing gap has been noted between amounts pledged and amounts dispersed, as well as delays between disbursement and implementation. Disbursements also remain inadequate: foreign aid disbursements since 2002 are estimated at US$83 per capita per year, whereas the need has been estimated at US$168.

Questions about the effectiveness of aid as structured and delivered by the international community have also arisen. At the local level, perceptions of development workers as receiving excessive wages, living in large homes, and generally living apart from the rest of society are not uncommon and result in local resentment and questions about the value derived from donor funding. Some of these views are reinforced by the inflationary effect of such a large, well-paid group on the local economy, making it that much more difficult for local residents to survive.

## Conclusions

The development and reconstruction of any war-torn society is immensely challenging. This is clearly true for Afghanistan. The prevalence of violence and the relationship between security and development continue to foster debate about basic approaches to development efforts. One view argues that such challenges present the very reason why the international community, including Canada, should stay committed to the endeavour and even increase its contributions to ensure positive results as soon as possible.

Another view, focusing on unfavourable conditions in Afghanistan that threaten to undo the small gains achieved thus far, argues for a reconsideration of development and reconstruction until these conditions change. Whatever the path taken, Afghanistan's future and that of the region hangs in the balance.

## TIMELINE FOR HUMANITARIAN ACTION IN POST-TALIBAN AFGHANISTAN

This chapter presents a plausible timelinefor the returnto their homes in Afghanistanof displaced persons and refugees after the Talibanhas lost the capacity togovern, andhas been supplanted by a differentpolitical arrangement.Thequestion of return implicates many aspects of humanitarian action, and Afghanistan's dislocated persons will clearly need considerable short-term humanitarian relief and longer-term relief and development assistance. This chapter recommends specific international and US government policies to enhance the effectiveness of humanitarian action.

The paper begins with a statement of assumptions, and thenaddresses three components: 1) immediate concerns (six months), 2) medium-term issues (12 to 18 months), and 3) longer-term prospects. In each part, the paper discusses the decisions that will have to be made, who will make them, what the obstacles will be, and how they can be overcome.

Prior to the horrific terrorist attacks in the US on September 11, 2001, Afghanistan was already in the midst of a humanitarian crisis. Over four million refugees were being aided by the United Nations High Commissioner for Refugees, mainly in Iran and Pakistan. Approximately one million internally displaced persons had been uprooted by conflict and hunger, and somesix million persons were dependent upon external humanitarian aidfrom the World Food Programme for subsistence. A well-established aid effort was slowly beingeroded by a difficult operational environment for humanitarian agencies imposed by the Taliban, which inhibited donor support.

After September 11,foreign humanitarian workers were evacuated in the face of military action by the US and its allies; information today about current conditions on the ground in

Afghanistan is fragmentary at best. Much of what little infrastructure there was will have been pulverized by a prolonged bombing campaign, although roads and smaller-scale infrastructure such as irrigation canals and wells are likely to remain intact to some degree.Nevertheless, there will be daunting challenges to the continuation and expansion ofrelief efforts and the prospect of sustainable return in a recovering Afghanistan.

### Assumptions

The US-led military campaign will continue, but the Taliban will not collapse all at once. Rather, there will be a piece-meal process of disintegration over a period of weeks or months. A fragile coalition government couldbe assembled shortly. But the post-Taliban coalition of political factions will not be able to establish a centralized government and authority will remain largely decentralized and localized. At the same time, the humanitarian needs of the Afghan people, already great, will continue to grow.

International aid will continue to be deployedby governmental donors on both a multi-lateral and bi-lateral basis to assist the people of Afghanistan, not only through this immediate emergency period, but also through a period of recovery and reconstruction.However, the level of funding may fall as the emergency eases, even though there may be political pressure to keep funding levels higher than would normally be the case in post-emergency recovery operations. This will place a premium on achieving a high degree of effectiveness in humanitarian action, an outcomethat will be crucial to shaping a future Afghanistan conducive to the return of refugees and displaced persons.

## TIMELINE

### Immediate Concerns (the first six months)

The overriding immediate concern will be to avoid further unnecessary displacement by providing basic humanitarian reliefto the Afghan people during thefirst six months, especially food, shelter, clothing and medical services.The logistics of delivering aid and relief operations will be more difficult than before, and will grow increasingly difficult. The Afghan winter is nowin its early stages. Temperatures will plunge, and snow falls will make already difficult delivery efforts nearly impossible in some remote locales. The logistical capacity of military forces may have to be used to meetthis objective.

Depending on local conditions, the means of delivering aid will vary from cross-border programs based in surrounding countries and landtransport, to deliveries by air. In particularly remote areas, airdrops may be required if it can be ensured that these airdrops actually reach needy people.

Nevertheless, things are likely to get worse before they get better. Even a partial collapse of the Talibancould precipitate large-scale internal and cross border movements if widespread anarchy ensues,particularly if there is fighting for the control of cities. This would again raise concerns about border closures and access by Afghans to the territories of Pakistan and Iran, and sharing the humanitarian burdens of the front line states.

While emergency relief operations will need to continue during the period of immediate concern, post-relief planning should begin and include programs to encourage Afghans to return to their homes and strive for self-sufficiency. The precise timeline for action relative to repatriation will be dictated by a variety of factors having to do with the security situation, the seasons, and the capacities of both returnees and the society to which they will return to absorb them.

Clearly the authorities in Pakistan and Iran will put pressure on Afghan refugees to return once the Taliban has been substantially supplanted. But it is highly unlikely that four million refugees and one million internally displaced persons will be able to return swiftly to their homes. Afghanistan has limited absorptive capacity and is likely to remain dependent upon external assistance and migrant remittances for the foreseeable future. Donor governments, including the United States and European Union, should ensure that aid to refugees is coordinated with, and supplemented by, development assistance to host governments.

The return of refugees and displaced persons is likely to be piecemeal. Refugee families are not likely to return on a wholesale basis during this period. Past experience has shown that it is more likely that young men will venture back to visit their former homes, and, if conditions permit, to plant crops, and repair or rebuild housing. Women, children and the elderly may remain in the relative safety of whatever refugee camp or internal refuge they have found. Only when the men are convinced that it is safe are whole families likely to relocate.

Agriculture will be a key determinant of repatriation. The exact period of the Spring planting season in Afghanistan varies from place to place. A variety of other factors will affect the prospects of cultivation, including whether the seed available is appropriate for the land parcels in question, depending on whether they are rain-fed or irrigated. Nor will the infrastructure likely to be adequate to support the distribution of large quantities of seeds, poultry, livestock and farming equipment. In addition, there will be an urgent need to rebuild agricultural irrigation systems and to repair roads in order to give farmers access to markets. But it would be necessary to work on the rehabilitation of irrigation systems when river levels are low. Work would be difficult in the Spring when rivers become flooded.

A premium will thus be placed on small-scale projects from the very outset. Similar projects were utilized in the past decade in places like Cambodia and Central America, where the United Nations High Commissioner for Refugees (UNHCR) and United Nations Development Programme (UNDP) undertook joint efforts.

The quality of public security will have particularly profound consequences for the delivery and distribution of humanitarian aid as well as refugee return. The history of Afghanistan shows that no external force is likely to be able to provide a sufficient degree of protection if the presence of that force is contested. An international protection force, whether based on paramilitary police or the military, could be needed to guard against banditry - but not as an occupation force. This would require UN Security Council authorization, and such an initiative would have to overcome a clear reluctance by many countries which are capable of contributing police or troops. But there may be little real choice if a minimal level of public security is to be established and maintained.Contingency planning on this issue should continue. The deployment of forces in Somalia in 1992 to protect the delivery of food assistance may be instructive. This is particularly so before the mission there evolved into a political objective and ended badly.

Afghanistan is afflicted with tens of thousands of land mines, a circumstance that clearly will inhibit the return of refugees and displaced persons.

Nor is this a new problem. A landmine clearance effort has been underway in Afghanistan for more than seven years, which has resulted in the clearing of 240 square kilometers. Another 350 square kilometers have been identified for clearing. One new feature is the new types of ordinance that have been dropped in the current campaign - namely, unexploded cluster bombs - which will necessitate new training for awareness and clearance. Also, a major focus in the future will be around the areas of the present front lines in northeast Afghanistan and in the Shomali plain north of Kabul. Planning for this should begin now. Problems associated with landmines in Afghanistan must be addressed early in any humanitarian action plan, with sufficient resources to undertake the task.

Cross-border relief and post-relief efforts will have to be launched, not just from Pakistan, but from all of the surrounding countries, including Iran and Uzbekistan. Diplomatic efforts should be undertaken now to strengthen the access of international organizations and NGOs to necessary facilities in these countries, including visas, travel permits, customs waivers, etc. The objective should be to secure a variety of routes for the delivery of humanitarian aid.

The importance of close coordination between the efforts to prepare and encourage refugees to return and the efforts to rehabilitate and reconstruct infrastructure in Afghanistan cannot be over-emphasized. Past Afghan refugee repatriation efforts show the utility of appointing a UN special envoy with authority and responsibility for planning the return of refugees in both the host countries and the country of return. This official should be associated with a broader UN recovery effort.

A consolidated humanitarian needs assessment will have to be undertaken as soon as access inside Afghanistan has been re-established. In order to promote accountability, the United Nations Office for the Coordination of Humanitarian Affairs (OCHA) should, as is normal, oversee this effort with a view to preparing a revised consolidated funding appeal. Governments and humanitarian NGOs should cooperate with this effort, but this outcome will depend ona closely coordinated group of donor governments, notably the US and European Union, to make this a disciplinedstrategic process.

In addition, US bilateral approaches will support particular foreign policy objectives. US objectives to eliminate terrorist networks with a global reach and to promote a stable post-Taliban Afghanistan which does not harbor and support them in the futurecould be served by particular assistance strategies. The design of these strategies will be informed by the ways in which the political and security situation evolves in Afghanistan. In order to achieve this goal, the US would have to play a serious role in the recovery of Afghanistan and the neighboring countries. Nevertheless, coordination with other donors and international institutions will be necessary.

An inclusive coordination structure for humanitarian work already exists in the region. Building on past experiences and existing structures, arecovery office should be established under the auspices of the United Nations, led by the UN humanitarian and development agencies under the overall coordination of OCHA. Abroad assemblage of agencies would be needed to address not only issues associated with refugee return, but also internally displaced persons and civilians who were never displaced but were trapped during the winter in remote locales. The leadership of the UN Secretary General with the concerted support of donor governments will be needed to overcome the policy coordination cacophony that typically characterizes the UN system in the midst and immediate aftermath of a humanitarian emergency. This is particularly so in relation tothe problem of linking together the work of agencies involved in relief and development assistance activities. An early endeavor of this recovery office would be to prepare and revise on a continuing basis a consolidated assessment and appeal process for recovery activities. A process is needed, not a static document, in order to ensure a sufficiently strategic element in the planning, implementation and evaluation of projects.

This has implications for the United Nations. The current integrated mission task force dealing with Afghanistan is limited to the UN system. Lakhdar Brahimi, the UN Secretary-General's special representative on Afghanistan, has assembled a small cadre of advisors. There is need for a broader process which systematically draws upon governments and the independent sector to think and pre-position ideas for the difficult policy formation and implementation tasks ahead with respect to the return of refugees and displaced persons.

Such an arrangementalso has implications for the US government.The merger of US AID over the past decade into the State Department and the erosion of the State Department's budget, including its planning functions, have weakened the capacity for development assistancepolicy coordination. Development "strategy" has given way to the necessity of handling immediate crises and managing food aid along with other humanitarian assistance.The thinking on the development-related aspects of refugee return must be strengthened on an urgent basis, including by establishing appropriate liaison relationships between those in government who are formulating and implementing policy with think tanks, NGOs, and scholars.

Besides designing and implementing recovery programs, a consolidated UNrecovery effort would facilitate communication and consensus-building between local leaders, NGOs and donors. One of the tools that could be very useful in Afghanistan is"quick impact projects". These are small projects which could be focused on improvements in things such as irrigation canals, seed distribution, income generation, education, and health infrastructure, etc.Such programs should pay particular attention to Afghan women because they have suffered systematic discrimination in their access to employment and social services.

While small projects do not address structural problems such as weak governance institutions or an undeveloped economy in

Afghanistan, they will not only be of genuine help, but they will also be a means towards confidence building for returning refugees and displaced persons as well as the surrounding local community. Such an approach would be particularly apt in Afghanistan which is likely to be without significant national-level infrastructure for the foreseeable future.

## *Medium-term Issues (12 to 18 months)*

Depending on local conditions, especially security, it may be possible to set in motion a large-scale voluntary repatriation program for Afghan refugees in Pakistan and Iran. To be successful, any such effort should include material incentives (seeds, oil, edibles, grain, farm implements, and money) to be given to refugee families as they return.

In this regard, it should be recalled that in the period 1992-93, some 2.9 million Afghan refugees returned from Pakistan and Iran. In 1992 alone, approximately 1.6 million Afghan refugees returned home, approximately 1.4 million of whom from Pakistan. In 1993, approximately 1.3 million returned to Afghanistan, more than one million of whom from Iran. UNHCR provided each returning family with 300 kilograms of wheat and $130 in cash.

This earlier repatriation effort was compromised by civil war that broke out between factions competing for political supremacy. Many Afghans who had returned once again went into exile where they remain to this day. In addition to an encashment program,well-crafted small-scale reintegration programs will also be needed to help sustain return.

A major new complication in the present Afghan displacement is the number of refugees and displaced persons who have fled their homes in urban areas in the wake of the bombing campaign. A significant commitment of funding as well as technical assistance and material aid will be essential if Afghan urban life is to be re-constituted. Not only homes but also hospitals, schools, public administration facilities and houses of worship will need to be re-constructedif the basic urban infrastructure is to be restored.

Once again, the recurrence of winter will highlight the most urgent needs of this recovering society; medical and food aid will be needed, depending on the drought. These medium-term recovery issues in Afghanistan should be addressed as well in the development of a strategic framework process administered by the UN.

### *Longer-term Prospects (18 months on)*

A substantial, multi-year program of reconstruction, rehabilitation, economic development and institution building will be critical to any effort to make refugee return in Afghanistan sustainable.In this connection, particular attention should be paid to the indigenous human resources that have emerged by reason of past international action. This would include men and womenfrom the Afghan Diaspora as well as refugees educated whilethey were in Pakistan or Iran, or introduced to organizational or business methods as members of the local staff of international humanitarian organizations. A highly participatory approach will be needed in Afghanistan in order to move from relief to recovery. This cohort of several thousand persons is likely to be a key resource for achieving a peaceful and stable future for Afghanistan.An inventory of the leadership and skills of these persons should be undertaken immediately. Special attention should be given to women in this exercise as they have been systematically excluded from public life in the past. The experience of the UN transitional mission in encouraging refugee repatriation and the growth of indigenous NGOs in Cambodia in the early 1990s could be instructive.

Afghanistan is one of the poorest nations in the world and has suffered through modern times as one of the last battlefields of the cold war. The largely subsistence agricultural sector has been depressed and increasingly devoted to drug production; men and boys have been recruited for war; health care and education for women and girls has been limited by the Taliban. Afghanistan's people have the lowest annual incomes anywhere. Millions of displaced persons and refugees have been exiles for over a decade.

Afghanistan and its people have been virtually ignored by development agencies (e.g., the World Bank does not include Afghanistan in the Tables of World Development Indicators that it provides for 130 economies because available data for Afghanistan is too sparse). A limited number of UN agencies and a handful of humanitarian NGOs have worked inside Afghanistan as well as with Afghan refugees, especially in Pakistan, and assisted with clearing landmines left by the Russians.

Development assistance and continuing humanitarian aid in post-Taliban Afghanistan will be difficult and daunting. US bilateral initiatives will be needed. Also, the World Bank, which is preparing a far-reaching reconstruction plan, anda variety of international organizations in the United Nations system (Office for the Coordination of Humanitarian Affairs, World Food Programme, United NationsHigh Commissioner for Refugees, United Nations Children's Fund, World Health Organization, United Nations Development Programme), as well as the International Committee of the Red Cross and a variety of NGOs, will be involved in the effort to re-build Afghanistan. Policy coordination will be a key determinant of effectiveness. United States leadership will be essential.

The international efforts for the recovery of Afghanistan are likely to be undertaken in a predominantly humanitarian mode. Humanitarian assistance will likely be accompanied by relatively light political, security and economic development deployment. These efforts would be assisted by re-animating anestablished international humanitarian policy coordination structure, the Afghan Support Group (ASG),a collection of donor governments, international organizations and NGOs supported by the UN (OCHA in particular).This would contribute to the enhancement of the effectiveness of longer-term relief and development assistance. The ASG is scheduled to meet shortly in Berlin. Again,leadership by the UN Secretary General and disciplined action by donor governments, particularly the United States and European Union, would be required to strengthen the ASG.

A consolidated longer-term needs assessment should be conducted under the auspices of the ASG in standard sectors for development activities, such as economic management, agriculture, infrastructure, social services, health, education, housing, water and sanitation, etc. This assessment should provide the baseline for longer-term strategic recovery efforts undertaken by the UN and World Bank.

To successfully create conditions conductive to the voluntary return of Afghan refugees and displaced persons, the international community will have to be willing to make long-term commitments. The people of Afghanistan have been brutalized by war, civil strife, oppression and draught for over 20 years. Past experience has shown that half-way measures of relief and rehabilitation do not sustain return.

The United States, which is taking the lead role effort to bring down the Taliban, has an equal lead role to take in creating the conditions for return and recovery. This will require a sustained commitment of financial and material aid, and support for the United Nations in coordinating, planning, and implementing the overall endeavor. There is no guarantee of success, but a determined and sustained effort by all parties will maximize the prospects for a satisfactory outcome.

## POLITICAL HISTORY OF AFGHANISTAN

The monarchy of Zahir Shah which began in the 1933 ended in 1973 with Mohammed Daud declaring himself as the first president of the Republic. Mohammed Daud's reign lasted till 1978, he was overthrown by the Saur revolution led by the Communist People's Democratic Party of Afghanistan, the uncertainty in the communist rule led to soviet occupation in 1979, Soviet entered the country with the Red Army and Barbarak Kamal was installed as the ruler in the year 1980.

The communist social reforms clashed with the long established social standards of Afghanistan and hence the support for the PDPA soon crumbled. To counter the Soviet invasion, the Mujahideen i.e. The guerilla fighters from the rural areas of Afghanistan organized themselves into an army and fought back the Soviet, this tumultuous period of struggle was characterized by bloodshed leading to the killing of a million of Afghans.

The Mujahideen were organized into many political factions, it was armed and supported by Saudi Arabia, Pakistan and the US. It was during this time that Osama Bin Laden had entered the politics of Afghanistan, he was leading the Mujahideen. It needs no mention that the Mujahideen was mainly supported by the US as a strategic foreign policy to check the spread of communist regime and have a control over the region.

In 1986, Najibullah was replaced as the head of the Soviet backed regime. And in 1988, when the war was ongoing, Afghanistan, USSR, the US and Pakistan had signed peace accords; subsequently, the Soviet Union of Russia began pulling out its troops. The last troop left in 1989, however the civil war still continued as the Mujahedeen tried to topple Najibullah's government. After the overthrowing of the Najibullah's government in 1992, the factions of the Mujahideen fought amongst themselves until the Taliban seized control of Kabul and solidified its rule in 1996. The Taliban ruled the country from 1996-2001.

Theoritical connections can be made to the "state of nature" proposed by Thomas Hobbes, he was the earliest philosophers, who witnessed the terrors of the English Civil War and thereby concluded that the inherent nature of the man is "short, brutish and nasty" hence he conceptualised the notion of a "Levaithan", whose purpose is to protect the man from spilling into the state of nature, ever since the communist coup in 1978, Afghanistan has been the ground for warring factions, this has allowed for the budding of extremist muslim groups, the international community's response to the chaos and the stringent rule of Taliban has been a Hobbesian's approach, this lead to the installation of Hamid Karzaia as the Levaithan in 2001.

How and why did this happen? In 1998, the USA launched missile strikes in the militant bases of Osama Bin Laden as he was accused of bombing the US embassies in Africa. It was followed by the UN imposing an embargo and financial sanctions on the Afghanistan to handover Osama Bin Laden, this was the beginning of USA's uncomfort with the Mujahiadeen. Later, as a response to the September 112001 Pentagon attacks, US led bombing started in Afghanistan, the pseudonym of the "global war against terror" had become the policy of the United States and hence it started targeting the Taliban. The Anti-Taliban Northern Alliance which fought a war against the Taliban entered during the same time.

The Taliban was over thrown in 2001. As the result of the negotiations that happened in Bonn, Germany; Afghan groups agreed for the establishment of an interim government. *Loya Jirga* elected Hamid Karzai as the interim head till 2004. In 2004 the *Loya Jirga* adopted the new constitution which provided for a strong presidency.

## CONSTITUTIONAL HISTORY OF AFGHANISTAN

Having tracked the political history, it is evident that Afghanistan's fragile politic barely gave any opportunity to actually implement the constitutional principles. However it had too many constitutions. Since the first constitution in 1923, Afghanistan had eight different sets of constitution. The first two constitutions of 1923 and 1931 were established by the monarchy but they barely had any public participation and were totally elitist conferring all the power on the monarchy without leaving any room for popular vote. In 1963, after thirty years of stability under the regime of King Zahir, he called in for the formation of the constitution. This constitution was drafted democratically over a period of eighteen months, it provided for a popularly elected parliament, provincial advisory councils, elected city councils, and an independent legislature. This era marked the beginning of democracy in the region, two parliamentary elections were also held, however it was short lived. In 1973, Sardar Daoud, took power by coup, Afghanistan was declared Republic and the constitution that was drafted in 1963 was suspended. A new constitution was promulgated in 1977 without popular consultation; again, during the communist coup, the 1977 constitution was suspended. Another constitution was put in place in 1980 by Babrak Karmal, this came to an end with the Soviet invasion, the government of Najibullah introduced yet another constitution in 1987, it only lasted till the exit of the Soviet union. After the Soviet withdrawal in 1992, the new interim Mujahideen government proposed a new constitution, but it never came into fore as the fighting broke out between the internal elements, and later on the Taliban never introduced a constitution at all.

Thus in this whole period, Afghanistan had three spells of unconstitutionalism between 1973-1977, 1980-1987 and 1992-2001.

Hence due to the instability in political structure and governance, people took to the local *Jirga* and *Shura* for their dispute resolution as there was no continuity in the legal system.

## LEGAL PLURALISM IN AFGHANISTHAN

*Jirga* and *Shura* fall outside the purview of state institutions, the chthonic law that is adjudicated upon in such institutions is diverse due to different ethnicities and varies with regions, it isn't a uniform system of law, however it plays a significant role in dispute resolution.

Prolonged conflict in the society, multiple constitutions and a lack of centralized authority propelled people, particularly people living in the rural areas to take up to non-state chthonic law, rural population constitutes eighty percent of the Afghan population and hence one cannot dismiss the pervasive and binding effect of chthonic law in Afghanistan.

Even today, Hamid Karzai's government is largely composed of the old war lords of Northern alliance, and hence due to the lack of separation of powers people are still dependent on the local non state entities for the purposes of security and justice.

The reasons as to why people prefer chthonic law over the state law boils down to the following:

a) Chthonic law focuses on substantive justice instead of procedural justice;
b) It focuses on compensation and reconciliation instead of punishment;
c) The parties have a sense of faith in the institution and hence are bound by it.

Pashtuns are the dominant ethnic tribe in Afghanistan, their chthonic law is the pasthunwali, it is an amalgamation of *Shari'a* law, customs and ethical values of the tribe. The decision making process in a *jirga* is driven by consensus rather than voting; parties to the dispute and the communities meet for the resolution of a dispute. It has an appeal procedure as well, the first level of appeal is taken to another *jirga* with more elder members, the second level of appeal is taken to a tribal assembly which has representatives of pashtuns from other lineages.

In a Shura, the *Shari'a* plays a significant role when compared to a *jirga,* it is composed of imams and the "local religious figures" for the resolution of dispute, the local practices of the geography play a major role in dispute resolution. Now, with the emergence of a constitution, there surfaces a problem of deeply embedded legal pluralism, the question then remains, how do we reconcile the state and non state entities? Specifically in a culture which lacks constitutional morality. The normative laws guiding a constitutionally validated judiciary would inevitably come into conflict with the diverse normative framework of a non state entity.

United States Institute of Peace proposes the interaction of both, in cases where chthonic law isn't in congruence with the state law, the state should ensure that the chthonic law doesn't violate "the basic human rights" or "principles within the law", thus the government should act as a bridge between the both, the model posits that the government should prescribe the areas where non state institutions can be beneficial and work positively, the state shall have supremacy on important realms such as criminal law and property law, the rationale for such supremacy is the conception that the state's objective is to further justice and hence it must have finality over issues of such issues of significance, the *jirgas* have their own conceptions of justice, but however the model ascribes finality and supremacy to the state conception's of justice.

Wardak on the other hand proposes for an active human rights unit along with *jirga/shura* and the formal legal institutions. The role of the human rights unit is to interact with the educational institutions at the local level for the production of material pertaining to issues that are culturally sensitive in nature and sensitise people on human rights abuses such as domestic violence and so on, thus it works at the ground level. The formal mechanism of the state on the other hand is to deal with civil issues that are usually not dealt by the informal mechanisms and other major criminal offences. It is to aid the informal institutions and the human rights unit in their functioning. In some way, both the models hierarchize the institutions at hand, despite giving due recognition to chthonic institutions, major powers are given to the state instilled formal legal institutions; however the ground reality remains that, even in the matters pertaining to major criminal offences, the mechanisms adopted by the informal institutions secure more authority.

Hence, the judge then, while assessing the decisions must weigh it in terms of two different normative frameworks: legal and chthonic. He must analyse the extent to which it is consistent or comes into contradiction with such frameworks. While doing so, he must also incorporate into his decisions, the universal principles of international human rights and the *shari'a* law. A standard set of priori rules will not be able to resolve the conflicts that arise due to legal pluralism; hence an assessment has to be done on a case-by-case basis depending upon the facts and circumstances of each case.

The constitution of Afghanistan also provides for fundamental rights such as the freedom of expression, presumption of innocence, right to liberty, right to form social organization, and the right to legal defence if accused of an offence under the law ; the philosophy of fundamental rights is to encapsulate human rights, the aim of the state is to protect the fundamental rights, thus the discourse of fundamental rights can also serve as a framework to evaluate the decisions of *jirga/shura*. A concern can be raised if there is a deviation of fundamental right.

The state may as well identify major avenues i.e. Issues related to women, major criminal offences etc. that could potentially give space for conflict and then oversee the rulings of*jirga/ shura* pertaining to such matters.

Judicial review needn't always be one sided, decisions can also be made from the vantage point of chthonic law. For an instance, in the south African case of Bangindawo and Other v Head of Nyanada Regional Authority & Another, the court while deciding on the role of a traditional ruler- who was a judge and the legislator, opined that such duality could hamper judicial independence, however, it was careful enough to not impose the western notion of separation of powers and held that, such duality can be allowed as the adherents of such customary law trust the impartiality of the ruler when he is a judge. Mechanisms have to be developed to provide for the working multiple legal systems, trying to annihilate entities outside the purview of state can turn counter productive.

Now, we are going to examine the legal history of Islamic law in Afghanistan and track the making of the current constitution.

## LEGAL HISTORY OF AFGHANISTAN

The population of Afghanistan is 80–85% *sunnis* and 15–20% *shei'ite.* The majority of*sunnis* in Afghanistan are followers of the *hanafi* school and the *Shias* follow the *jafari*jurisprudence.

In the 1950's and 1960's the rulers started to modernize the justice system in line with the Western world, hence during this process of consolidation, *Hanafi* version of *Shari'a* law along with the customary laws provided the foundation for the legal system in Afghanistan. Islamic scholars acted as Judges in the state courts. During the process of modernization, a lot of these laws were also codified, since then, the state law rather than the Islamic law began to be the primary source of the law.

Thus, Afghanistan substantially altered its structure of governance through the 1964 constitution, the political atmosphere during the time was relatively peaceful and hence there was public participation at the time of making the constitution.

In the 1964 constitution, Article 69 explicitly stated that in the event of no codified law, the*Hanafi* jurisprudence of the *Shari'a* law will be considered as the law. Thus this justice system tried to reconcile between the Islamic *Shari'a* law and the modern state law, it regulated the interaction between the both. State law was recognized as the primary source of law and the Shari'a law to be the secondary source of law. The impact of this transition in reality is minimal; the corruption embedded in the legal system and the lack of faith in the state authority distanced people from formal legal structures.

Later, the reforms that were introduced during the communist regime were totally at odds with both Islam and Afghan traditions, hence the whole system of governance and its judicial reforms (decrees) were rejected by the people, and instead they took to the local traditional institutions for the purposes of dispute resolution.

After the collapse of the Marxist government, the Mujahideen government (1992–1996) declared*Shari'a* as the substructure of their "Islamic State of Afghanistan". They attempted to impose a totalitarian theocracy. The Taliban'stheocratic regime (1996–2001) imposed an even more regressive version of *Shari'a*

## BONN AGREEMENT AND THE 2004 CONSTITUTION: AN ANALYSIS

Thus owing to the relevance of *Shari'a* in the justice system, the Bonn agreement emphasized on rebuilding the justice system in accordance with Islamic principles, the rule of law and the Afghan legal traditions. In other words, it tried to put in *Shari'a* that is compatible with the Afghan traditions and the fundamental principles of human rights that are in vogue in the contemporary international arena.

Article 3 of the Constitution makes it explicit that no statute can be contrary to the "beliefs and rulings" of the sacred religion of Islam, it is important for us to mark the phrase "beliefs and rulings" as it awards the Supreme Court with ample discretion so as to decide on what a belief is, *Shari'a* law has been given a due constitutional recognition, fears were expressed that this clause can have the potentiality to introduce Taliban like theocratic regime.

Under the new constitution, the Supreme Court, "can review compliance of laws, legislative decrees, international treaties and international conventions with the Constitution and interpret them, in accordance with the law." The constitution grants the Supreme Court in Article 121, the power of judicial review i.e. "power to reject virtually any law or treaty as un-Islamic.

On the other hand Article 7 states that "The state shall abide by the UN charter, international treaties, international conventions that Afghanistan has signed, and the Universal Declaration of Human Rights."

The constitution has been aspirational to include relevance of the Universal declaration of Human Rights and make it a mandate to abide by it. But, if a law has to pass through the filters of Article

3 it is subject to much skepticism as to whether both the Articles can be reconciled and implemented.

Thus, it is important for us to examine whether article 3 is justiciable or non justiciable. Most of the Islamic constitutions have a *Shari'a* clause of this kind in their constitution and had explicitly made it non justiciable, which means that the Supreme Court cannot enforce it, or otherwise the courts have read the clauses to be non justiciable;

When it comes to Afghanistan, it is not explicit in the constitution as to whether this clause is justiciable or non justiciable, all Afghan judges and scholars believe that the clause is justiciable, if so, then it is important to arrive at a mechanism as to how the review of laws has to be done so that they are in consonance with Islam. Due to multiple ethnicities, and different Islamic jurisprudential schools in place, there is no consensus on the interpretative mechanism in Afghanistan.

Article 130 states that the court would decide in accordance with *Hanafi* jurisprudence in the instance when there is no provision in the Constitution or other laws pertaining to the ruling on an issue. Majority of *Sunnis* follow the *Hanafi* school of jurisprudence and hence the *Hanafi* school of jurisprudence has been given a priority in the constitution.

However, the Article merely makes a reference to the instance when there is no particular ruling on an issue but doesn't prescribe for the interpretation of laws in general. Article 130 is problematic as not all *Sunni* Muslims follow the *Hanafi* school and this is not agreeable to the minority *Shias* either, moreover Article 3 doesn't make any reference to the adherence to*Hanafi fiqh, it merely states "beliefs and rulings" of the sacred religion of Islam.* It is important to give space for these concerns and hence while evaluating the "islamicness" of any legislation, it is advisable for the courts to not stick to one classical school but instead they have to take to the broader principles that reinforce the protection of human rights. Now, it is important for us to make a reference to the interpretation of Islamic law, the difference between classical view and the modern view; this would help us in understanding how Islamic principles are to be synchronized with liberal values of a democratic state. A reference is made to Egypt so as to examine how modern Islamic jurisprudence has evolved.

*Shari'a* is basically an Arabic word which simply means "the path to follow".

The primary sources of *Shari'a* are the Quran and the *Sunnahs;*

Quran is the Holy book and the *Sunnahs* are the Statements and Deeds of the Prophet Mohammed which are used to interpret the Quran.

The secondary sources for the Islamic law are the *Qiyas,* anological reasoning i.e. Reasoning deduced from the cases in Quran and *Ijma* is the consensus of Islamic jurists.

The science of interpreting *Shari'a* is called *'ilm usul al-fiqh,* a scholar's interpretation of it is known as *fiqh.*

Classical jurists adopted two methods to interpret *Shari'a* and develop *fiqh.*

Namely, *Ijitihad* and *taqlid.*

*Ijtihad* understands God's law through four sources, namely the.

The Qur'an,

The *hadith* literature: Account of events in Prophet's life.

The juristic logic *(qiyas)* and

The juristic consensus (*ijma*).

*Taqlîd* entails adopting the jurist's rulings despite having no evidence; it is the personal religious view of the jurist and is trusted to be correct.

Using the sources, a scholar had to look at the scripture and then evaluate the authenticity of the text and the clarity of its command. Thus only few scriptures were finalized to be certain with respect to authenticity and clarity, these came to be known as "*qat'i*", the rest are presumptive in nature, and are believed to be "*Zanni*".

Whenever there is no evidence, the classical jurists using the *Taqlid* form of interpretation believed that the principles of *Zanni* also highly reflect God's will and hence are presumptively binding, the modern jurists deviate from such a conception, they believe that the classical interpretation of Islamic law must be only relied to the extent of *"qat'i"*. This departure gives the leverage for the modern jurists to interpret Islamic law from a utilitarian perspective and also accommodate the customs of the State. The benchmark that was set to be achieved by the modern jurists are the "goals of *Shari'a*"

On this note, a reference must be made to the Egyptian constitution; Article 2 of the Egyptian constitution requires all the legislations to be consistent with the Islamic principles. The constitutional court in Egypt while resorting to modern jurisprudence required the laws to be furthering the principles of "justice" and "public utility", it advocated legal liberalism and thus protected negative liberties in the arena of human rights and economic regulation. Through this, the court expanded the scope of Islamic review and tried to harmonize the liberal values with Islamic principles.

Country's system for implementing a *Shari'a* Clause reflects the country's institutional, political and social environment. Hence when such an interpretation as like in Egypt is advocated by the Supreme Court in Afghanistan, it would build judicial power and bolster the constitutionalist culture that protects many liberal rights.

The power of judicial review in Afghanistan is subject to debate, it doesn't rest solely with the Supreme Court, the constitution through its article 157 created a constitutional commission to supervise the implementation of the constitution. However like in Egypt it doesn't have specialized constitutional benches to deal with the issues of *Shari'a.*

Now, let us look at the political structure in the country and the rationale for adopting such structure.

## THE CURRENT POLITICAL STRUCTURE IN AFGHANISTAN AND ITS RATIONALE

### *The Separation and Balance of Powers in the Government*

Afghanistan's political system is presidential in nature with a directly elected President, two vice presidents, a bicameral legislature, and an independent judiciary. The president can choose his cabinet but it is subject to the approval of the legislature. The legislature and the judiciary also have a significant role to play in the constitution. The lower house of the bicameral legislature requires a minimum of 68 members to be women out of the total 249 members, this is to safeguard and ensure the political participation of women and is constitutionally mandated by Article 83 of the constitution. This is definitely a progressive step towards the empowerment of the women especially after the regressive policies towards women in the Taliban regime for a period of ten years.

However in a country like Afghanistan, it is skeptical as to how much a meaningful political choice can people make as to the direct election of president as the electoral politics are still in the budding state and the means of communication to be able to approach people is still underdeveloped. The concentration of power in the hands of a single person is dangerous especially in an unstable political situation as the rewards for illegitimate capture of the presidency stands high, and thus increases the risk of it happening. The President cannot even be impeached by the legislature which can make him a strong Monarch. Moreover, in a Presidential system, the executive and the legislature usually belong to two different parties and hence the legislature's control over the budget can be a medium to brake the executive and hence lead to dead lock between the both and delay the decision making process. The president has been given wide discretionary powers to pick and choose members for the purposes of allocating ministries, the ground reality remains that the key ministries in the post Taliban government have been given to the anti taliban Northern alliance leaders who were once involved in pillaging Kabul. Nepotism, institutional abuse of power fructuate the promises of reconstruction, protection of human rights and the progress of democracy in the country.

On the other hand, given the atomic structure of the Afghanistan's society, when we think of the political structure in terms of a parliamentary system, it is highly probable that no one party would attain majority in the legislature and it would be composed of multiple political parties, the executive would be a fragile coalition leading to slow decision making process.

People of the Country wanted a system where in there would be strong prime minister and the President as the ceremonial head acting as a mediator; this is more akin to India and is a partial parliamentary system. The political considerations of USA which was a party in the constitution making cannot be denied, it has a significant role to play in determining the political structure of the country, to have a control over the region, presidential system in Afghanistan is best suited to its interests rather than a strong parliament, because presidential system entails dealing with a single person and the executive is under the control of the President.

Fear that the country would break apart lead to the creation of a centralized authority having firm control at the top. The tragedy of policy making in Afghanistan is that it has largely been Hobbesian, Jefferson's Republican vision of decentralized authority, checks and balances on power or the Gandhian vision of village level panchayat justice system didn't inform the constitution making.

Usually, the Supreme Court acts as the check to the power of the constitution through its power of the judicial review and interpretation. The Supreme Court of Afghanistan has been awarded with the same power, through the power to interpret the constitutionality of laws and treaties and may even review them; however the nascent judges interpret it according to their own religious view which can be often conservative owing to the Taliban regime in the region.

For instance, ten days after the constitution had been ratified, the Supreme Court announced that airing a female singer on Kabul TV is unislamic and hence unconstitutional, the Supreme Court had neither a case before it nor a law which could back such an order. Hence the court's decree wasn't enforced; this sort of makes the legality of the Supreme Court a little shaky.

### Unitary State

The State to be a "unitary state" owing to the fragmented nature of the country in the past. Ethnic groups that were disenfranchised in the past now have autonomous military and political, structures. The party structures that came up during Jihad times (the war with the Russian government) almost functioned as mini state governments and indulged in activities like issuing the visas, carrying foreign relations and printing currency. The interference of the foreign neighbor states that is leading to the disintegration of the country also prompted the constitution makers to call it an "independent, indivisible and a unitary state."

Owing to the historical past of authoritarianism and brutality, the local populations always resented the decisions made by the centre and thus they have developed their own independent social organization and a culture of self governance, the country even lacked the requisite infrastructure to run the government from the Centre. The war period created the Gap between the Centre and the local provinces, Among Pashtun tribe, the *jirga* or tribal assembly is consensus-building device for resolving disputes and for non pastuns councils called as (*shura*) However, without consolidation of the State, establishment of fiscal control and legitimate power structures, there is high probability of the country being torn apart and hence despite the circumstances in the past, Afghanistan aspired to be a unitary structure.

### Elements of Consociationalism in Afghanistan's Constitution

Consociationalism gives space for the recognition, representation and political participation of all major social segments in the governance of the Country. Afghanistan is an ethnically divided society and the period during the Taliban regime witnessed the division of the society on ethnic lines and of their own political consciousness. For instance during the Taliban regime, "Jihad" was declared on the minority Shia Hazaras, they were severely persecuted, and other minorities like the Tajik, Uzbek who formed a part of Northern Alliance which aimed at overthrowing the Taliban were also badly targeted by the Taliban and severe human right violations had been perpetrated on them. Hence giving them a constitutional recognition would help in assuaging their fears of the tyranny of majoritarian democracy.

Recognizing this need, Article 4 of the Afghanistan's constitution makes it explicit that "The nation of Afghanistan is comprised of the following ethnic groups: "Pashtun, Tajik, Hazara, Uzbak, Turkman, Baluch, Pashai, Nuristani, Aymaq, Arab, Qirghiz, Qizilbash, Gujur, Brahwui and others." This is understood to be the constitutional recognition of minorities and guaranteeing them citizenship in Afghanistan.

Moreover, Article 6 of the Constitution makes it an obligation on the part of the state to ensure "equality among all ethnic groups and tribes and to provide for balanced development in all areas of the country."

Liberal consociational rules aim at broadening the spirit of inclusion and leave the decision to the electorate to decide upon the terms of such inclusion. On the other hand, corporate rules perceive individuals as group members and make explicit provisions for power sharing, like the case of Bosnia and Herzegovina. Afghanistan in such sense can be called a liberal consociation as it allows for diverse participation through its provisions but doesn't make explicit provisions for power sharing among the ethnicities.

Moreover, the 2004 Afghanistan constitution contains several components that could induce power-sharing, such as the Single Non-Transferable Vote electoral system for legislative elections and the proviso for two vice-presidents, this could be utilized to provide for ethnic diversity in the executive, however, the discretion rests with the President.

2

# The Taliban in Afghanistan

The Taliban is a predominantly Pashtun, Islamic fundamentalist group that ruled Afghanistan from 1996 until 2001, when a U.S.-led invasion toppled the regime for providing refuge to al-Qaeda and Osama bin Laden. The Taliban regrouped across the border in Pakistan, where its central leadership, headed by Mullah Mohammed Omar, leads an insurgency against the Western-backed government in Kabul. Both the United States and Afghanistan have pursued a negotiated settlement with the Taliban, but talks have little momentum as international forces prepare to conclude combat operations in December 2014 and withdraw by the end of 2016.

## RISE OF THE TALIBAN

The Taliban was formed in the early 1990s by an Afghan faction of mujahideen, Islamic fighters who had resisted the Soviet occupation of Afghanistan (1979–89) with the covert backing of the U.S. Central Intelligence Agency and its Pakistani counterpart, the Inter-Services Intelligence directorate (ISI). They were joined by younger Pashtun tribesmen who studied in Pakistani madrassas, or seminaries; *taliban* is Pashto for "students." Pashtuns comprise a plurality in Afghanistan and are the predominant ethnic group in much of the country's south and east.

The movement attracted popular support in the initial post-Soviet era by promising to impose stability and rule of law after four years of conflict (1992–1996) among rival mujahideen groups. Talibs entered Kandahar in November 1994 to pacify the crime-ridden southern city, and by September 1996 seized the capital, Kabul, from President Burhanuddin Rabbani, an ethnic Tajik whom they viewed as anti-Pashtun and corrupt. The Taliban regime controlled some 90 percent of the country before its 2001 overthrow, analysts say.

The Taliban imposed its brand of justice as it consolidated territorial control. Taliban jurisprudence was drawn from the Pashtuns' pre-Islamic tribal code and interpretations of sharia colored by the austere Wahhabi doctrines of the madrassas' Saudi benefactors. The regime neglected social services and other basic state functions even as its Ministry for the Promotion of Virtue and Prevention of Vice enforced prohibitions on behavior the Taliban deemed un-Islamic, requiring women to wear the head-to-toe *burqa,* or *chadri;* banning music and television; and jailing men whose beards it deemed too short.

The regime was internationally isolated from its inception. Two UN Security Council resolutions passed in 1998 urged the Taliban to end its abusive treatment of women. The following year the council imposed sanctions on the regime for harboring al-Qaeda. Only Saudi Arabia, the United Arab Emirates, and Pakistan recognized the government. Many analysts say Islamabad supported the Taliban as a force that could unify and stabilize Afghanistan while staving off Indian, Iranian, and Russian influence.

## LEADERSHIP AND SUPPORT

Mullah Omar, a cleric and veteran of the anti-Soviet resistance, led Taliban-ruled Afghanistan from 1996 to 2001 as *amir al-mu'minin,* or "commander of the faithful." He granted al-Qaeda sanctuary on the condition that it not antagonize the United States, but bin Laden reneged on their agreement in 1998 when he orchestrated bombings of U.S. embassies in East Africa. The episode was indicative of tensions that emerged between the two groups, analysts say. The Taliban was fundamentally parochial while al-Qaeda had its sights set on global jihad—yet after 9/11, Omar rejected U.S. demands that he give up bin Laden. Ethnic minority Tajiks, Uzbeks, and Hazaras in northern Afghanistan opposed to

Taliban rule formed the Northern Alliance, which assisted U.S.-led forces in routing the Taliban after 9/11. Though the regime was dismantled during the occupation, Mullah Omar and many of his top aides escaped to the frontier territories of Pakistan, where they reconstituted the Taliban's central leadership.

Dubbed the "Quetta Shura" for the capital of Balochistan province, where they are believed to have taken refuge, they maintain a degree of operational authority over Afghan Taliban fighters, but appear "unwilling or unable to monopolize anti-state violence," a UN Security Council monitoring team foundin September 2013.

Many experts suspect the Pakistani security establishment continues to provide Taliban militants sanctuary in the country's western tribal areas in an effort to counter India's influence in Afghanistan. Islamabad dismisses these charges. (Tehrik-i-Taliban Pakistan, commonly known as the Pakistani Taliban, is an insurgent group distinct from its Afghan namesake; it coalesced in response to the Pakistani military's incursions into that country's tribal areas. The Afghan Taliban, by contrast, views Pakistan as a benefactor.)

The Taliban's post-2001 resurgence has partially been financed by narcotics production and trafficking, though Mullah Omar issued injunctions against opium production, and the Taliban eradicated much of the poppy crop during its rule. Insurgents and other strongmen extort *ushr*, an agricultural tithe, from farmers and levies at roadside checkpoints. Revenues from illicit mining also contribute to Taliban coffers, whichnet some $400 million a year, the UN estimated in 2012.

## Public Opinion of the Taliban

More than a decade since its fall from power, the Taliban enjoys continued, if declining, support. The Asia Foundation found that in 2013, a third of Afghans—mostly Pashtuns and rural Afghans—had sympathy for armed opposition groups (AOGs), primarily the Taliban. Nearly two-thirds of Afghans, the survey found, believed that reconciliation between the government and AOGs would stabilize the country.

Afghan support for the Taliban and allied groups stems in part from grievances directed at public institutions. While the Asia Foundation survey found the Afghan National Army and Afghan National Police garner high public confidence, many civilians see government institutions such as the militia-like Afghan Local Police as predatory. Likewise, international forces' support for warlords and strongmen, an expedient in securing territory, likely also alienated many rural Afghans from Kabul, analysts say.

Many rural Afghans have come to trust the Taliban's extensive judicial network over government courts to "solve disputes in a fair war, without tribal or ethnic bias, or more commonly, without having to pay bribes," says Graeme Smith, a Kabul-based senior analyst at the International Crisis Group.

## A Resilient Insurgency

As the Obama administration wound down the war in Iraq, it recommitted the United States to counterinsurgency operations against the Taliban and allied groups in Afghanistan, authorizing a surge that brought peak troop levels to about one hundred thousand in June 2011 and redoubled civilian efforts. Pakistani safe havens stymied U.S. counterinsurgency efforts, though the CIA's targeted-killing program there has sought, in part, to fulfill a "force protection" mission where the U.S. military cannot operate.

But as the Pentagon withdrew the surge troops in 2012, further drew down its military footprint in 2013, and handed lead security authority over to Afghan forces in June of that year, the Taliban-led insurgency escalated.

The United Nations Assistance Mission in Afghanistan (UNAMA) documented 8,615 civilian deaths and injuries in 2013, a 14 percent increase over the previous year and the highest toll since it began keeping these records in 2009. UNAMA attributed the vast majority of these casualties to insurgents who deliberately targeted civilians or used such indiscriminate tactics as improvised explosive devices; other civilians were caught in the crossfire between insurgents and government forces.

In some outlying districts, Afghan forces and local insurgents have reached informal ceasefires that effectively cede a degree of authority to the Taliban. The UN reported in 2014 that the Taliban maintained outright control of four districts, out of 373 nationwide, but the insurgency's reach extends much further: Afghan security forces judged in late 2013 that some 40 percent of districts had a "raised" or "high" threat level.

## AN ELUSIVE ENDGAME IN AFGHANISTAN

Afghan forces have taken over nearly all combat operations, but some military analysts question whether they can keep the insurgency at bay as coalition forces draw down. Though NATO's combat mission expires at the end of 2014, a consultative *loya jirga,* a traditional grand assembly of tribal elders and community leaders, overwhelmingly endorsed a longer-term role for the U.S. military and its partners in helping secure the country.

That role is likely to be narrowly circumscribed, however. The United States has articulated a post-2014 mission focused exclusively on training Afghan forces and conducting counterterrorism operations against "the remnants of al-Qaeda." In May 2014, President Barack Obama announced a timetable calling for a complete U.S. withdrawal by the end of 2016. (This residual force is contingent on the Afghan government concluding agreements with the U.S. government and NATO; both candidates vying for the presidency have promised they would sign them.)

Some Afghans and U.S. military analysts see the U.S. withdrawal from Iraq in late 2011, which followed Washington and Baghdad's failure to agree on a renewed status-of-forces agreement, as a cautionary tale. After the last U.S. troops departed Iraq, Sunni insurgents unleashed levels of violence not seen since the height of the civil war several years prior, and made territorial gains across large swathes of the country.

Meanwhile, as an outright battlefield victory appeared unattainable, the United States came to believe by 2010 that political reconciliation "is the solution to ending the war". But talks between the Taliban and the central government have suffered repeated setbacks. Most notably, in September 2011, Kabul's chief negotiator, former president Rabbani, was assassinated. The Taliban has so far shown little interest in accepting the constitution and laying down its arms, while some civil society groups also oppose a negotiated settlement, fearing a backslide on women's rightsand other gains made in the past decade.

U.S.-Taliban talks have not fared better than those carried out by Kabul. Prospective negotiations mediated by Qatar in July 2013 were quickly scuttled after Afghan president Hamid Karzai objected to the manner in which the Taliban opened its office in Doha. The Obama administration had originally explored the prisoner swap of U.S. Army Sgt. Bowe Bergdahl for five Taliban officials as a potential confidence-building measure tethered to broader peace talks, but no such deal was in the works by the time the exchange went through in June 2014; it appears to have taken place as a one-off event.

Some of the White House's detractors contend that the surge's rigid timetable undermined U.S. leverage at a moment when maximum military pressure was brought to bear on the insurgency, and that the anticipated withdrawal has likewise diminished the Taliban's incentives to negotiate.

As coalition forces draw down, the Taliban has recast its mission from one resisting foreign occupation to one that is confronting a government it considers a Western pawn. Meanwhile, its battlefield position and financial interests further reduce its incentives to negotiate, analysts say. The UN says the Taliban and Afghan forces are at a "military stalemate." Other analyses are less optimistic about the central government's ability to hold its ground. The International Crisis Group reports that insurgents are increasingly confident as "ongoing withdrawals of international soldiers have generally coincided with a deterioration of Kabul's reach in outlying districts." An independent assessment of Afghan security forces commissioned by the Pentagon predicts that the Taliban will pick up the tempo of its operations and expand areas under its control between 2015 and 2018.

Meanwhile, strong revenues from a bumper poppy harvest in 2013 and other illicit trade have further reduced the Taliban's incentives to reach a negotiated settlement. Some Taliban factions have become less an ideology-driven armed opposition group than a profit-driven mafia, according to the UN. But while the insurgency remained formidable, the Taliban failed at one of its chief strategic objectives of 2014: mass disruption of Afghanistan's provincial and presidential elections.

## ECONOMIC, SOCIAL, POLITICAL AND SECURITY CONTEXT

To understand DFID's work in Afghanistan and its future strategy it is necessary to understand the economic, social, political and security context in which it currently works within country and what could potentially happen in the future.

### *Economic Context*

Afghanistan is one of the poorest countries in the world. A third of the population lives on less than 60p per day. Aid has supported much of its economic progress since 2001 and the Afghan Government remains heavily aid dependent. While the withdrawal of international combat forces will have its own economic impact, the World Bank also projects "an expected decline in civilian aid as international attention shifts elsewhere." The average growth rate has been 9% over the past nine years but it is expected to decrease to 5-6% from 2011 to 2018. Given that 70% of the population is under 25 years old and population growth is expected to continue at 2.8% annually, this is likely to mean continued high unemployment among the youth and little progress in reducing poverty.

The Afghan economy is largely dependent on agriculture and rural trade; around 85 % of the population is entirely reliant on income from agriculture and livestock. This is despite the fact that only 12 % of the country's land is arable and only half of that is currently under cultivation. Agricultural growth over the past decade has been volatile, in part due to Afghanistan's vulnerability to disasters, and improvements remain limited. Agriculture and livestock based livelihoods remain largely dependent upon the success of rain-fed crops and pasture. Afghanistan experienced its eighth drought in eleven years in 2011, devastating rural families and threatening any potential progress in alleviating rural poverty.

Afghanistan's agricultural economy is under developed. The British and Irish Agencies Afghanistan Group (BAAG) highlighted the lack of market knowledge and modern agricultural and business skills in Afghanistan. We heard while we were in Afghanistan that many agricultural products were sent to Pakistan to be processed or stored and then sold back to Afghanistan at much higher prices.

The illicit economy, particularly around opium, remains significant. The income from opium production in 2011 was estimated to be roughly equivalent to 9% of the GDP. Afghanistan is believed to supply roughly 93% of the opium on the world market and 90% of the heroin trafficked into the UK originated in Afghanistan. While poppy eradication and alternative livelihood programmes have had mixed results, a UN Office on Drugs and Crime report finds a "strong association" between insecurity, lack of agricultural assistance and poppy cultivation.

The big hope for the future Afghan economy is its potential mineral wealth. Initial estimates from the US Geological Survey have suggested a possible $3 trillion in mineral assets, based on a partial survey of the country. However, mining profits are not likely to come online for another decade and it is an industry that generally does not result in widespread national employment. It also requires a skilled and mobile workforce and infrastructure to exploit resources that are largely located in remote or mountainous areas of the country—none of which are currently evident in Afghanistan.

## AFGHAN TALIBAN

The Taliban were largely founded by Pakistan's Interior Ministry under Nasrullah Barbar and the Inter-Services Intelligence (ISI) in 1994. In 1999, Nasrullah Baber who was the minister of the interior under Bhutto during the Taliban's ascent to power admitted, "we created the Taliban".

William Maley, Professor at the Australian National University and Director of the Asia-Pacific College, writes on the emergence of the Taliban in Afghanistan:

"In 1994, with the failure of [Gulbuddin Hekmatyar's alliance] attempt to oust [the Afghan] Rabbani [administration], Pakistan found itself in an awkward position. Hekmatyar had proved incapable of seizing and controlling defended territory: in this respect he was a bitter disappointment to his patrons.... In October 1994, [Pakistani interior minister] Babar [took] a group of Western ambassadors (including the US Ambassador to Pakistan John C. Monjo) to Kandahar, without even bothering to inform the Kabul government, even though it manned an embassy in Islamabad.... On 29 October 1994, a convoy of trucks, including a notorious ISI officer, Sultan Amir... and two figures who were later to become prominent Taliban leaders, entered Afghanistan."

The ISI used the Taliban to establish a regime in Afghanistan which would be favourable to Pakistan, as they were trying to gain strategic depth. Since the creation of the Taliban, the ISI and the Pakistani military have given financial, logistical, military including direct combat support.

According to Pakistani Afghanistan expert Ahmed Rashid, "between 1994 and 1999, an estimated 80,000 to 100,000 Pakistanis trained and fought in Afghanistan" on the side of the Taliban. Peter Tomsen also stated that up until 9/11 Pakistani military and ISI officers along with thousands of regular Pakistani armed forces personnel had been involved in the fighting in Afghanistan.

*Human Rights Watch* wrote in 2000: "Of all the foreign powers involved in efforts to sustain and manipulate the ongoing fighting [in Afghanistan], Pakistan is distinguished both by the sweep of its objectives and the scale of its efforts, which include soliciting funding for the Taliban, bankrolling Taliban operations, providing diplomatic support as the Taliban's virtual emissaries abroad, arranging training for Taliban fighters, recruiting skilled and unskilled manpower to serve in Taliban armies, planning and directing offensives, providing and facilitating shipments of ammunition and fuel, and... directly providing combat support."

In 1998, Iran accused Pakistani commandos of "war crimes at Bamiyan". The same year Russia said, Pakistan was responsible for the "military expansion" of the Taliban in northern Afghanistan by sending large numbers of Pakistani troops including ISI personnel some of whom had subsequently been taken as prisoners by the anti-Taliban United Front (Northern Alliance).

In 2000, the UN Security Council imposed an arms embargo against military support to the Taliban, with UN officials explicitly singling out Pakistan. The UN secretary-general criticized Pakistan for its military support and the Security Council stated it was "deeply distress[ed] over reports of involvement in the fighting, on the Taliban side, of thousands of non-Afghan nationals." In July 2001, several countries including the United States, accused Pakistan of being "in violation of U.N. sanctions because of its military aid to the Taliban." The Taliban also obtained financial resources from Pakistan. In 1997 alone, after the capture of Kabul by the Taliban, Pakistan gave $30 million in aid and a further $10 million for government wages.

"The Taliban are not Islam - the Taliban areIslamabad. " After the 9/11 attacks, Pakistan claimed to have ended its support to the Taliban. But with the fall of Kabul to anti-Taliban forces in November 2001, ISI forces worked with and helped Taliban militias who were in full retreat. In November 2001, Taliban and Al-Qaeda combatants as well as Pakistani ISI and other military operatives were safely evacuated from the Afghan city of Kunduz on Pakistan Armycargo aircraft to Pakistan Air Force bases in Chitral and Gilgit in Pakistan's Northern Areas in what has been dubbed the "Airlift of Evil"

A range of officials inside and outside Pakistan have stepped up suggestions of links between the ISI and terrorist groups in recent years. In fall 2006, a leaked report by a British Defense Ministry think tank charged, "Indirectly Pakistan (through the ISI) has been supporting terrorism and extremism—whether in London on 7/7 [the July 2005 attacks on London's transit system], or in Afghanistan, or Iraq." In June 2008, Afghan officials accused Pakistan's intelligence service of plotting a failed assassination attempt on President Hamid Karzai; shortly thereafter, they implied the ISI's involvement in a July 2008 Taliban attack on the Indian embassy. Indian officials also blamed the ISI for the bombing of the Indian embassy. Numerous U.S. officials have also accused the ISI of supporting terrorist groups including the Afghan Taliban. U.S. Defense Secretary Robert Gates said "to a certain extent, they play both sides." Gates and others suggest the ISI maintains links with groups like the Afghan Taliban as a "strategic hedge" to help

Islamabad gain influence in Kabul once U.S. troops exit the region. U.S. Chairman of the Joint Chiefs of Staff Admiral Mike Mullen in 2011 called the Haqqani network (the Afghan Taliban's most destructive element) a "veritable arm of Pakistan's ISI". He further stated, "Extremist organizations serving as proxies of the government of Pakistan are attacking Afghan troops and civilians as well as US soldiers."

From 2010, a report by a leading British institution also claimed that Pakistan's intelligence service still today has a strong link with the Taliban in Afghanistan. Published by the London School of Economics, the report said that Pakistan's ISI has an "official policy" of support for the Taliban. It said the ISI provides funding and training for the Taliban, and that the agency has representatives on the so-called Quetta Shura, the Taliban's leadership council. The report, based on interviews with Taliban commanders in Afghanistan, was written by Matt Waldman, a fellow at Harvard University. "Pakistan appears to be playing a double-game of astonishing magnitude," the report said. The report also linked high-level members of the Pakistani government with the Taliban. It said Asif Ali Zardari, the Pakistani president, met with senior Taliban prisoners in 2010 and promised to release them. Zardari reportedly told the detainees they were only arrested because of American pressure. "The Pakistan government's apparent duplicity – and awareness of it among the American public and political establishment – could have enormous geopolitical implications," Waldman said. "Without a change in Pakistani behaviour it will be difficult if not impossible for international forces and the Afghan government to make progress against the insurgency." Amrullah Saleh, director of Afghanistan's intelligence service until June 2010, told Reuters in 2010 that the ISI was "part of a landscape of destruction in this country".

In March 2012, the Commander of NATO forces in Afghanistan, General John Allen, told the United States Senate that as of 2012 there was still no change in Pakistan's policy of support for the Afghan Taliban and its Haqqani network. When asked by U.S. Senator John McCain whether the ISI had severed its links with the Afghan Taliban, General Allen testified: "No."

### Recruitment

The Pakistani army through ISI have been accused of recruiting fighters and suicide bombers for the Afghan Taliban among the 1.7 million registered and 1-2 million unregistered Pashtun Afghan refugees living in refugee camps and settlements along the Afghan-Pakistan border in Pakistan many of whom have lived there since the Soviet war in Afghanistan.

Abdel Qadir, an Afghan refugee who returned to Afghanistan, says Pakistan's Inter-Services Intelligence had asked him to either receive training to join the Afghan Taliban or for him and his family to leave the country. He explains: "It is a step by step process. First they come, they talk to you. They ask you for the information.... Then gradually they ask you for people they can train and send [to Afghanistan].... They say, 'Either you do what we say, or you leave the country.'"

Janat Gul, another former refugee who returned to Afghanistan, told the UN Office for the Coordination of Humanitarian Affairs, that Afghan refugees which had been successfully recruited by the ISI were taken to Pakistani training camps which had previously been used during the times of the Soviet war in Afghanistan.

According to an investigative report among Afghan refugees inside Pakistan by the *New York Times*, people testified that "dozens of families had lost sons in Afghanistan as suicide bombers and fighters" and "families whose sons had died as suicide bombers in Afghanistan said they were afraid to talk about the deaths because of pressure from Pakistani intelligence agents, the ISI."

Pakistani and Afghan tribal elders also testified that the ISI was arresting or even killing Taliban members which wanted to quit fighting and refused to re-enlist to fight in Afghanistan or to die as suicide bombers. One former Taliban commander told the *New York Times* that such arrests were then sold to the Westerners and others as part of a supposed Pakistani collaboration effort in the War against Terror.

### Provision of Safe Haven

Gen. James L. Jones, then NATO's supreme commander, in September 2007 testified in front of the U.S. Senate Foreign Relations

Committee that the Afghan Taliban movement uses the Pakistani city of Quetta as their main headquarters. Pakistan's minister for information and broadcasting, Tariq Azim Khan, mocked the statement by saying, if there were any Taliban in Quetta, "you can count them on your fingers."

### *Training*

From 2002 until 2004, without major Taliban activities, Afghanistan witnessed relative calm with Afghan civilians and foreigners being able to freely and peacefully walk the streets of major cities and reconstruction being initiated. The 2010 testimonies of former Taliban commanders show that Pakistan through its Inter-Services Intelligence was however "actively encouraging a Taliban revival" from 2004-2006.

The effort to reintroduce the Afghan Taliban militarily in Afghanistan was preceded by a two-year, large-scale training campaign of Taliban fighters and leaders conducted by the ISI in several training camps in Quetta and other places in Pakistan. From 2004-2006 the Afghan Taliban consequently started a deadly insurgency campaign in Afghanistan killing thousands of civilians and combatants and thereby renewing and escalating the War in Afghanistan (2001-present). One Taliban commander involved in the Taliban resurgence said that 80 percent of his fighters had been trained in an ISI camp.

## HAQQANI NETWORK

The ISI have close links to the Haqqani network and contribute heavily to their funding. U.S. Chairman of the Joint Chiefs of Staff Admiral Mike Mullen in 2011 called the Haqqani network (the Afghan Taliban's most destructive element) a "veritable arm of Pakistan's ISI". He further stated:

"Extremist organizations serving as proxies of the government of Pakistan are attacking Afghan troops and civilians as well as US soldiers." —Former U.S. Chairman of the Joint Chiefs of Staff Mike Mullen, *2011*

Mullen said, the U.S. had evidence that the ISI directly planned and spar-headed the Haqqani 2011 assault on the U.S. embassy, the June 28 Haqqani attack against the Inter-Continental Hotel in Kabul and other operations. It is widely believed the suicide attack on the Indian embassy in Kabul was also planned with the help of the ISI A report in 2008 from the Director of National Intelligence stated that the ISI provides intelligence and funding to help with attacks against the International Security Assistance Force, the Afghan government and Indian targets.

### Al Qaeda

Besides supporting the Hezb-e Islami of Gulbuddin Hekmatyar, the ISI in conjunction with Saudi Arabia strongly supported the faction of Jalaluddin Haqqani (Haqqani network) and allied Arab groups such as the one surrounding financier Bin Laden, nowadays known as Al-Qaeda, during the war against the Soviets and the Afghan communist government in Afghanistan in the 1980s.

In 2000, British Intelligence reported that the ISI was taking an active role in several Al Qaeda training camps from the 1990s onwards. The ISI helped with the construction of training camps for both the Taliban and Al Qaeda. From 1996 to 2001 the Al Qaeda of Osama Bin Laden and Ayman al-Zawahiri became a state within the Pakistan-supported Taliban state. Bin Laden sent Arab and Central Asian Al-Qaeda militants to join the Taliban's and Pakistan's fight against the United Front (Northern Alliance) among them his Brigade 055.

It is believed that there is still contact between Al-Qaeda and the ISI today. The former Afghan intelligence chief Amrullah Saleh has repeatedly stated that Afghan intelligence believed and had shared information about Osama Bin Laden hiding in an area close to Abbottabad, Pakistan, four years before he (Bin Laden) was killed there. Saleh had shared the information with Pakistani President Pervez Musharraf who had angrily brushed off the claim taking no action.

In 2007, the Afghans specifically identified two Al-Qaeda safe houses in Manshera, a town just miles from Abbottabad, leading them to believe that Bin Laden was possibly hiding there. But Amrullah Saleh says that Pakistani President Pervez Musharraf angrily smashed his fist on a table when Saleh presented the information to him during a meeting in which Afghan President Hamid Karzai also took part. According to Saleh, "He said, 'Am I the president of the Republic of Banana?' Then he turned to President Karzai and said, 'Why have you brought this Panjshiri guy to teach me intelligence?'"

A December 2011 analysis report by the Jamestown Foundation comes to the conclusion that "in spite of denials by the Pakistani military, evidence is emerging that elements within the Pakistani military harboured Osama bin Laden with the knowledge of former army chief General Pervez Musharraf and possibly current Chief of Army Staff (COAS) General Ashfaq Pervez Kayani. Former Pakistani Army Chief General Ziauddin Butt (a.k.a. General Ziauddin Khawaja) revealed at a conference on Pakistani–U.S. relations in October 2011 that according to his knowledge the then former Director-General of Intelligence Bureau of Pakistan (2004–2008), Brigadier Ijaz Shah (retd.), had kept Osama bin Laden in an Intelligence Bureau safe house in Abbottabad." Pakistani General Ziauddin Butt said Bin Laden had been hidden in Abbottabad "with the full knowledge" of Pervez Musharraf. But later Butt denied making any such statement.

### Assassination of Pivotal Afghan Leaders

The ISI has been involved in the assassination of major Afghan leaders which have been described as pivotal for the future of Afghanistan. Among those leaders are the main anti-Taliban resistance leader and National Hero of Afghanistan Ahmad Shah Massoud and the prominent Pashtun anti-Soviet and anti-Taliban resistance leader Abdul Haq. The ISI has also been accused of having been involved in the murder of former Afghan president and chief of the Karzai's administration High Peace Council Burhanuddin Rabbaniand several other anti-Taliban leaders.

In the case of Ahmad Shah Massoud, who was killed by two Arab suicide bombers two days before September 11 attacks in the United States in 2001 ("9/11"), the Arab suicide assassins - supposed journalists - were granted with multiple entry visas valid for a year in early 2001 by Pakistan's embassy in London. As author and Afghanistan expert Sandy Gall writes such multiple visas for a year are "unheard of for journalists normally". The ISI subsequently facilitated the two men's passage through Pakistan over the Afghan border into Taliban territory. Afghan journalist Fahim Dashty says, "Al-Qaida, the Taliban, other terrorists, the Pakistan security services — they were all working together... to kill him."

Abdul Haq, who was killed by the Taliban on October 26, 2001, enjoying strong popular support among Afghanistan's Pashtuns wanted to create and support a popular uprising against the Taliban - also dominantly Pashtuns - among the Pashtuns. Observers believe that the Taliban were only able to capture him with the collaboration of the ISI.

Ahmad Shah Massoud had been the only resistance leader able to defend vast parts of his territory against the Taliban, Al-Qaeda and the Pakistani military and was sheltering hundreds of thousands of refugees which had fled the Taliban on the territory under his control. He had been seen as the leader most likely to lead post-Taliban Afghanistan. After his assassination, Abdul Haq was seen as one of the main contenders for that position. He had private American backers which had facilitated his re-entry into Afghanistan after 9/11. But journalists reported about tensions between the CIA and Haq. Former CIA director George Tenet reports that, at the recommendation of one of Haq's private American lobbyists Bud McFarlane, CIA officials met with Abdul Haq in Pakistan but after assessing him urged him not to enter Afghanistan. Both leaders, Massoud and Haq, were recognized for being fiercely independent from foreign especially Pakistani influence. Both, two of the most successful anti-Soviet resistance leaders, were rejecting the Pakistani claim of hegemony over the Afghan mujahideen.

Abdul Haq was quoted as saying during the anti-Soviet period: "How is that we Afghans, who never lost a war, must take military instructions from the Pakistanis, who never won one?" Massoud during the Soviet period said to the Pakistani Foreign Minister who had asked him to send a message to the Russians through the Pakistanis who were conducting talks "on behalf of our Afghan brethren": "Why should I send a message? Why are you talking on our behalf? Don't we have leaders here to talk on our behalf?"

Khan replied "This is how it has been and how it will be. Do you have a message?" Massoud told the foreign minister that "nobody who talks on our behalf will have any kind of result." Consequently, neither Massoud nor Abdul Haq were consulted before and neither participated in the Battle of Jalalabad (1989) in which the ISI tried but failed to install Gulbuddin Hekmatyar as the post-communist leader of Afghanistan.

### *Allegations of Drug Running*

It is alleged that the ISI have control over opium production and refining and also control all smuggling operations between Afghanistan and Pakistan. Wendy Chamberlin in testimony before the United States House of Representatives International Relations Committee stated that the ISI involvement in the drug trade was substantial.

## U.S. STRATEGY TOWARD THE TALIBAN DURING ITS RULE

The Clinton Administration opened talks with the Taliban after it captured Qandahar in 1994, and engaged the movement after it took power. However, the Administration was unable to moderate its policies and relations worsened throughout the Taliban period of rule. The United States withheld recognition of Taliban as the legitimate government of Afghanistan, formally recognizing no faction as the government. The United Nations continued to seat representatives of the Rabbani government, not the Taliban. The State Department ordered the Afghan embassy in Washington, DC, closed in August 1997. U.N. Security Council Resolution 1193 (August 28, 1998) and 1214 (December 8, 1998) urged the Taliban to end discrimination against women.

Women's rights groups urged the Clinton Administration not to recognize the Taliban government. In May 1999, the Senate-passed S.Res. 68 called on the President not to recognize an Afghan government that oppresses women.

The Taliban's hosting of Al Qaeda's leadership gradually became the Clinton Administration's overriding agenda item with Afghanistan. In April 1998, then-U.S. Ambassador to the United

Nations Bill Richardson (along with Assistant Secretary of State Karl Inderfurth and NSC senior official Bruce Riedel) visited Afghanistan, but the Taliban refused to hand over Bin Laden. They did not meet Mullah Umar. After the August 7, 1998, Al Qaeda bombings of U.S. embassies in Kenya and Tanzania, the Clinton Administration began to strongly pressure the Taliban to extradite him, imposing U.S. sanctions on Taliban-controlled Afghanistan and achieving adoption of some U.N. sanctions as well. On August 20, 1998, as a response to the Africa embassy bombings, the United States fired cruise missiles at alleged Al Qaeda training camps in eastern Afghanistan, but Bin Laden was not hit. Some observers assert that the Administration missed several other opportunities to strike him, including a purported sighting of him by an unarmed Predator drone at the Tarnak Farm camp in Afghanistan in the fall of 2000. Clinton Administration officials said that domestic and international support for ousting the Taliban militarily was lacking.

### The "Northern Alliance" Congeals

The Taliban's policies caused different Afghan factions to ally with the Tajik core of the anti-Taliban opposition—the ousted President Rabbani, Ahmad Shah Masud, and their ally in the Herat area, Ismail Khan. Joining the Tajik factions in the broader "Northern Alliance" were Uzbek, Hazara Shiite, and even some Pashtun Islamist factions. Virtually all the figures mentioned remain key players in politics in Afghanistan, sometimes allied with and at other times adversaries of President Hamid Karzai.

- Uzbeks/General Dostam. One major faction was the Uzbek militia (the Junbush-Melli, or National Islamic Movement of Afghanistan) of General Abdul Rashid Dostam. Frequently referred to by some Afghans as one of the "warlords" who gained power during the anti-Soviet war, Dostam first joined those seeking to oust Rabbani during his 1992-1996 presidency, but later joined him and the other Northern Alliance factions opposed to the Taliban.
- Hazara Shiites. Members of Hazara tribes, mostly Shiite Muslims, are prominent in Bamiyan, Dai Kundi, and Ghazni provinces (central Afghanistan) and are always fearful of,

and subject to some extent to, repression by Pashtuns and other larger ethnic factions. The Hazaras have tended to serve in working class and domestic household jobs, although more recently they have been prominent in technology jobs in Kabul, raising their economic status. They are also increasingly cohesive politically, leading to gains in the September 2010 parliamentary elections. During the various Afghan wars, the main Hazara Shiite militia was Hizb-e-Wahdat (Unity Party, composed of eight different groups). Hizb-e-Wahdat suffered a major setback in 1995 when the Taliban captured and killed its leader Abdul Ali Mazari. One of Karzai's vice president's Karim Khalili, is a Hazara. Another prominent Hazara faction leader, Mohammad Mohaqeq, is a Karzai critic.

- Pashtun Islamists/Sayyaf. Abd-i-Rab Rasul Sayyaf, now a leading Islamic conservative in parliament, headed a Pashtun-dominated hardline Islamist *mujahedin* faction (Islamic Union for the Liberation of Afghanistan, *Ittihad Islami*) during the anti-Soviet war. Even though he is an Islamist conservative, Sayyaf viewed the Taliban as selling out Afghanistan to Al Qaeda and he joined the Northern Alliance.

## Strategy Pre-September 11, 2001

Throughout 2001, but prior to the September 11 attacks, Bush Administration policy differed little from Clinton Administration policy—applying economic and political pressure on the Taliban while retaining some dialogue with it, and refraining from militarily assisting the Northern Alliance. The September 11 Commission report said that, in the months prior to the September 11 attacks, Administration officials leaned toward such a step. The report added that some officials wanted, in addition, to assist ethnic Pashtuns who were opposed to the Taliban. Other covert options were reportedly under consideration as well. In accordance with U.N. Security Council Resolution 1333, in February 2001 the State Department ordered the Taliban representative office in New York closed, although Taliban representative Abdul Hakim Mujahid continued to operate informally. In March 2001, Administration officials received a Taliban envoy to discuss bilateral issues. In one significant departure from Clinton Administration policy, the Bush Administration stepped up engagement with Pakistan to try to reduce its support for the Taliban. At that time, there were widespread but unconfirmed allegations by U.S. experts that Pakistani advisers were helping the Taliban in their fight against the Northern Alliance.

Even though the Northern Alliance was supplied with Iranian, Russian, and Indian financial and military support—all of whom had different motives for that support—the Northern Alliance nonetheless continued to lose ground to the Taliban after it lost Kabul in 1996. By the time of the September 11 attacks, the Taliban controlled at least 75% of the country, including almost all provincial capitals. The Alliance suffered a major setback on September 9, 2001 (two days before, and possibly an integral part of, the September 11 attacks), when Ahmad Shah Masud was assassinated by Al Qaeda operatives posing as journalists. He was succeeded by his intelligence chief, Muhammad Fahim, a veteran figure but one who lacked Masud's undisputed authority.

## SEPTEMBER 11 ATTACKS AND PROCESS ENDURING FREEDOM

After the September 11 attacks, the Bush Administration decided to militarily overthrow the Taliban when it refused a final U.S. offer to extradite Bin Laden in order to avoid military action. President Bush articulated a policy that equated those who harbor terrorists to terrorists themselves, and judged that a friendly regime in Kabul was needed to enable U.S. forces to search for Al Qaeda personnel there. The Administration sought and obtained U.N. backing: U.N. Security Council Resolution 1368 of September 12, 2001, said that the Council "expresses its readiness to take all necessary steps to respond (implying force) to the September 11 attacks."

This was widely interpreted as a U.N. authorization for military action in response to the attacks, but it did not explicitly authorize Operation Enduring Freedom to oust the Taliban. Nor did the Resolution specifically reference Chapter VII of the U.N. Charter, which allows for responses to threats to international peace and security.

In Congress, S.J.Res. 23 (passed 98-0 in the Senate and with no objections in the House, P.L. 107-40, signed September 18, 2011), was somewhat more explicit than the U.N. Resolution, authorizing "all necessary and appropriate force against those nations, organizations, or persons he determines planned, authorized, committed, or aided the terrorist attacks that occurred on September 11, 2001 *or harbored such organizations or persons*."

Major combat in Afghanistan (Operation Enduring Freedom, OEF) began on October 7, 2001. It consisted primarily of U.S. air-strikes on Taliban and Al Qaeda forces, facilitated by the cooperation between reported small numbers (about 1,000) of U.S. special operations forces and Central Intelligence Agency operatives. The purpose of these operations was to help the Northern Alliance and Pashtun anti-Taliban forces by providing information to direct U.S. air strikes against Taliban positions. In part, the U.S. forces and operatives worked with such Northern Alliance contacts as Fahim and Amrollah Saleh, who during November 2001-June 2010 served as Afghanistan's intelligence director, to weaken Taliban defenses on the Shomali plain north of Kabul (and just south of Bagram Airfield, which marked the forward position of the Northern Alliance during Taliban rule). Some U.S. combat units (about 1,300 Marines) moved into Afghanistan to pressure the Taliban around Qandahar at the height of the fighting (October-December 2001), but there were few pitched battles between U.S. and Taliban soldiers.

The Taliban regime unraveled rapidly after it lost Mazar-e-Sharif on November 9, 2001, to forces led by Dostam. Northern Alliance (mainly the Tajik faction) forces—the commanders of which had initially promised then-Secretary of State Colin Powell that they would not enter Kabul— entered the capital on November 12, 2001, to popular jubilation. The Taliban subsequently lost the south and east to U.S.-supported Pashtun leaders, including Hamid Karzai. The end of the Taliban regime is generally dated as December 9, 2001, when the Taliban surrendered Qandahar and Mullah Umar fled the city, leaving it under Pashtun tribal law.

Subsequently, U.S. and Afghan forces conducted "Operation Anaconda" in the Shah-i-Kot Valley south of Gardez (Paktia Province) during March 2-19, 2002, against 800 Al Qaeda and Taliban fighters. In March 2003, about 1,000 U.S. troops raided suspected Taliban or Al Qaeda fighters in villages around Qandahar (Operation Valiant Strike). On May 1, 2003, then-Secretary of Defence Rumsfeld announced an end to "major combat."

## *Post-Taliban Governance-Building hard Work*

The Bush Administration argued that leaving the region after the 1989 Soviet pullout allowed Afghanistan to degenerate into chaos, and it decided to try to build a relatively strong Afghan central government and economy, both of which were devastated by decades of war. The effort, which many outside experts described as "nation-building," was supported by the United Nations, international institutions, and U.S. partners in several post-Taliban international meetings.

The Obama Administration's strategy review in late 2009 narrowed official U.S. goals to preventing terrorism safe haven in Afghanistan and Pakistan. However, the elements of Obama Administration strategy during 2009-2011 continued, and in some cases expanded, the nation-building programs put in place by the Bush Administration. No matter how expansively the U.S. mission has been defined, building the capacity of and reforming Afghan governance— particularly reducing governmental corruption— have been consistently and widely judged to be key to the success of U.S. policy. This has been stated explicitly in each Obama Administration policy review, strategy statement, and report on progress in Afghanistan, as well as all major international conferences on Afghanistan, including the major conference in Bonn on December 5, 2011. That was held at the 10th anniversary of the Bonn Agreement that began the post-Taliban political transition.

## *U.S. and global Civilian Policy Structure*

Building the capacity of the Afghan government, and helping it develop economically, is primarily, although not exclusively, the purview of U.S. and international civilian officials and institutions.

In line with the prioritization of Afghanistan policy, in February 2009, the Administration set up the position of appointed "Special Representative for Afghanistan and Pakistan" (SRAP), occupied first by Ambassador Richard Holbrooke, reporting to Secretary of State Clinton. Holbrooke died on December 13, 2010, but his team at the State Department, led as of February 2011 by Ambassador Marc Grossman, remains largely intact, consisting mainly of members detailed from several different agencies.

At the U.S. Embassy in Kabul, Ambassador Ryan Crocker replaced Karl Eikenberry on July 25, 2011. There is a "deputy Ambassador" and separate Ambassador rank officials to manage U.S. economic assistance issues and to oversee Embassy operations. Another official of Ambassador rank coordinates U.S. rule of law programs. Under various programs, U.S. civilian and coalition military personnel are assigned to various Afghan ministries in advisory capacities. Some of those programs were briefly interrupted in late February—early March 2012 after the killing of two U.S. military personnel at the Afghan Interior Ministry by a ministry employee angered by the mistaken U.S. burnings of several Qurans on February 20, 2012.

The U.S. Embassy has progressively expanded its personnel and facilities to accommodate the additional civilian hires and Foreign Service officers who have been posted to Afghanistan since 2009: As mentors and advisers to the Afghan government. U.S. officials say there are more than 1,130 U.S. civilian officials in Afghanistan, as of late 2011, up from only about 400 in early 2009. Of these at least 400 serve outside Kabul as part of initiatives such as the 32 "District Support Teams" and the "District Working Groups." That is up from 67 outside Kabul in 2009.

On February 7, 2010, in an effort to improve civilian coordination between the United States, its foreign partners, and the Afghan government, a NATO "Senior Civilian Representative" in Afghanistan, UK Ambassador Mark Sedwill, took office. This official works not only with U.S. military officials but with representatives of the embassies of partner countries and with a special U.N. Assistance Mission-Afghanistan. In April 2011 Sedwill was replaced by the former British Ambassador to Iran, Sir Simon

Gass. The contribution of the United Nations to enhancing governance and coordinating donors.

Afghan Ambassador to the United States Sayed Tayib Jawad served as Ambassador from 2004 until his recall in August 2010. Then deputy Foreign Minister Eklil Hakimi replaced him on February 23, 2011.

### *Security Policy, 2011-2014 "Transition, and Beyond"*

The formal Obama Administration policy goal is to prevent Afghanistan from again becoming a safe haven for global terrorism, but the U.S. criteria for judging achievement of that goal have generally included the degree to which the Afghan government and security force can defend itself, govern effectively, and develop economically. U.S. plans discussed by Defence Secretary Panetta in early 2012 envision an accelerated transition to Afghan security lead, with the U.S. and partner forces adopting a mentoring "overwatch" role by mid-2013. This raises questions as to whether the Administration might be reducing some of its goals in the interests of more rapidly winding down U.S. involvement in Afghanistan. Still, the basic pillars of U.S. and NATO security strategy that have been in place since 2001 remain intact.

### *Who Is "The Enemy"? Taliban, Haqqani, Al Qaeda, and Others*

Security in Afghanistan is being challenged by a confluence of related and, to varying degrees, cooperating armed groups whose tactics continue to evolve based on experiences from previous fighting. There has not been agreement about the relative strength of insurgents in all of the areas where they operate. The top commander in Afghanistan, General John Allen, told journalists in October 2011 that the numbers of insurgents may be far fewer than the 25,000 previously assessed.

### *Groups: The Taliban ("Quetta Shura Taliban")*

The core of the insurgency remains the Taliban movement loyal, for the most part, to Mullah Umar, who led the Taliban regime during 1996-2001. He and many of his top advisers reportedly operate from Pakistan, probably the city of Quetta but possibly also Karachi, thus accounting for the term usually applied to Umar and his aides: "Quetta Shura Taliban" (QST). Still, the exact level of Mullah Umar's control over insurgent ranks is unclear, and little precise information exists on Mullah Umar's remaining inner circle. In recent years, he has lost some of this top aides to U.S.-led military action, including Mullah Dadullah and Mullah Usmani.

Umar has been making appointments to replenish the QST leadership ranks. When his top deputy, Mullah Bradar, was arrested in Pakistan in February 2011, Umar replaced him with younger and reputedly hardline, anti-compromise leaders Mullah Abdul Qayyum Zakir, a U.S. detainee in Guantanamo Bay, Cuba until 2007; and Akhtar Mohammad Mansoor, a logistics expert. The Taliban has several official spokespersons still at large, including Qari Yusuf Ahmadi and Zabiullah Mujahid, and it operates a clandestine radio station, "Voice of Shariat" and publishes videos.

Some believe that Umar and his inner circle blame their past association with Al Qaeda for their loss of power. Others believe the Taliban is unlikely to completely sever its ties to Al Qaeda and other terrorist groups, but the death of Al Qaeda founder Osama Bin Laden on May 1, 2011, has perhaps strengthened the arguments of those in the movement advocating distance from Al Qaeda. U.S. officials argue that the successes produced by the U.S. "surge" in Afghanistan are causing some Taliban leaders to at least consider the concept of a political settlement, and in the process causing a reported split in its ranks over the issue. Suggesting he may be leaning toward those urging compromise, Mullah Umar released a statement on the 10th anniversary of the September 11 attacks on the United States (September 11, 2011) acknowledging there have been some talks, although only over prisoner exchanges. His subsequent statement marking a Muslim holiday on November 10, 2011 admonished Taliban commanders to avoid causing civilian casualties.

## AFGHAN NATION-STATE

Mir Wais Hotak, seen as Afghanistan's George Washington, successfully rebelled against the Persian Safavids in 1709. He overthrew and killed Gurgin Khan, and made the Afghan region independent from Persia. By 1713, Mirwais had decisively defeated two larger Persian armies, one was led by Khusraw Khán (nephew of Gurgin) and the other by Rustam Khán. The armies were sent by Sultan Husayn, the Shah in Isfahan (now Iran), to re-take control of the Kandahar region.Mirwais died of a natural cause in 1715 and was succeeded by his brother Abdul Aziz followed by his son Mahmud. In 1722, Mahmud led an Afghan army to the Persian capital of Isfahan, sacked the city after the Battle of Gulnabad and proclaimed himself King of Persia. The Persians were disloyal to the Afghan rulers, and after the massacre of thousands of religious scholars, nobles, and members of the Safavid family, the Hotaki dynasty was ousted from Persia after the 1729 Battle of Damghan.

In 1738, Nader Shah and his Afsharid forces captured Kandahar from Shah Hussain Hotaki, at which point the incarcerated 16 year old Ahmad Shah Durrani was freed and made the commander of Nader Shah's four thousand Abdali Afghans.

From Kandahar they set out to conquer India, passing through Ghazni, Kabul, Lahore and ultimately plundering Delhi after the Battle of Karnal. Nader Shah and his army abandoned Delhi but took with them huge treasure, which included the Koh-i-Noor andDarya-ye Noor diamonds. After the death of Nader Shah in 1747, the Afghans chose Ahmad Shah Durrani as their head of state. Regarded as the founder of modern Afghanistan, Durrani and his Afghan army conquered the entire present-day Afghanistan, Pakistan, Khorasan and Kohistanprovinces of Iran, along with Delhi in India. He defeated the Sikhs of the Maratha Empire in thePunjab region nine times, one of the biggest battles was the 1761 Battle of Panipat.

In October 1772, Ahmad Shah Durrani died of a natural cause and was buried at a site now adjacent to the Shrine of the Cloak in Kandahar. He was succeeded by his son, Timur Shah Durrani, who transferred the capital of Afghanistan from Kandahar to Kabul in 1776. After Timur Shah's death in 1793, the Durrani throne was passed down to his son Zaman Shah followed by Mahmud Shah, Shuja Shah and others.

The Afghan Empire was under threat in the early 19th century by the Sikhs in the east and the Persians in the west. The western provinces of Khorasan and Kohistan were taken by the Persians in 1800. The biggest blow to Afghans however came on 13th July 1813, when the Vizier of Afghanistan Fateh Khan and his brother Dost Mohammad Khan came face to face with Sikh armies atAttock(Battle of Attock). The Sikh armies as usual were led by their famous Hindu General Diwan Mokham Chand who was 70 years old at that time, the battle saw the gruesome massacre of Afghan armies, over 9,000 Afghan soldiers laid their lives in this battle, Dost Mohammad Khan save himself with great difficulty whereas Vizier Fateh Khan fled back even before the Afghans were defeated.. The defeat created a sensation in Kabul the capital of Durrani Empire, the defeat of the Wazir of Afghanistan by Mohkam Chand roused fear in Afghans that Sikhs may now march upon Kabul. However the grand victory of Sikh Armies coincided with the Holy Festival of Diwali which is celebrated by Hindu, Sikhs, Jains and Buddhists which resulted in the return of victorious Sikh armies and their Famous Hindu General Mohkam Chand back to Lahore(Now In Pakistan). This defeat ended the Afghans dream of regaining Panjab and instead push Afghans on more defensive approach. Post this defeat Afghans mostly fought defensive battles. Another Hindu General Diwan Misr Chand plundered Afghan general Jabbar Khan in Kashmir in 1819 which saw the end of Muslim rule over Kashmir(1339-1819).

The Sikhs of Punjab, under Ranjit Singh, invaded Afghanistan's Khyber Pakhtunkhwa region and in 1834 captured its second capital, Peshawar. The regions of Multan, Kashmir, Sindh and Balochistan were also lost. Fateh Khan, leader of the Barakzai tribe, had installed 21 of his brothers in positions of power throughout the Afghan Empire. After his death, they rebelled and divided up the provinces of the empire between themselves. During this turbulent period, Afghanistan had many temporary rulers until 1826 when Dost Mohammad Khan rose to power. In 1837, Akbar Khan and the Afghan army crossed the Khyber Pass to defeat the Sikhs at the Battle of Jamrud, killing Sikh Commander Hari Singh Nalwa .. However, the arrival of the Sikh army under Wazir Dhyan Singh Dogra and his elder brother Maharaja Gulab

Singh in the vicinity of Jamrud didn't allow the Afghans to occupy the Jamrud fort. Akbar Khan and his Afghan army fled back to Kabul. By this time the British were advancing to the area from the east and the First Anglo-Afghan War or better known as the Great Game was initiated.

### Western Influence

Following the 1842 Battle of Gandamak that was fought between Akbar Khan and William Elphinstone, the British established diplomatic relations with the Afghan government but withdrew all forces from the country. They returned during the Second Anglo-Afghan War in the late 1870s for about two year military operations, which was to defeat Ayub Khan and assist Abdur Rahman Khan establish authority. The United Kingdom began to exercise a great deal of influence after this and even controlled the state's foreign policy. In 1893,Mortimer Durand made Amir Abdur Rahman Khan sign a controversial agreement in which the ethnic Pashtun and Baloch territories were divided by the Durand Line. This was a standard divide and rule policy of the British and would lead to strained relations, especially with the later new state of Pakistan.

After the Third Anglo-Afghan War and the signing of the Treaty of Rawalpindi in 1919, KingAmanullah Khan declared Afghanistan a sovereignand fully independent state. He moved to end his country's traditional isolation by establishing diplomatic relations with the international community and, following a 1927–28 tour of Europe and Turkey, introduced several reforms intended to modernize his nation. A key force behind these reforms was Mahmud Tarzi, an ardent supporter of the education of women. He fought for Article 68 of Afghanistan's 1923 constitution (declared through a loya jirga), which made elementary education compulsory.

Some of the reforms that were actually put in place, such as the abolition of the traditionalburqa for women and the opening of a number of co-educational schools, quickly alienated many tribal and religious leaders. Faced with overwhelming armed opposition, Amanullah Khan was forced to abdicate in January

1929 after Kabul fell to rebel forces led by Habibullah Kalakani. Prince Mohammed Nadir Shah, Amanullah's cousin, in turn defeated and killed Kalakani in November 1929, and was declared King Nadir Shah. He abandoned the reforms of Amanullah Khan in favor of a more gradual approach to modernisation but was assassinated in 1933 by Abdul Khaliq, a Hazara school student.

Mohammed Zahir Shah, Nadir Shah's 19-year-old son, succeeded to the throne and reigned from 1933 to 1973. Until 1946 Zahir Shah ruled with the assistance of his uncle, who held the post of Prime Minister and continued the policies of Nadir Shah. Another of Zahir Shah's uncles, Shah Mahmud Khan, became Prime Minister in 1946 and began an experiment allowing greater political freedom, but reversed the policy when it went further than he expected. He was replaced in 1953 by Mohammed Daoud Khan, the king's cousin and brother-in-law. Daoud Khan sought a closer relationship with the Soviet Union and a more distant one towards Pakistan. Afghanistan remained neutral and was neither a participant inWorld War II, nor aligned with either power bloc in the Cold War. However, it was a beneficiary of the latter rivalry as both the Soviet Union and the United States vied for influence by building Afghanistan's main highways, airports and other vital infrastructure. By the late 1960s, many Western travelers were using these as part of the hippie trail. In 1973, while King Zahir Shah was on an official overseas visit, Daoud Khan launched a bloodless coup and became the first President of Afghanistan.

## MARXIST REVOLUTION AND SOVIET WAR

In April 1978, a prominent member of the People's Democratic Party of Afghanistan (PDPA),Mir Akbar Khyber, was mysteriously killed. Leaders of the PDPA feared that the government was planning to dismantle them because many were being arrested. Hafizullah Amin along with other PDPA members managed to remain at large and organised an uprising. The PDPA, led by Nur Mohammad Taraki, Babrak Karmal and Hafizullah Amin, overthrew the regime of Daoud by assassinating the President along with his family and relatives. Taraki quickly took over and moved to carry out an ill-conceived land reform, which was misunderstood by virtually all Afghans. The PDPA began imprisoning, torturing and murdering thousands of members of the traditional elite, the religious establishment, and the intelligentsia. On the other hand, they prohibited usury, made statements on women's rights by declaring equality of the sexes and introducing women to political life.Anahita Ratebzad was one of several female Marxist leaders and a member of the Revolutionary Council.

As part of its Cold War strategy, the United States strengthened political ties with Pakistan although Zbigniew Brzezinski, National Security Advisor to U.S. President Jimmy Carter, has warned that this might prompt a Soviet intervention. The Central Intelligence Agency (CIA) began using Pakistan's Inter-Services Intelligence (ISI) as a proxy network to recruit, finance and arm the multinational Mujahideen fighters inside Pakistan, which was aimed to prevent the Soviet Union from reaching the oil-rich Persian Gulf through Balochistan. In March 1979, Hafizullah Amin took over as Prime Minister of Afghanistan, retaining the position of field marshal and becoming Vice-President of the Supreme Defence Council. Taraki remained the president and in control of the army until he was killed in September 1979.

To bolster the Parcham faction and as part of its Cold War strategy to ultimately reach Gwadar in Balochistan, the Soviet Union decided to invade Afghanistan in December 1979 by sending 100,000 soldiers of the Red Army to its southern neighbor. In the meantime, Hafizullah Amin was killed and replaced by Babrak Karmal. In response to all these, theReagan administration in the U.S. increased arming and funding of the Mujahideen, thanks in large part to the efforts of Charlie Wilson and CIA officer Gust Avrakotos.

Early reports estimated \$6–20 billion but more recent reports suggest that up to \$40 billion were provided by the U.S. and Saudi Arabia to Pakistan. This was in the forms of cash and weapons, which included over two thousand FIM-92 Stinger surface-to-air missiles. The money and weapons were directly given to Pakistani Armed Forces, which was distributed by its ISI network to various Mujahideen groups although much of it was secretly kept for Pakistan's own defense and other purposes. Despite receiving only minor aid compared to leaders of other Mujahideen groups, Ahmad Shah Massoud was named "the Afghan who won the Cold War" by *The Wall Street Journal*.

The 10-year Soviet war resulted in the deaths of over 1 million Afghans, mostly civilians and due to land-mines. About 6 million fled to Pakistan and Iran, and from there tens of thousands began emigrating to the European Union, United States, Australiaand other parts of the world. Faced with mounting international pressure and great number of casualties, the Soviets withdrew in 1989 but continued to support Afghan President Mohammad Najibullah until 1992.

## UNDERMINING HUMANITARIAN PRINCIPLES

Humanitarian aid is based on the principles drawn in the humanitarian code of conduct in which all NGHAs are committed to act accordingly. The essence of these principles – Humanity, Neutrality and Impartiality – is to deliver humanitarian assistance to the vulnerable and needy population regardless of race, ethnic, nationality and political background. Since the PRTs are deployed in Afghanistan for a military and political purpose, therefore; they cannot be perceived as humanitarian actors. The humanitarian actors expressed their concerns continuously about the issue. Save the Children Fund, for instance, declared the humanitarian involvement of military as: "*inappropriate and contrary to the fundamental humanitarian principles of independence and impartiality*" (Hugh, 2004). Some may argue that the military occupying power has a mandate to ensure the safety and security of the civilian population or NGHAs in the unstable and unsecure environments based on International Humanitarian Law and the 4$^{th}$ Geneva Convention. This never means that the occupying military power can deliver humanitarian aid directly, nor it can legally justify involvement of military in relief operations. In contrast, the present military involvement in delivering humanitarian and development assistance is in violation of international humanitarian principles.

In another instance, a press release by NATO/ISAF on December 2007, declared that: "Humanitarian assistance operations are helping both the people of Afghanistan and coalition forces to fight the global war on terror" (ISAF, 2007). The integration of humanitarian assistances with a political agenda of war on terror has significantly undermined the principle of neutrality of NGHAs among the local Afghan population. Moreover, according to Donini (2009, p.2) ICRC is the only international organization that is able to operate neutrally, impartially and independently on both sides of the warring parties. However, thousands of NGHAs are operating in Afghanistan after the fall of Taliban.

## Overlapping Interventions

In principle, the roles and responsibilities of PRTs and NGHAs are sharply different, however; in practice these responsibilities are extremely blurred. Under this circumstance, development and humanitarian actors have expressed their concerns about the overlapping of certain implemented projects in the field (Hugh, 2004).

An assessment conducted by the Asian Development Bank (ADB) on Security of ADB Projects in Afghanistan in 2007 revealed a couple of substantial PRT interventions that contradict Article 32.4 of the United Nations Guideline for Civil-Military Cooperation. Here, the paper quotes some of the ADB assessment findings:

"*Some PRTs include projects linked to health care, education, water supply or waste clearance, in this, there is an overlap with NGO programmes*" (Marsden & Arnold, 2007; p.30)

"*There is some evidence that some PRTs have provided cash to power holders or individual villagers in an effort to win influence*" (Marsden & Arnold, 2005; p.31).

"*Some PRTs, including those led by Spain and Italy, use military personnel for development work*" (Marsden & Arnold, 2007, p.30).

As a result of PRT's constant intrusions without respecting the enacted civil-military cooperation guidelines, the United Nations Office for the Coordination of Humanitarian Aid (UNOCHA) described the increasing influence of military in humanitarian activities as follows:

"*In NATO and elsewhere there has been an evolution of the doctrine of military–civilian operations, with an increasing tendency for military forces being used to support the delivery of humanitarian aid, and sometimes even to provide this aid directly* (Barry and Jefferys,2001, p. 1).

Moreover, another critique against the PRTs involvement in the development and humanitarian sphere is their unprofessionalism. The military actors are not well-trained to implement complex cross-cutting and mutually reinforcing projects at the community level. This awkwardness is bolded in the areas of rebuilding the political institutions and effectively engaging with civil society actors (Jenny, 2007).

### *Fuelling Violence*

Increased violence against humanitarian aid workers is another consequence of the current ineffective civil-military cooperation in Post-Taliban Afghanistan. In the list of fragile countries where the level of violence against aid workers is enormously high, Afghanistan is positioned in third place. Relief operations by PRTs notably raised acts of violence against NGHAs. In 2004, for instance, five employee of Médecins Sans Frontières (MSF) were targeted and killed by insurgent. As a result, MSF evacuated its staff and stopped operating in Afghanistan. Moreover, an assessment conducted by the German Institute for International and Security Affairs, revealed that the security environment in northern provinces of Afghanistan has deteriorated and level of violence against aid workers has increased since the deployment of the German Military (Lange, 2008). It is noteworthy that the northern provinces of Afghanistan were considered highly secured regions after the fall of Taliban regime.

Appendix one is produced by Afghanistan NGO Security Organization (ANSO) which shows a 60% increase in the abduction of aid workers over the year 2009 (ANSO Annual Report, 2011). According to the Afghanistan NGO Safety Office (ANSO) the increased nature of insurgents' attacks on NGHAs, are functionally linked with a misperception that NGHAs have political and military agendas (Cornish & Glad, 2008). Such views were strongly publicised by the various international high officials like Colin Powell, the former US Secretary of States, who said: "NGOs are the force multiplier" (Runge, 2007). Ultimately, the consequences of such publications were the death of 1500 civilians who were targeted by different insurgency attacks in 2010. Furthermore, a report by UNAMA contrasts the level of violence in 2001 with the level of violence in 2007. According to the report, in 2001 only 3 suicide attacks were carried out in Afghanistan, while after five years of international military presence in Afghanistan, this figure increased 53 times. In other words, 160 suicide bombing attacks were conducted by insurgents in 2006 (UNAMA, 2007).

### *Reducing Humanitarian Space*

The increased level of violence, is a restricting factor for the presence of NGHAs in most of the local Afghan communities. Humanitarian actors need "Humanitarian Space" (Runge, 2007) in the conflict affected areas to independently and impartially identify conflict victims to assist them. This humanitarian space is getting limited, especially when PRTs interfere in providing aid by wearing civilian uniforms and driving unmarked vehicles in the local communities. This humanitarian nature of the military posed another serious threat to the security of NGHAs since there is no distinguishing indicator left between them and the PRTs. MSF, for instance, was among those NGHAs that found itself in an eroded humanitarian space. The justification given by MSF, after evacuating its staff and stopping all its operations in Afghanistan, was increased level of violence against their employees as a consequence of military involvement in providing humanitarian aid in the ground. In another instance, a UK quartered NGO left its projects and withdrew from Kamdesh District because a US armed team visited the community without informing the local authorities in advance and prior consultation with the NGO (Afghanistan Group, 2008, p. 22).

In appendix two, the figures shown in the circles are the total number of armed NATO forces in each province. Regions that are coloured in red means a 50% of growth in Armed Opposition Groups (AOG) attacks. It is interesting to see in Herat Province, for instance, the number of NATO forces is fewer – 6,700 forces – compared to Helmand – 31,000 forces – but still the level of violence in Helmand had a 50% growth over the year 2009. This shows that the presence of military in the local Afghan communities have contributed to the growth of violence.

To condemn the erosion of humanitarian space in Afghanistan, The Agency Coordinating Body for Afghan Relief (ACBAR) released a statement in 2007, mentioning that:

*"Humanitarian actors are increasingly unable to provide adequate protection and assistance to displaced people and other populations at risk in the south and east of Afghanistan due to the significant deterioration in the security situation. Humanitarian space and humanitarian access continues to be seriously limited"* (ACBAR, 2007).

Moreover, existence of great insecurity against the NGHAs significantly decreased the possibilities of accessing the needy population in most of the Afghan communities. Studies carried out by UNHCR and ICRC demonstrates that large part of the country is inaccessible by NGHAs. UNHCR claimed that in 2008, they only had access to 55% of the country and ICRC declared that the humanitarian access situation was the worst in the last 27 years in Afghanistan in 2008 (Norton-Tylor, 2008).

3

# Afghan-Pakistan Border Rules

## BORDER TENSIONS

Following the U.S. military intervention in the fall of 2001, the Afghan Taliban, along with some members of al-Qaeda and other foreign Islamist fighters, established sanctuaries in northwest Pakistan, specifically in the Federally Administrative Tribal Areas (FATA). This region has long enjoyed substantial autonomy from Pakistan's central government based in Islamabad, but lacks equal political representation and social development. The region has been a buffer zone operating under its own paramilitary forces and police and ruled directly by the President of Pakistan via the Governor of the North West Frontier Province, now known as Khyber Pakhtunkhwa. The FATA consists of Bajaur, Mohmand, Khyber, Kurram, North Waziristan, and South Waziristan. The presence of large ethnic Pashtun tribes on both sides of the 2,430-kilometer (1,510 mile) Afghan-Pakistan frontier facilitates the infiltration of Taliban insurgents, many of whom are ethnic Pashtuns. An estimated 40-50 million Pashtuns (some 29 million in Pakistan and 12.5 million in Afghanistan) live on either side of the Durand Line, which formally divided the territory of Afghanistan and

Pakistan (then part of the British Raj) in 1893. The Pakistani government considers the line a formal international border, but the government of Afghanistan does not. From the perspective of the Afghan Taliban and other terrorists, the FATA has several advantages: the region is remote and largely under the control of sympathetic tribal leaders who exercise considerable autonomy. It provides a sanctuary where they can recruit, train, and supply their fighters. The porous borders permit easy infiltration of men and material into Afghanistan or into other areas of Pakistan where they can attack the coalition supply lines that traverse Pakistani territory. In the eyes of many Pashtuns, Pakistan's Punjabi majority clearly dominates the Pakistani regime, while Afghanistan's minority ethnic groups – Uzbeks, Hazaras, and Tajiks – exert greater influence over Afghanistan's central government than their minority status would seem to warrant. These circumstances allow the Taliban to claim to represent the aspirations of the Pashtuns better. Pakistan has made a greater effort than Afghanistan to seal the border, having established many more border checkpoints and at times suggesting that the border be mined or fenced. The Afghan government has always rejected such proposals as likely to aggravate Pashtun anger over the division of their tribal units.

The Afghan Taliban are presently divided into three main groups: the Mullah Omar group, known to the West as the Quetta Shura because of the belief that its leadership has found refuge near the city of Quetta in Pakistani Balochistan; the Haqqani Network of Jalaluddin and his son Sirajuddin Haqqani, which operates out of North Waziristan and the bordering Afghan provinces of Paktia, Paktika, and Khost; and the Hizb-i-Islami of Gulbuddin Hekmatyar, a former Mujahideen leader now operating from the Nuristan area. The Tehreek-e-Taliban of Pakistan (TTP) is the strongest member of the Pakistan Taliban. The Haqqani movement is reported to be the most violent group, engaged in criminal operations such as smuggling and kidnapping. It also conducts guerrilla operations in eastern Afghanistan, and is suspected of having extremely close ties with the Pakistani intelligence service. There is hope that the Haqqanis might be bought off for the right price. The Afghan government has already sought to negotiate with the leaders of the other two groups and reintegrate any of their members who decide to lay down arms and reenter civilian life. Both these initiatives have met with minimal success. Following the assassination of the head of the Afghan government's peace commission in September 2011 by a suicide bomber claiming to be a Taliban peace envoy, President Hamid Karzai announced that he was focusing his peace efforts on the Pakistani government pending more credible evidence that the other groups would be willing to negotiate in good faith. He has also launched new diplomatic outreach initiatives to India and Iran.

Starting around 2005, Hamid Karzai and Pervez Musharraf repeatedly clashed over who was responsible for the deteriorating security situation along their joint border. Karzai advocated the expanded use of air strikes and ground raids into Pakistan, while Musharraf called on Karzai to get his own house in order. Proposals to seal the border were raised, but are impractical.

The Pashtun population is located on both sides of the border and has enjoyed the right to cross the Afghan-Pakistan border on a routine basis without a visa. Some 80,000 people can also legally cross the border on special permits. Pakistan still hosts more than 3 million Afghan refugees that can readily cross back home. Meanwhile, alarmed U.S. officials became aware of the growing evidence that al-Qaeda was re-establishing its main base of operations in the FATA. They warned that any future 9/11-style attack against the United States from al-Qaeda would probably originate from the group's new safe haven in the FATA. In 2008, the Chairman of the Joint Chiefs of Staff, Admiral Michael Mullen, singled out the terrorist camps in northwest Pakistan as one of the most serious threats confronting the next U.S. presidential administration: "Al-Qaida is there. Its leadership is there. We know that. And it continues to plan against the West, including against our homeland."

U.S. policy makers recognize that overt U.S. military incursions into Pakistan can prove counterproductive by antagonizing the local population and making the friendly Pakistani government look weak. For this reason, they have employed other tools for countering terrorism in northwest Pakistan. Since 2001, the United States has provided the Afghan and Pakistani governments and militaries with considerable money, training, equipment, and other security assistance. In addition, the United States has targeted some of its economic aid to the border region directly. Furthermore, the United States exchanges intelligence data directly with the Afghan and Pakistani governments. Finally, the United States has sought to enhance cooperation between the Afghan and Pakistani governments regarding security along their mutual border. For example, the Bush administration helped convene the innovative "Joint Peace Jirga" that took place in Kabul from August 9-12, 2007. More than 600 representatives from Afghanistan and Pakistan attended this unprecedented council of tribal and government leaders. In addition, Washington also helped establish a Joint Intelligence Operations Centre in Kabul. The centre provides a forum where analysts from Afghanistan, Pakistan and the NATO-led International Security Assistance Force (ISAF) can share and evaluate data about terrorist activities along the Afghan-Pakistani border.

Unfortunately, none of these instruments appears to have proven very effective at reconciling Afghanistan and Pakistan or curbing the flow of men and material across their joint border. In its November 2010 progress report to Congress on the Afghan war, the Pentagon acknowledges that efforts to prevent the Taliban from sending men and material across the Afghanistan-Pakistan border "have not produced measurable results."

### *Rules of Engagement*

Pentagon spokespeople have always declined to comment on the U.S. rules for using military force on Pakistan's side of the border region, but from time to time information on this issue surfaces. In August 2007, while reviewing more than one thousand pages of documents released in the course of the Army's investigation of the death of Ranger Pat Tillman, the media discovered information regarding the rules of engagement that governed U.S. military operations along the Afghanistan-Pakistan border at the time of his death in April 2004. As expected, the rules indicated that the U.S. Secretary of Defense, then Donald Rumsfeld, could order a major military incursion into Pakistan if he deemed such action necessary. In practice, the Secretary presumably would consult with his cabinet colleagues and the president before doing so. The head of U.S. Central Command could also, according to the released documents, authorize direct military action against

"The Big Three" (al-Qaeda leader Osama bin Laden; his deputy, Ayman al-Zawahiri; and the head of the Taliban, Mullah Omar). U.S. intelligence analysts and other observers erroneously believed that all three men probably resided in the Afghan-Pakistan border region.

More controversially, the documents specify that U.S. field commanders could, on their own authority, authorize units to "penetrate no deeper than 10km" into Pakistan in three cases: (1) during "hot pursuits" of al-Qaeda, Taliban, or other terrorist operatives fleeing into Pakistan from Afghanistan; (2) as part of U.S. Special Forces operations to recover crews of U.S. planes and helicopters that have crashed inside Pakistan; and (3) in the event that American troops are engaging hostile targets located on the Pakistani side of the border.

The documents do not indicate that U.S. commanders had to seek approval from – or even inform – Pakistani authorities before conducting incursions into their territory. Over the years, certain U.S. commanders have apparently expanded the concept to justify either pre-emptive or preventive strikes designed to disrupt an attack before it occurs, which expands the notion of "hot pursuit" considerably.

U.S. and Afghan units that have come under attack by mortars and other fire from attackers in Pakistan have engaged in retaliatory counterfire on the grounds of self-defense. They have extended this concept to encompass both the tactical (disrupting the immediate attack) and the operational (impeding the cross-border movement of the insurgents and their supplies).

U.S. military commanders noted a sharp deterioration in border security after the Pakistani government began negotiating a series of peace deals with local tribal leaders and with various extremist groups, which effectively allowed the militants to operate in Afghanistan without Pakistani impediments. These agreements took effect in South Waziristan in April 2004 and February 2005, in North Waziristan in September 2007, and the Swat Valley district of the North West Frontier province in 2009. After several of these ceasefire agreements began entering into force, the number of monthly U.S. combat deaths in Afghanistan began to exceed those in Iraq, despite the fact that five times as many U.S. troops were in Iraq than Afghanistan at the time.

Even after these agreements collapsed in 2009, and the military drove the Islamists out of the Swat Valley, NATO officers complained that the Pakistani military was only attacking the Pakistani Taliban, and not the Afghan Taliban or the al-Qaeda hideouts in the autonomous tribal areas of northwest Pakistan that threatened U.S. interests. Because the Afghan Taliban have not generally attacked Pakistanis, the Pakistani government and military have wanted to maintain a truce or nonaggression pact with these groups while concentrating their resources on the threat from the Pakistani Taliban, as well as maintaining robust defenses against India. Some members of the Pakistani national security community even see these groups as potential allies against India. In addition, many more Pakistanis believe that since the Western militaries are planning to withdraw from the region in the next few years, the Taliban could well return to power in Kabul, making it important for Pakistan not to antagonize them. U.S. analysts sometimes complain that some members of the Pakistani

intelligence services continue to provide aid to the Taliban, including alerting them to imminent U.S. air strikes on Pakistani territory. For this reason, the U.S. rules of engagement appear not to require advanced U.S. notification to Pakistani authorities of impending attacks inside the country's territory.

The Central Intelligence Agency (CIA) assigns a small number of American civilians and paramilitary troops to operate alongside the Pakistani military, but primarily as advisors. The United States also maintains a liaison relationship with the director, staff, and operational levels of Pakistan's Inter-Services Intelligence (ISI), which originally sponsored the Afghan Taliban and reportedly still maintains some contacts with it. U.S. and Pakistani intelligence and law enforcement services have conducted more than one hundred joint raids against suspected Taliban, al-Qaeda, or other Islamist extremists. The Americans provide Pakistanis with various types of intelligence, especially analyses of intercepted communications and imagery data from U.S. planes and spy satellites, in addition to hundreds of millions of dollars in military equipment and training annually. In return, the Pakistanis share their superior human intelligence about militant activities in the tribal areas and other terrorist plots.

### *The Trust Deficit*

One problem is the high level of distrust among all three parties. Obama administration representatives consider the Afghan central government corrupt and ineffective. They would have preferred that someone more energetic and effective replace Karzai as president but could not find a suitable replacement during the most recent Afghanistan presidential election. Despite extensive foreign training programs and other support, the Afghan National Army and Afghan National Police have little capacity to defeat the Taliban insurgents without continued direct U.S. assistance. The expansion of their size in recent years has compounded the problem that the Afghan government lacks the budget to sustain a large security establishment. Their persistent weaknesses is one of the main reasons why the Obama administration felt compelled to send tens of thousands of additional

U.S. troops to Afghanistan after assuming office. Relations between Washington and Islamabad are worse. Many Pakistanis erroneously believe that the United States favors India over Pakistan and is seeking to work with New Delhi and Israel to constrain Pakistan's regional influence and hobble Pakistan's nuclear arsenal. They also mistakenly argue that the rise of suicide terrorism within Pakistan is due to Islamabad's support for

U.S. counterterrorism policies, such as sending in the army to fight Islamists in the FATA, and not to their own sponsorship and mistaken belief that they can separate "good" from "bad" terrorists. Some extremist groups originally sponsored by the state as proxy forces against India have shown evidence of acting on their own against Pakistani targets. Extremist influences were evident in several recent developments, including the January 2011 assassination of the Punjab's secular governor by his police guard.

In this regard, both Americans and Pakistanis have a perception that the other is ungrateful. Whereas Americans resent the fact that Pakistanis hate them despite the billions in aid they have provided, Pakistanis gripe that Americans fail to appreciate all the sacrifices they have incurred in fighting terrorism. Pakistanis blame their financial losses and other costs on Islamabad's decisions to join Washington's war on terror after 9/11; though the number of suicide attacks and Pakistani government and civilian casualties has only soared since the July 2007 military operation against the Red Mosque in Islamabad, following the kidnapping of several Chinese citizens. Pakistanis note that U.S. aid covers only a small percentage of those costs, and that even now the U.S. Congress is cutting back on earlier aid pledges, many of which remain unimplemented. They see the current criticism as simply an Afghan-U.S. effort to "scapegoat" Pakistan for their inability to reverse what looks to be a losing war.

### *Drone Wars*

Former Pakistani President Musharraf, while rejecting proposals to conduct joint missions with U.S. forces inside Pakistan and downplaying the need for Pakistani troops to suppress the growing strength of the Pakistani Taliban in the FATA and Swat Valley, reportedly privately agreed that the United States could conduct drone and hot pursuit operations. Since assuming office in 2008, however, Pakistan's new civilian government has never publicly authorized U.S. military operations on its territory, even as cross-border operations. Instead, it has insisted that Pakistani regular troops and paramilitary forces can deal with the Taliban insurgents and any high-value al-Qaeda terrorist targets. When it negotiated controversial peace agreements with the insurgents soon after assuming office, the civilian government argued that it had only negotiated with the Pakistani Taliban, not their Afghan counterparts or international terrorist groups using Pakistani territory as a safe haven. Still, it is widely known that the unmanned aerial vehicles (UAVs) operate from Pakistani territory and that the Pakistani government provides some of the intelligence used to select their targets and assess the damage inflicted. The most obvious sign of Pakistani consent is that the government has never ordered the Pakistani Air Force to shoot down the drones, which they could easily do. In recent years, drone strikes have constituted the principle U.S. military activity inside Pakistani territory.

According to various media and think tank reports, CIA and Department of Defense drones, such as the Predator and Reaper, armed with Hellfire missiles have killed hundreds of people in northwest Pakistan. These numbers have reportedly surged in 2010 and 2011 as the Obama administration has been seeking to complement the increase in U.S. combat troops inside Afghanistan with intensified operations in the Taliban sanctuary in neighbouring Pakistan.

The drone strikes are controversial, but are still considered the best of a bad set of options by both U.S. and Pakistani officials. Human rights groups criticize drone strikes as extrajudicial killings, since the suspected terrorists are killed outright rather than given trials. Since U.S. officials decline to comment on the UAV operations in Pakistan, the Taliban and others are free to exaggerate to the media the number of innocent victims they cause. Polls show that the UAV attacks are not popular with the Pakistani people, though the inhabitants of the tribal areas who are oppressed by the foreign Islamist radicals are not really free to express their opinion for fear of retaliation. Experts believe that the number of civilian casualties has declined in recent years due to improved intelligence, stricter rules of engagement, and the use of less powerful missile warheads. Still, the UAVs cannot capture terrorist suspects for further interrogation and cannot gather additional intelligence at the attack site such as documents and computer files. Confirming deaths also is difficult due to the absence of credible witnesses or physical evidence at the site. Several prominent targets have been proclaimed dead only to turn up alive later.

Members of the Pakistani Taliban also cite the continuing UAV strikes to justify their terrorist campaign against the Pakistanis living outside the tribal zone. They describe their bombings as retaliation for the Pakistani government's allowing the UAVs to operate. Although most Pakistanis have little sympathy for the militants, polls indicate that they blame the Americans and their own government for antagonizing the Islamists, whose operations had originally been focused on the Afghan-Pakistan border region. The drone strikes have also led the jihadists to kill many other tribal inhabitants whom they suspect of providing targeting data to the Americans or their Pakistani partners. A more recent development has been that the Pakistani Taliban has cited the U.S. drone attacks as the reason why they have started to attack Western targets, such as the torching of the trucks delivering fuel through Pakistan to the NATO forces in Afghanistan. The Pakistani government has come to support them more since their range of targets has been extended to those Pakistani Taliban leaders who are harming the Islamabad government and Pakistani civilians. UAV-launched missiles have reportedly killed several anti-Islamabad guerilla leaders. Although the Pakistani Taliban cite the drone strikes as the reason for their efforts to attack the Pakistani government, Pakistani civilians, and now civilians in NATO cities, it is unlikely that ending the UAV strikes would lead the terrorists to curtail their operations. These advantages explain why industry analysts expect the global market for UAVs to grow from $5 billion to a cumulative total of more than $70 billion during the next decade. The U.S. Air Force plans to increase its number of UAVs from 250 to 450 units.

Perhaps the most important argument in favor of using drone strikes in northwest Pakistan is that the two main alternative options for attacking the terrorists are worse. The Pakistani military has made clear that they cannot repress the terrorists in the tribal regions. Although the controversial ceasefire accords negotiated earlier have formally collapsed, the Pakistani Army has repeatedly postponed announced plans to occupy North Waziristan, home to Afghan insurgents and the foreign fighters supporting them, as well as al-Qaeda and other terrorists having more global ambitions. A military occupation of North Waziristan would meet fierce resistance from the region's population, which has traditionally enjoyed extensive autonomy. The recent floods have also forced the military to divert its assets to humanitarian purposes, helping the more than ten million displaced people driven from their homes.

Yet, sending in U.S. combat troops on recurring raids or a protracted occupation of Pakistani territory would provoke widespread outrage in Pakistan and perhaps in other countries as well, since the UN Security Council mandate for ISAF only authorizes military operations in Afghanistan. On one such occasion, when U.S. Special Forces conducted a ground assault in the tribal areas in 2008, the Pakistanis reacted furiously. On September 3, a U.S. Special Forces team attacked a suspected terrorist base in Pakistan's South Waziristan region; killing over a dozen people. These actions evoked strong Pakistani protests. Army Chief of Staff, Gen. Ashfaq Kayani, who before November 2007 had led the ISI, issued a written statement denying that any agreement or understanding existed with the coalition forces in Afghanistan that permitted them to attack targets inside Pakistan. The general pledged to defend Pakistan's sovereignty and territorial integrity at all cost. Prime Minister Yousaf Raza Gilani and President Asif Ali Zardari also criticized alleged U.S. military operations on Pakistani territory. On September 16, 2008, the Pakistani army announced it would shoot at U.S. forces attempting to cross the Afghan-Pakistan border. On several occasions since then, Pakistani troops and militia have fired at what they believed to be American helicopters flying from Afghanistan to deploy Special Forces on their territory. Further large cross-border U.S. military operations could easily rally popular support behind the Taliban and al-Qaeda in Pakistan. It might even precipitate the collapse of the Islamabad government and its replacement by a regime in nuclear-armed Pakistan that is less friendly to Washington.

### New Border Incidents

The cross-border situation deteriorated again in late September and early October 2010, when Western intelligence agencies intercepted evidence that terrorists were preparing to conduct mass murder in major European cities along the lines of the November 2008 Islamist terrorist attacks in Mumbai, India. Concerned about evidence that the likely attackers were undergoing training in the terrorist safe havens of the tribal areas of northwest Pakistan – especially North Waziristan – the United States stepped up its UAV attacks on targets in Pakistan, conducting a record number of drone strikes in September, and even launching controversial air strikes using helicopter gunships operating from Afghanistan. At the same time, U.S. helicopters assigned to ISAF were engaging in a more aggressive campaign to defend Afghan border outposts. Taliban and Haqqani guerrillas would sally forth from their sanctuaries in Pakistan and attack Afghan army outposts in eastern Afghanistan, then flee back across the border with NATO aircrews in hot pursuit. Even before the recent incidents, NATO commanders had been justifying the cross-border attacks by citing the failure of the Pakistani army to occupy and suppress the guerrilla and terrorist bases in the tribal regions, especially in North Waziristan. The White House and the Pentagon became increasingly frustrated by the presence of the insurgent sanctuaries on Pakistani territory and the failure of the Pakistani government to establish control there. The Obama administration eventually authorized a more "proactive" air campaign against the Pakistani-based militants. While still declining to send U.S. ground forces across the border into Pakistan, the Pentagon increased the use of both manned helicopter attacks along the border and unmanned aerial vehicles for striking targets deeper inside Pakistani territory.

In one of these operations, two ISAF Apache helicopters attacked a site from which the insurgents were reportedly preparing to fire a mortar at a coalition base in Afghanistan's Paktia province. After attacking this target, which resulted in their briefly crossing into Pakistani territory, the U.S. crews concluded that they were taking small-arms fire from the Mandat Kandaho border patrol post, located some 200 meters inside Pakistan in the Kurram Agency. In self-defense, the helicopters reentered Pakistani airspace and fired two missiles that destroyed the post, killing three members of Pakistan's paramilitary Frontier Corps and wounding three others in the process. The whole affair was marked by confusion. The incident occurred before dawn, which made it even harder to avoid straying across the Afghan-Pakistan border. According to the Pakistani military, the Frontier Corps troops, a poorly trained and equipped tribal patrol force, fired "warning shots" to caution the helicopter crew that they had entered the territory of Pakistan's upper Kurram Agency. A joint NATO-Pakistani inquiry concluded that the two helicopter crews misinterpreted the shots as an attack against them and fired back. Coalition officials considered this approach dangerous considering that NATO interpreted the existing rules of engagement as allowing coalition forces to engage targets across the border without seeking advanced permission in cases of self-defense. In Kabul, NATO staff criticized the border guards' decision to fire at the helicopters rather than use established procedures to protest the border overflight, while in Washington, defense officials wondered why the Pakistanis did not simply try to communicate with NATO by car or radio. U.S. officials initially resisted apologizing for the incident or offering to pay compensation to the victims' relatives since those killed had opened fire first on U.S. forces.

However, the Pakistani Ministry of Foreign Affairs termed these overt border violations and attacks on its territory a "clear violation and breach of the UN mandate," which authorized ISAF combat operations only in Afghanistan. Interior Minister Rehman Malik said that an investigation was needed to assess the reasons for the attack, in effect to determine in NATO eyes "whether we are allies or enemies." Prime Minister Gilani told members of Pakistan's National Assembly that his government would defend Pakistani national sovereignty at all costs: "We can never allow you [NATO] to infringe on Pakistan's sovereignty and security. And if you will not explain your actions, compensate us and apologize for this, we can use other means. And we have other options." More importantly, the Pakistani officials denied that agreed rules of engagement existed that permitted coalition forces to attack and even enter Pakistani territory in reaction to insurgent threats. A Foreign Ministry statement insisted that, "there are no agreed 'hot pursuit' rules" and that, "Such violations are unacceptable." In addition to the rhetorical flourishes, the Pakistani government closed the Torkham Gate at the Afghan border for more than a week. Simultaneously, various groups of militants, perhaps with the complicity of the local Pakistani authorities, torched dozens of the oil tankers and other vehicles at various locations in Pakistan that were transporting supplies to ISAF.

But Pakistani officials kept other logistics routes, including the Chaman crossing, open to NATO's convoys. In the end, NATO officials decided to resolve the crisis by issuing various forms of regret and apologies.

Despite the apologies from NATO officials and reopening of the border crossing on October 10, 2010, the incident came at an unfortunate time in the relationship between the United States and Pakistan, which had been on the upswing in previous months. By early October, frustrated American officials were worrying that the incident had negated whatever goodwill the United States achieved by enacting billions of dollars in aid, including a five-year, $7.5 billion civilian aid package aimed to show that Washington wanted a long-term nonmilitary commitment to Pakistan extending beyond the war on terror. Additionally, the U.S. government spent more than $100 million on Pakistani flood relief partly, as Morrell noted, for "enhancing our reputation and our image in Pakistan."

### *The Current Crisis*

The recent intensified fighting in Afghanistan has led U.S. officials to adopt a less tolerant attitude toward the Pakistan-based Islamists who conduct cross-border attacks. Thus far, Afghan, U.S., and NATO forces have relied primarily on attacks by unmanned drones as well as search and destroy operations against Pakistani-based insurgents whenever they move into Afghan territory. U.S. officials are now considering more vigorous action to counter the threat presented by the cross-border attacks from Pakistan.

2011 was a terrible year in the U.S.-Pakistan relationship, beginning with the Raymond Davis affair. Davis was a CIA contractor working under the cover of the U.S. Embassy in Islamabad who shot two Pakistani men in January claiming they meant to rob him. The affair highlighted the complex relationship between the two intelligence agencies, whose members distrust one another even as they work together in joint operations. Not only does the CIA work with the Pakistani government to identify and apprehend suspected terrorists, but they also collaborate to identify targets for the U.S. drone strikes on Pakistani territory. Although a Pakistani court released Davis after compensation was paid to the victims' families, the affair badly strained relations, with the Pakistani government refusing to support U.S. claims that Davis enjoyed immunity from prosecution. Many Pakistanis complain the incident exposed problems inherent in the large U.S. intelligence presence in their country. During his April 2011 visit to Washington, ISI head Lt. Gen. Ahmed Shuja Pasha asked the CIA to withdraw intelligence operatives from Pakistan and curtail its unpopular drone strikes. Mullen made clear that the UAV operations in Pakistan would continue, describing the Afghanistan-Pakistan border region as the "epicenter of terrorism in the world." The White House then ordered the May 2 attack on bin Laden's compound in central Pakistan without seeking Pakistani permission or notifying Pakistani authorities in advance. In response, on May 14, 2011, a joint session of both houses of Pakistan's parliament unanimously enacted a resolution to defend Pakistan's sovereignty, security, and territorial integrity against U.S. military actions.

Shortly before retiring as Chairman, Mullen made some explosive comments about the continuing links between Pakistan's Inter-Services Intelligence and the Haqqani terrorist network whose members, thought to number some 10,000 to 15,000 fighters, operate in Afghanistan from bases in Pakistan. The support for the Haqqani network has been known in Washington though not publicized. A leaked State Department cable dated December 5, 2008, records the National Intelligence Officer for South Asia briefing NATO representatives that the ISI "provides intelligence and financial support to insurgent groups – especially the Jalaluddin Haqqani network out of Miram Shah, North Waziristan – to conduct attacks in Afghanistan against Afghan government, ISAF, and Indian targets." What was unusual about Mullen's September 22 testimony before the Senate Armed Services Committee was his explicit claim that the ISI had directed and supported Haqqani attacks on

U.S. targets in Afghanistan. After noting the difficulty of winning an insurgency when the guerrillas enjoy sanctuary in a neighbouring country, Mullen added that official Pakistani support for the Afghan insurgents "represent[s] a growing problem that is undermining U.S. interests and may violate international norms, potentially warranting sanction." The ISI confirms supporting the Haqqani and other terrorist groups during the 1990s, but claims to have severed all operational ties with these networks during the last decade since the 9/11 terrorist attacks. At most they acknowledge maintaining liaison ties with these groups to exchange information and simply follow their activities. Observers differ on whether the Pakistani armed forces have the capacity to suppress the Haqqani network even if they wanted to, with many suspecting that Pakistani commanders either support its activities or fear that attempting to suppress the group would lead it to retaliate against Pakistani targets.

The timing was right for airing these differences in public. There is widespread frustration that the Pakistani government is playing a "double game," aligning with the United States in public while cultivating terrorist ties in private. Mullen's imminent retirement afforded him with a license to make more controversial statements than in the past. In addition, the U.S. and NATO forces are being dramatically downsized. Pakistanis have undoubtedly begun to consider a post-NATO Afghanistan, and the potential value of relying on their terrorist proxies to exercise influence there. Given this context, Mullen's words were appropriately blunt: "In choosing to use violent extremism as an instrument of policy, the government of Pakistan, and most especially the Pakistani army and ISI, jeopardizes not only the prospect of our strategic partnership but Pakistan's opportunity to be a respected nation with legitimate regional influence," he said. "They may believe that by using these proxies, they are hedging their bets or redressing what they feel is an imbalance in regional power. But in reality, they have already lost that bet. By exporting violence, they've eroded their internal security and their position in the region. They have undermined their international credibility and threatened their economic well-being."

### Whither the War

Secretary of Defense Leon Panetta agreed with Mullen that the Pakistani authorities "must take steps to prevent the safe haven that the Haqqanis are using," adding that, "We simply cannot allow these kinds of terrorists to be able to go into Afghanistan, attack our forces and then return to Pakistan for safe haven." Yet, Panetta was coy about how the United States would respond to the continuing attacks on its troops. The expectation is that the drone strikes against the Haqqani network could escalate, despite Pakistani objections. U.S. commanders rightly insist that they cannot allow Afghanistan insurgents and international terrorists unimpeded use of safe havens on Pakistani soil to support attacks on American soldiers. That said, the long-standing U.S. view has been that the best way to make enduring progress in weaning Pakistan away from supporting international terrorism is by continuing to partner with Pakistan rather than berating Islamabad in public or openly embarrassing its civilian government through overt cross-border attacks that violate Pakistani sovereignty.

It is possible the United States would launch airborne forces, like the helicopter-enabled commando attack against bin Laden's headquarters in central Pakistan. But these Special Forces operations would rouse strong Pakistani feelings and might prove counterproductive. Pakistani Interior Minister, Rehman Malik, said his government would "not allow" U.S. forces to attack the claimed Haqqani strongholds in North Waziristan. "Our government is already cooperating with the U.S. ? but they also must respect our sovereignty."

The Congress is likely to respond to the latest crisis by cutting back on some aid and imposing restrictions on other U.S. assistance to Pakistan. For example, future aid might require executive branch certification for release of the funds. The Obama administration already employed this approach earlier this year by withholding hundreds of millions of dollars in Coalition Support Funds in response to Pakistani restrictions on the number and movement of U.S. government security personnel in Pakistan. Pakistanis saw the restrictions as an affirmation of Washington's transactional view of their relationship in which Pakistanis would only receive assistance when Islamabad met Washington requirements. When Senator Susan Collins asked Panetta about making such aid conditional on administration certification that Pakistan was cooperating with the United States in the war on terror, the Defense Secretary agreed that, "Anything that makes clear to them that we cannot tolerate their providing this kind of safe haven to the Haqqanis, and that they have to take action – any signal that we can send to them – I think would be important to do." Congress applied the same kinds of restrictions during the 1990s, after the joint U.S.-Pakistani campaign against the Soviet occupation of Afghanistan had ended and concerns about Pakistan's nuclear proliferation activities increased, culminating in the 1998 detonation of several nuclear weapons by India and Pakistan. There is also strong congressional support for having the State Department add the entire Haqqani network to its list of foreign terrorist organizations, which would restrict the movement of its members and perhaps disrupt their foreign financing. At present, only a few of the network's leaders have been sanctioned as terrorists.

Pakistan's civilian government is in a difficult situation. On the one hand, its members must show Pakistani nationalists that they are not American lackeys and will resist Washington's pressure. Pakistani public opinion is clearly hostile to the United States in general and U.S. military operations within their country in particular. Pakistanis note that whatever consent Musharraf gave lapsed with his retirement and the end of military rule. Pakistanis widely blame the U.S. war against the Taliban and other Muslim militants for bringing terrorism to Pakistan, which has suffered from suicide bombings and other civil strife in recent years, and for seeking to use the Pakistani army as Washington's mercenary force. Pakistanis calculate that they have incurred enormous financial losses and other costs in terms of the elevated terrorist violence Pakistan has experienced since Islamabad's decisions to side with Washington and support the U.S.-led Operation Enduring Freedom after 9/11. They note that the Pakistani armed forces have suffered more casualties fighting Islamist militants than have coalition forces on the other side of the Afghan-Pakistan border. In their view, more U.S. drone and cross-border attacks would further increase Pakistani military causalities and terrorist victims.

On the other hand, Pakistan receives billions of dollars of assistance from the United States – originally focused on security assistance but increasingly encompassing nonmilitary aid as well – and the civilian government is genuinely opposed to terrorism. Breaking with the United States and NATO would benefit India in the diplomatic competition between the two nations. Pakistani officials have sought to limit U.S. military operations in their country by affirming their commitment to reign in extremist activity in Pakistan and across the border. The Pakistani army has also resumed military operations against the Pakistani Taliban; though the recent floods have disrupted whatever plans might have existed to expand operations throughout the remaining tribal areas. Despite the government's formal opposition to the drone attacks, it is understood that the UAVs operate within Pakistan with the government's approval and, reportedly, with its intelligence assistance – vitally important given the limited U.S. human assets in the region – now that the drones target the Pakistani Taliban as well.

From the perspective of the Pakistani government, the problem with the recent helicopter attacks was that they deviated from the standard rules of engagement, as well as their killing of three Pakistani soldiers. Pakistani authorities regularly overlook occasional incursions across their border as long as these incidents do not attract much public attention. The Pakistani government even rapidly overcame the negative fallout from the June 2008 incident in which an ISAF air strike killed 11 Frontier Corps members manning a border checkpoint, leading to an exchange of fire with other Pakistani forces. But in late September, U.S. helicopters fired missiles into Pakistani territory four times in one week. Additionally, the U.S. government addressed these incidences publically. Pakistani officials originally said nothing about the September 24 and 25 helicopter missile strikes on their territory, but the September 30 attack killed three paramilitary soldiers located inside Pakistan, making it hard to conceal. One of the cross-border helicopter attacks that occurred a few days before the attack on the Frontier Corps members killed as many as 60 fighters who had been attacking an Afghan border post; by the time the attacks were perpetrated the militants had fled to the Pakistani side of the border. Rather than remain silent, moreover, NATO officials confirmed the media reports that its manned helicopters had crossed into Pakistani territory and killed Pakistanis, actions that alliance representatives justified as legitimate acts of self-defense.

Misperceptions regarding each other's capabilities and intentions is also an enduring problem in the U.S.-Pakistani relationship. U.S. officials and their NATO and Afghan allies believe that the Pakistani military could suppress the Afghan Taliban insurgents in the border areas if they really made an effort to do so. Meanwhile, Pakistani officials think that if the coalition really got its act together it could easily employ its overwhelming capabilities to crush the Taliban guerrillas and secure the Afghan-Pakistan border.

The failure to do so gives rise to all sorts of suspicions that the United States is secretly sustaining the insurgency in order to justify its continued military presence in the region. They also believe that ineffective Afghan and NATO policies have contributed to the rise of the Afghan Taliban, and believe that some anti-Islamabad terrorists have been attacking Pakistani forces while using Afghan territory as a sanctuary. The parties' clashing perceptions have been manifest in their firefights along the Afghan-Pakistan border, which involves their troops alternately cooperating and combating one another.

## Concluding Observations

Geography and other factors will force Afghanistan, Pakistan, and the United States to collaborate despite their differences over the border region. Pakistan needs financial and diplomatic support from Washington to complement that provided by China, which has placed firm limits on its annual aid levels. The United States gives Pakistan billions of dollars in direct assistance to Islamabad, as well as considerable revenue to Pakistanis involved in the shipping of U.S. military supplies to Afghanistan. U.S. diplomats have also helped dampen Indian desires to retaliate militarily against Pakistan for earlier terrorist attacks.

The United States in turn needs Pakistani support to transit military supplies to its troops in Afghanistan. Efforts to develop an alternative supply route through Russia and other former Soviet bloc states have made considerable progress, but these shipments are more expensive and make the NATO war effort excessively dependent on Moscow. Washington must have some Pakistani support to achieve a favorable regional environment for an eventual peace settlement in Afghanistan. The United States is also very eager to collaborate with the Pakistani military to secure the country's growing nuclear weapons arsenal.

One task is to clarify the rules of engagement under the new conditions of a departing Western military presence, a resurgent Taliban, and a Pakistani government and military frustrated with the United States and Afghanistan but yet still open to some cooperation. When President Zardari met Marc Grossman, the new U.S. Special Representative for Afghanistan and Pakistan who replaced Richard Holbrooke, he said they needed "clear terms of engagement" in the battle against Islamist militants to avoid further damaging bilateral security ties.

Zardari's office subsequently explained that, "In the absence of well-defined and documented terms of engagement, wrong plugs may be pulled at the wrong times by any side that could undermine the bilateral relations." The statement added that, "The president said that terms of engagement should be clearly defined and specified so that any dispute could be settled amicably."

## TALIBAN RULE (SEPTEMBER 1996-NOVEMBER 2001)

The Taliban regime was led by Mullah Muhammad Umar, who held the title of Head of State and "Commander of the Faithful." He remained in the Taliban power base in Qandahar and almost never appeared in public, although he did occasionally receive high-level foreign officials. Al Qaeda leaders Osama bin Laden relocated from Sudan to Afghanistan, where he had been a recruiter of Arab fighters during the anti-Soviet war, in May 1996. He at first was located in territory in Nangarhar province controlled by Hezb-i-Islam of Yunus Khalis (Mullah Umar's party leader) but then had free reign in Afghanistan as the Taliban captured nearly all the territory in Afghanistan. Umar reportedly forged a political and personal bond with Bin Laden and refused U.S. demands to extradite him. Like Umar, most of the senior figures in the Taliban regime were Ghilzai Pashtuns, which predominate in eastern Afghanistan. They are rivals of the Durrani Pashtuns, who are predominant in the south.

The Taliban lost international and domestic support as it imposed strict adherence to Islamic customs in areas it controlled and employed harsh punishments, including executions. The Taliban authorized its "Ministry for the Promotion of Virtue and the Suppression of Vice" to use physical punishments to enforce strict Islamic practices, including bans on television, Western music, and dancing. It prohibited women from attending school or working outside the home, except in health care, and it publicly executed some women for adultery. In what many consider its most extreme action, and which some say was urged by Bin Laden, in March 2001 the Taliban blew up two large Buddha statues carved into hills above Bamiyan city, considering them idols.

## BEYOND 2014: LIKELY OUTCOMES AND SIZE OF RESIDUAL FORCE

Assessing that Afghan forces will continue to need direct military support after 2014 to prevent the Taliban from advancing, the United States and its NATO partners are attempting to formulate plans for a "residual force" that would remain in Afghanistan to continue to train and assist the ANSF and likely also conduct operations against high-value targets such as Al Qaeda. The residual force is intended to ensure sustainable stability until the Afghans can provide entirely for their own security.

Mainstream post-2014 options have been reported in various news stories. In November 2012, General Allen reportedly presented to the White House three options: 6,000, 10,000, or 20,000 forces—with decreasing levels of risk to U.S. gains associated as the number of troops increase with each option. The option providing for the fewest forces envisions mainly Special Operations forces remaining to help combat high-value targets.

The mid-range option also provided for training of Afghan security forces. The largest option would provide for some continued U.S. patrols in highly contested areas. U.S. briefings at a February 21, 2013, NATO meeting in Brussels suggested that the Administration is leaning toward a post-2014 international force of approximately 8,000 to 12,000 trainers and mentors—of which about two-thirds would be U.S. forces and one third would be non-U.S. force contributions—plus a still unspecified number of mostly U.S. counterterrorism forces. This option comports with an August 2013 recommendation from former NATO commander Admiral James Stavridis for a residual force of 9,000 U.S. and 6,000 partner forces. U.S. officials assert that the residual force is to support the ANSF, and that it is not a "bridging force" to bear security responsibility until Afghan forces are more capable. There is continuing debate about whether any U.S. air assets remaining in Afghanistan in 2014 would support not only international troops but also the ANSF; this debate appears to take into account the ANSF deficiencies in aircraft and medical evacuation capabilities. Other reports say the United States will transfer to the ANSF mortars, long-range artillery, and unarmed remotely piloted vehicles.

Secretary of State Kerry stated on May 16, 2013, that President Obama will likely announce the size of the post-2014 U.S. force in late May or early June 2013.

However, that announcement has been delayed, possibly because General Dunford said he wanted to assess the performance of the ANSF through the summer 2013 "fighting season." However, in press comments in July 2013, Gen. Dunford indicated the size of the post-2014 U.S. force needs to be determined by "late fall" of 2013 because of the planning process. The timing of the announcement could be dependent on finalization of the bilateral security agreement.

Some U.S. partner countries appear to be growing impatient about the U.S. post-2014 announcement because of the need to plan for post-2014 deployments.

Germany announced in late April 2013 that it will keep about 800 forces in Afghanistan after 2014, mostly in the northern sector where Germany now leads the international contingent. At a June 4-5, 2013, NATO meeting, it was announced that Italy would also join a post-2014 force, continuing to lead in the western sector, and that Turkey is considering continuing its leadership in the Kabul area beyond 2014.

That NATO meeting also reportedly decided that post-2014 NATO trainers would deploy in the northern, western, eastern, southern, and Kabul sectors. The United States and its partners reportedly are discussing retaining NATO leadership over the post-2014 international force under a mission name "Resolute Support."

## CONTINGENCY ON THE BILATERAL SECURITY AGREEMENT

U.S. officials say the post-2014 U.S. deployment is contingent on finalizing a Bilateral Security Agreement (BSA) with the Afghan government that provides legal immunities for U.S. forces in Afghanistan (Status of Forces Agreement). On October 3, 2012, deputy SRAP James Warlick was named lead U.S. negotiator for the BSA; Afghan Ambassador to the United States Hakimi leads the talks for the Afghan side. The negotiations formally began on November 15, 2012, and Chairman of the Joint Chiefs of Staff Gen. Dempsey said in July 2013 that the United States wants an agreement to be in place by the end of October 2013. That date, according to U.S. officials, is intended to remove the BSA issue from Afghanistan's presidential election campaign, and to allow U.S. commanders ample time to plan for the residual force.

In recent months, the negotiations had appeared to be stalled by disagreements over the U.S. demand for legal immunities for U.S. troops, the authorities of U.S. troops, and President Hamid Karzai's demands for security guarantees against what Karzai sees as a potentially hostile threat from neighboring Pakistan. The stalling of the negotiations had led outside experts to assess that the Administration might, as happened in Iraq, decide to withdraw all U.S. troops from Afghanistan when the current international security mission concludes at the end of 2014 (known as the "zero option"). The zero option had been mentioned by Administration sources in press articles since mid-2013, possibly as a means of building U.S. negotiating leverage with Afghan leaders.

During October 11-12, 2013, Secretary of State John Kerry held intensive discussions in Kabul with President Karzai in an attempt to revive progress in the negotiations. At the conclusion of their meetings on October 12, Karzai and Kerry announced that they had resolved U.S.-Afghan differences on the key issues of U.S. operations authority and security guarantee. Karzai apparently relented on the demand that the United States protect Afghanistan from Pakistan, and the United States reportedly agreed to coordinate with the Afghan security forces on post-2014 anti-Al Qaeda operations in Afghanistan. Left open was the issue of legal immunities for U.S. troops in Afghanistan after 2014, which the United States asserts is a non-negotiable requirement if U.S. forces are to remain. Karzai stated that the decision on legal immunities would be placed before the Afghan National Assembly (parliament) and a special *loya jirga* - a traditional Afghan assembly composed of about 2,000 notables convened to consider major issues. That *loya jirga* is tentatively scheduled for November 19, 2013. However, the government selects many of the participants, and Karzai's tentative agreement with Kerry on the other outstanding major issues suggests that Karzai will lobby the *loya jirga*, probably successfully, to approve the legal immunity. A U.S.-Afghanistan BSA will likely serve as a model for similar agreements between Afghanistan and partner countries. U.S. forces currently operate in Afghanistan under "diplomatic notes" between the United States and the interim government of Afghanistan—primarily one that was exchanged in November 2002. The notes give the United States legal jurisdiction over U.S. personnel serving in Afghanistan.

### Debate Over Mission Success At Likely Post-2014 Troop Levels

There is debate over how the ANSF will fare after 2014 with the levels of support currently receiving the most discussion (about 10,000 U.S. forces plus about 5,000 partner forces). According to some experts, this level of international support will succeed in encouraging the Taliban to seek a political settlement rather than face likely indefinite combat. Apparently factoring in a residual presence into their analysis, General Dempsey and General Dunford said in early 2013 that the Taliban will be a persistent, though not an "existential" threat, over the longer term.

However, some commanders and experts believe the relatively small residual force contemplated would enable the Taliban to make gains in the south and east and potentially unravel the Afghan security forces and government. On March 5, 2013, then Commander of U.S. Central Command General James Mattis told the Senate Armed Services Committee that he had recommended a total post-2014 force of about 20,000, of which 13,600 would be U.S. forces.

Whatever the level of post-2014 international forces, it is likely that, as international forces thin out sharply after 2014, local militias will re-form to deter or prevent Taliban gains. This was illustrated in a November 2012 meeting organized by Herat leader Ismail Khan, in which he reportedly began taking steps to reorganize his Soviet and Taliban-era militia. Vice President Muhammad Fahim has also discussed potentially reconstituting the Northern Alliance force in anticipation of the need to assist Afghan government forces against the Taliban. And, Uzbek leader Dostam, is also reportedly trying to reorganize his loyalists in northern Afghanistan. These and similar moves could spark ethnic and communal conflict from an all-out struggle for power and a reversion to Afghan rule by faction leaders rather than elected leaders.

### Strategic Partnership Agreement

The BSA is being negotiated pursuant to the broader "Strategic Partnership Agreement" (SPA) signed by President Obama and President Karzai in Afghanistan on May 1, 2012. That broad agreement signaled that the United States is committed to Afghan stability and development for many years after the transition is complete. The SPA was completed after more than one year of negotiations that focused on resolution of two disagreements in particular— Afghan insistence on control over detention centers and a halt to or control over nighttime raids on insurgents by U.S. forces. The SPA agreement also demonstrated U.S.-Afghan ability to overcome public Afghan discomfort over such issues as the March 2011 burning of a Quran by a Florida pastor; the mistaken burning by U.S. soldiers of several Qurans on February 20, 2012; and the March 11, 2012, of 16 Afghans by a U.S. soldier, Sergeant Robert Bales, who was arrested and tried in the United States. On September 17, 2012, several hundred Afghans demonstrated near a U.S.-Afghan training facility east of Kabul city (Camp Phoenix) to protest a video made in the United States, "The Innocence of Muslims." About 40 Afghan police reportedly were wounded preventing the crowd from reaching the facility.

Other disputes were mostly, but not completely resolved, by the time the SPA was signed. The night raid issue was resolved in April 2012 when the United States agreed to give Afghans more control over night raids, including requiring an Afghan court warrant to hold any raid captives for more than 48 hours. The detainee issue was partly resolved on March 10, 2012, with a U.S. agreement to accelerate the transfer of imprisoned insurgents to Afghan control, to occur over six months. However, a dispute over the transfer to Afghan control of the detention center at Bagram Airfield lingered, particularly because the facility holds about 50 non-Afghans ("enduring security threats") that the United States believed must not be released. An initial agreement fell apart during the March 10, 2013, visit to Afghanistan by Defense Secretary Chuck Hagel, but subsequent talks produced an Afghan commitment to consult the United States on any releases of the enduring security threats, and the detainees at Bagram came under Afghan control on March 25, 2013. A related issue arose in March 2013 when Karzai demanded U.S. special forces withdraw from Wardak Province after he alleged that they were abusing Afghans there. An agreement was reached on March 20, 2013, under which the U.S. forces withdrew over several months.

The strategic partnership agreement represents a broad outline of the post-2014 relationship, with details to be filled in subsequently. It has a duration of 10 years. The major provisions include the following:

- A commitment to continue to foster U.S.-Afghan "close cooperation" to secure Afghanistan. This strongly implies, but does not state outright, that U.S. troops will remain in Afghanistan after 2014, and no troop numbers are mentioned in the document. The document provides for negotiations on the Bilateral Security Agreement.
- The U.S. administration will request appropriations to provide training and arms to the Afghan security forces. The agreement does not stipulate dollar amounts or which systems are to be provided.
- The United States will designate Afghanistan as a "Major Non-NATO Ally," a designation reserved for close U.S. allies. In keeping with that pledge, on July 7, 2012, then Secretary Clinton stopped in Afghanistan and announced

that designation. It opens Afghanistan to receive (sale, donation) U.S. weaponry of the same level of sophistication as that sold to U.S. NATO allies, and facilitates provision of training and funds to leasing defense articles.

- There will be no "permanent" U.S. bases or the use of Afghan facilities for use against neighboring countries, but the agreement would apparently allow long-term U.S. use of Afghan facilities. Over the past several years, successive National Defense Authorization Acts have contained a provision explicitly prohibiting the U.S. establishment of permanent bases in Afghanistan.
- The Administration will request economic aid for Afghanistan for the duration of the agreement (2014-2024). No amounts were specified in the document. The Afghan government reportedly wanted a $2 billion per year commitment written into the agreement but the United States told Afghanistan that amounts can only be determined through the appropriations process.

In October 2011, Karzai called a *loya jirga* to endorse the concept of the SPA as well as his insistence on Afghan control over detentions and approval authority for U.S.-led night raids. A November 16-19, 2011, traditional *loya jirga* (the *jirga* was conducted not in accordance with the constitution and its views are therefore non-binding), consisting of about 2,030 delegates, gave Karzai the approvals he sought, both for the pact itself and his suggested conditions. The final SPA was ratified by the Afghanistan National Assembly on May 26, 2012, by a vote of 180-4.

The SPA replaced an earlier, more limited strategic partnership agreement established on May 23, 2005, when Karzai and President Bush issued a "joint declaration." The declaration provided for U.S. forces to have access to Afghan military facilities, in order to prosecute "the war against international terror and the struggle against violent extremism." Karzai's signing of the declaration was supported by the 1,000 Afghan representatives on May 8, 2005, at a consultative *jirga* in Kabul. The *jirga*supported an indefinite presence of international forces to maintain security but urged Karzai to delay a firm decision to request such a presence.

## TRANSITION PILLAR: BUILDING AFGHAN FORCES AND ESTABLISHING RULE OF LAW

Key to the transition to Afghan lead—and the post-2014 future of Afghanistan—is the effectiveness of the Afghan National Security Forces (ANSF), consisting primarily of the Afghan National Army (ANA) and Afghan National Police (ANP). The forces have expanded considerably since 2002, but some experts doubt the ANSF's capability to secure Afghanistan after 2014. ANSF strengths and weaknesses, including performance ratings for its components, is contained in the semi-annual DOD reports on Afghanistan stability.

Among the concerns about the ANSF is that about 35% of the force does not re-enlist each year, meaning that about one-third of the force must be recruited to replenish its ranks. Many believe that the force has been expanded too quickly to allow for thorough vetting or for recruitment of the most qualified personnel. Incidents of ANSF attacks on coalition personnel increased during 2011-2012, causing reduced interaction between Afghan forces and their U.S.-led mentors. Many units also suffer from a deficiency of weaponry, spare parts, and fuel. The Special Inspector General for Afghanistan Reconstruction (SIGAR) reported in October 2012 that the Afghan government will likely prove incapable of sustaining ANSF installations after 2014, mainly because of a lack of skilled maintenance personnel.

U.S. commanders frequently note concerns about the ANSF's deficiency of logistical capabilities, such as airlift, medical evacuation, resupply, and other associated functions. It is these deficiencies that are a particular focus of U.S. planning for a residual support force after 2014. Some of the deficiency throughout the ANSF is due to illiteracy, which prompted an increasing focus on providing literacy training. To date, the large majority of the ANSF force has received literacy training and has at least first grade literacy.

U.S. forces, along with partner countries and contractors, train the ANSF and will likely continue to do so after 2014. In February 2010, the U.S.-run "Combined Security Transition Command-Afghanistan" (CSTC-A) that ran the training was subordinated to the broader NATO Training Mission—Afghanistan (NTM-A). CSTC-A's mission was reoriented to building the capacity of the Afghan Defense and Interior Ministries, and to provide resources to the ANSF.

### Current and Post-2014 Size of the ANSF

On January 21, 2010, the joint U.N.-Afghan "Joint Coordination and Monitoring Board" (JCMB) agreed that, by October 2011, the ANA would expand to 171,600 and the ANP to about 134,000, (total ANSF of 305,600). Both forces reached that level by September 2011. In August 2011, a larger target size of 352,000 (195,000 ANA and 157,000 ANP) was set, to be reached by November 2012. The gross size of the force reached approximately that level by the end of September 2012, and remain at levels just below their targets. A higher target level of 378,000 was not adopted because of the concerns about the Afghan ability to sustain so large a force. About 1,700 women serve in the ANSF, of which about 1,370 are police.

In the run-up to the May 20-21, 2012, NATO summit in Chicago, which focused on long-term financial and military sustainment of the ANSF, there was initial agreement to reduce the total ANSF to 228,500 by 2017. However, based on assessments of the difficulty of securing Afghanistan, the February 21, 2013, NATO meeting tentatively reversed the decision to shrink the force, and it will stay at the 352,000 level until at least 2018.

### ANSF Top Leadership/Ethnic and Factional Considerations

In the immediate aftermath of the 2001 ousting of the Taliban regime, Northern Alliance figures took key security positions and weighted recruitment for the new ANSF toward ethnic Tajiks. Many Pashtuns, in reaction, refused recruitment, but the naming of a Pashtun, Abdul Rahim Wardak, as Defense Minister in December 2004, mitigated that difficulty. The problem was further alleviated with better pay and more close involvement by U.S. forces, and that the force is ethnically integrated in each unit and representative. According to the July 2013 DOD report, the overall ANSF force continues to come into line. Tajiks are slightly overrepresented in the ANA (33.3% versus about 25% of the population) and Uzbeks are slightly underrepresented (6% versus

10% of the population). And, those Pashtuns who are in the force are disproportionately eastern Pashtuns (from the Ghilzai tribal confederations) rather than southern Pashtuns (mostly Durrani tribal confederations).

Until 2010, the chief of staff of the ANA was General Bismillah Khan, a Tajik and former Northern Alliance commander. He was replaced by a Pashtun, Lieutenant General Sher Mohammad Karimi. Khan then served as Interior Minister until his ouster by the National Assembly in August 2012; in that position, he reportedly promoted his Tajik allies to key Interior Ministry and ANP positions. In September 2012, Karzai appointed Khan as Defense Minister, and Khan has earned U.S. and partner country praise for his performance as Defense Minister, to date.

The same day he appointed Khan, Karzai appointed professional police commander Gen. Ghulam Mojtaba Patang as Interior Minister. Patang entered his position with high respect as the first professional officer to be appointed to the top police slot and the July 2013 DOD report credits Patang with appointing competent professionals throughout the Interior Ministry and ANP ranks.

However, the National Assembly voted to remove him in July 2013 for failing to improve security along the Kabul-Qandahar highway. After seeking advice on the matter from the Afghan Supreme Court, Karzai replaced him on September 1, 2013 with Umar Daudzai, Karzai's former chief of staff, a Pashtun, who was serving as Ambassador to Pakistan. A highly respected Tajik figure, Kabul police chief Gen. Mohammad Ayub Salangi, was simultaneously appointed deputy Interior Minister.

Also in September 2012, Karzai named as intelligence director (National Directorate of Security, NDS) Asadullah Khalid, former Qandahar governor and a close Karzai ally, replacing Rehmatullah Nabil.

Khalid was wounded by a potential assassin in December 2012, but he resumed his duties after undergoing several months of treatment in the United States. His predecessor, Nabil, was returned to the post on September 1, 2013.

## ANSF Funding

On the assumption that the post-2014 ANSF force would shrink to 228,000, it was determined that sustaining a force that size would cost $4.1 billion annually. The United States pledged $2.3 billion yearly; the Afghan government pledged $500 million yearly; and allied contributions constituted the remaining $1.3 billion. The Afghan contribution was to rise steadily until 2024, at which time Afghanistan is expected to fund its own security needs. However, the apparent decision to keep the ANSF force at 352,000 necessitates revised funding levels of about $6 billion per year. Donor pledges to fund the force at that level have not been announced to date.

Even the $4.1 billion figure was considered difficult to raise. The GAO estimated in February 2013 that there was a $600 million per year discrepancy between allied donor pledges and the $1.3 billion requirement.

The specific known yearly pledges have included Germany ($190 million per year), Britain ($110 million per year), and Australia ($100 million per year). Other countries that are confirmed to have made pledges, but of unspecified amounts, include Denmark, Italy, Estonia, and the Netherlands. The Special Inspector General for Afghanistan Reconstruction (SIGAR) issued an audit in October 2012 saying the Afghan government will have major difficulty meeting its obligations to fund the force as donor countries wind down their involvement. According to a SIGAR audit (13-4), CSTC-A plans to provide about $1 billion directly to the Afghan government during 2013-2019 to pay for fuel for the ANSF.

The U.S. costs to train and equip the ANSF are provided in the aid table at the end of this chapter. As of FY2005, the security forces funding has been DOD funds, not State Department funds (Foreign Military Financing, FMF).

## NATO Trust Fund for the ANA

In 2007 ISAF set up a trust fund for donor contributions to fund the transportation of equipment donated to and the training of the ANA; the mandate was expanded in 2009 to include sustainment costs. In November 2010 a further expansion was agreed on to support literacy training for the ANA. As of March 2013, donor contributions and pledges to the ANA Trust Fund total about $700 million. U.S. funding for the ANA is provided separately, not through this fund.

### Law and Order Trust Fund for the ANP

There is also a separate "Law and Order Trust Fund for Afghanistan" (LOTFA), run by the U.N. Development Program (UNDP), which is used to pay the salaries of the ANP and other police-related functions. The United States donates to that fund, for the purpose of paying ANP salaries and food costs. From 2002-2012, donors contributed $2.75 billion to the Fund, of which the United States contributed about $1 billion. Japan's 2009 pledge to pay the expenses of the Afghan police for at least six months (about $125 million for each six month period) is implemented through the LOTF. The EU pledged $175 million for the fund from January 2011-March 2013.

In May 2012, there were reports of misfeasance at the fund. UNDP began to investigate the allegations and immediately terminated the contracts of three personnel and placed two others on administrative leave. UNDP is continuing to investigate the issue.

### Other Bilateral Donations

The DOD reports discuss other bilateral donations to the ANSF, both in funds and in arms and equipment donations. There is a "NATO Equipment Donation Program," through which donor countries supply the ANSF with equipment. Since 2002, about $2.9 billion in assistance to the ANSF has come from these sources. As an example, in October 2011, Croatia and Slovenia donated a total of over 20,000 AK-47 assault rifles to the ANP. Australia contributed $40 million to relocate the ANA's 205th Corps, and South Korea contributed $30 million for medical and communications equipment.

There is also a NATO-Russia Council Helicopter Maintenance Trust Fund. Launched in March 2011, this fund provides maintenance and repair capacity to the Afghan Air Force helicopter fleet, much of which is Russian-made.

## A WEAVING PROJECT FOR AFGHAN TURKMEN

The citizens of Afghanistan face numerous obstacles in their quest to return to and resettle in their homeland, not the least of which is a means of self-support in a country that has been greatly devastated. Some 30 million land mines, most of them plastic and difficult to detect, cover the countryside - a serious problem for a people who earn their livings primarily off the land. Carpet weaving has always been a major means of livelihood, particularly among the Turkmen of northern Afghanistan. During the current extended period of exile from their homeland the Turkmen have not by any means abandoned this traditional activity. They have, on the other hand, even expanded it, it is one of the few forms of labour that is both practical and profitable in a refugee camp environment. The pool of available and experienced weavers is even larger than before the war, and includes boys and young men as well as women. (In the past, women did most of the weaving).

Because of the heavy reliance on carpet weaving during this period of refugee status, every effort has been made to expand the market by incorporating new, non-traditional designs and colours. Upon a return to Afghanistan the marketability of the Turkmen's carpets will be of even greater importance because weaving will be of even greater importance because weaving will be one of the few practical and ready means of self-support in a devastated countryside. Thus, although a market almost certainly will exist, every possible niche of it must be exploited.

One portion of the market in the West - where almost all of these carpets are headed - is the market for traditional carpets woven with natural dyes. A project under the name of DOBAG was initiated in northwest Anatolia in Turkey eight years ago with the aim of producing these kinds of rugs. It has been a major success; the weaving of vegetable dye rugs has now expanded to hundreds of villages outside the bounds of the original project, in both the same and in different regions. The original project now comprises only a very small proportion of the vegetable dye rugs being woven in Turkey; private entrepreneurs and individual families in a number of different regions of Turkey produce most of these rugs.

Such a project could succeed in Afghanistan, too. The Afghan people, and the Turkmen in particular, have certainly not been remiss in their own efforts to increase the market for their carpets, however, this possibility has not occurred spontaneously from within the community, and it may need some impetus in this direction. Once the community recognizes the potential for this market, local entrepreneurial instinct will take over, to a large extent.

To establish the project at this time, it must be in the refugee camp setting, in Pakistan. We cannot work in Afghanistan, and most of the people are in Pakistan. Because almost all of the weavers will be from the Akcha region in northern Afghanistan, the cohesiveness of the project could be maintained when the weavers eventually return to Afghanistan.

This project must overcome a number of problems in its initial stages. The first is the location of an economical, not-too-distant source for madder root, the origin of the red family of natural dye colours. Madder root can be collected without great difficulty in the region of northern Afghanistan inhabited by the Turkmen. Under normal circumstances and even during the war, transporting the required amount from Afghanistan to Pakistan would not have been too difficult. However, as the war now enters its final stage with the siege of Jalalabad and Kabul, all roads from Afghanistan to Pakistan have been cut. Even if madder root can be found in Afghanistan, it will have to be brought over the mountains by donkey or camel.

Another problem is wool. The lustrous, oily wool of Afghanistan used for the traditional Turkmen rugs of this region would be ideal. However, even discounting transportation problems to Pakistan, the severe depopulation of Afghanistan - both of people and of animals - means that this wool is not available at any price. We must instead settle for one of the blends of imported (Australian or New Zealand) and local wool. We have rejected the pure merinos Australian wool, which is the most expensive locally available wool, because although it is quite lustrous, it is too soft - a characteristic inconsistent with the feel of the original carpets. We have opted instead for a blend of local and imported wool called Rayhan, which is reasonably lustrous while also being reasonably hard. Many Turkmen weaving in the refugee camps use this wool; however, invariably the wool yarns employed are machine spun (in Pakistan). In order to reproduce rugs with the look and feel of the nineteenth-or early twentieth-century originals, handspun wool yarn must at least be used for the warps and preferably for the pile as well. Provisions must be made for hand spinning of the wool, then," which will also be done in the refugee camps.

Most Turkmen women have been hand spinning recently enough that they are not likely to have forgotten this skill, Dyeing with plant dye sources, however, is another question. The use of such dye sources in Afghanistan was largely abandoned at least 40 years ago, in most cases, only the oldest generation will have retained any of this knowledge and experience. We have located two individuals who claim experience in this regard - whether their experience will prove adequate in obtaining the range of colours we need is something we will have to explore.

Remember that the ultimate arm of this project is only to serve as a model and as a tool for opening up new market possibilities for the Afghan Turkmen weavers. It is not intended to corner the market on this type of rug production. We only hope to receive and market those rugs for which we have paid the actual material and labour costs. Hopefully, the success of this project will inspire other Turkmen entrepreneurs and families to carry on independently in a similar vein. In such cases we will, of course, lose control over the product in regard to dye quality, wool quality and the traditional nature of the design. We can only hope and assume that, as in Turkey, the market itself will dictate a demand for quality and tradition on various levels. Within six months of this writing we hope to have the first sample rugs, probably small, off of the loom and ready for sale in Cambridge, Massachusetts.

It could be almost anywhere in rural northern Pakistan: a small, crowded bazaar lines both sides of a dirt road with countless shop fronts made of mud. Only the people are different - the faces, the clothing, indeed the entire feeling - because this is not Pakistan, but Afghanistan in exile. The faces are all Central Asian and the behaviour is reserved, not aggressive. These people are all Turkmen. You get the clear and unmistakable feeling that you have entered a Turkmen village or small own somewhere in Central Asia.

This is Faisal Camp, the Turkmen subdivision of greater Sawabi Camp (the Afghan refugee camps are generally divided according to ethnicity and local origin, just as was Afghanistan). Yet there is no village in the world like this. It goes on and on, 600,000 people living in this amorphous, infinitely extendable Central Asian village sitting in the Pakistani Panjab plain.

Today is the 15th of February, a long-awaited date. Indeed, the last Russian soldier does leave Afghanistan on this day. But the mood here in the camp is decidedly low key; if a war has been won, still nobody seems to be celebrating. Or perhaps the feeling is simply one of realism: the struggle is not over until the Afghan Communist regime falls - which everyone fully expects to happen - and until the parties of the Mujahideen agree on some type of consensus government. In any case, no one is talking about packing up and heading for home - not for the time being, anyway.

Everyone, then, continues to do what they've been doing for the last five or eight years, which for the Turkmen is weaving carpets. Since carpet weaving is their primary means of livelihood here, the Turkmen have tried to exploit almost every conceivable riche of the market. Rug sizes range from 2 by 2 inches (to be put under drinking glasses?) to approximately 10 by 14 feet. From traditional Turkmen designs, they have branched out into Persian city and village designs as well as Caucasian designs. "War rugs" - that is, rugs with tank, helicopter and gun designs - seem to be quite a hit in the West, and are being knocked off the looms in prodigious numbers. One may hope that this is a passing phase, but it is, for now, very much a commercial enterprise, not an individual's eccentric inspiration. Another new item is bicycle seat covers - carpets woven in the shape of a bicycle seat (probably for the Pakistani market).

Peshawar can be considered the capital of Afghanistan in exile: it is the central command post of the Mujahideen, the locus of most of the relief organizations and also the largest market for Afghan carpets, both new and old. The flood of refugees has turned this always crowded but previously moderate-sized city into an unplanned metropolis of some 2 million, plagued by noise, dust and air pollution - in short, a city bursting at the seams. Even so, given these conditions and the somewhat intimidating number of weapons on display it is probably one of the more interesting places remaining in the East to do business. There are no large dealers here, just hundreds of small-scale Afghan dealers, most of them either Turkmen or Persian-speaking Afghans.

The other aspect that makes doing business here interesting is the presence of older rugs, an increasingly rare commodity in the East these days. Although you cannot find any real antiques in Peshawar, there are at least semi-antique rugs - say, 15-50 years old-available in numbers that have not been seen in Turkey for at least five years. Even these, however, are quickly drying up.

A surprise to me on this trip was the amount of Iranian goods now on the market in Pakistan. What with the current shortage in the Afghan supply, the numbers are almost pushing those of Afghan goods available. Most of what can be seen are semi-antique southern and western Iranian village rugs and kilims - Shiraz, Qashqai, Afshar and the like. Almost anything woven in Iran seems to turn up here, including the finer town rugs. Most of these rugs are smuggled into Pakistan through Baluchistan. This activity exists on such a large scale because of the great discrepancy between the official Iranian bank-export rate and the black market rate for hard currency. Although I refrained from buying these rugs because of the US embargo on Iranian goods, the dealers hero say that many of them are destined for the United States. The majority probably go to Europe, particularly the kilims, which are very hot now on the Italian and Spanish markets.

# 4

# The Taliban Stakes of Pakistan

As Ahmad Rashid has described so well, the Taliban (Islamic student) movement sprang from Pushtun refugees in Pakistan, concentrated in temporary camps in western Pakistan. Pushtun young men who had grown up in these camps were drawn back to the Afghan homeland after the Soviet exit, but under civil war conditions in their country. These youths had been trained in the use of small arms (carrying weapons was a natural legacy of their culture) and taught to believe they could impose a peaceful, Islamic moral order on their country. Most had no deep memory of traditional social life in Afghanistan itself, many had lost their parents and, being displaced, few were accustomed to the valued roles women played in Afghan society. The Taliban religious outlook was a product of the free, but largely Quranic, obscurantist education available to boys in the austere camp environments. Their teachers themselves typically were religious leaders (*maulvis* or *mullahs*) from Deobandi or Wahabi brands of fundamentalist Islam who ran traditional religious schools (*madrassas*) with hostels, frequently using them as recruiting grounds for political ends.

When the Soviet forces withdrew from Afghanistan in 1989, the United States essentially washed its hands of responsibility for the future of that debilitated country. Having defeated Soviet power and installed a weak Islamic republic under Tajik cleric Burhanuddin Rabbani in Kabul, Afghan mujahideen groups increasingly quarreled among themselves on ethnic and tribal lines and most of Afghanistan succumbed to internal warfare. Pakistan's elected, bureaucratic and armed leaders could not so easily ignore this turbulence and groped for a strategy that would restore civil order beyond Pakistan's borders in Afghanistan.

Under liberal Prime Minister and Interior Minister in 1993, the government of Pakistan worked out a two-fold strategy toward Afghanistan: (a) to support the revival of traditional Pushtun rule in the hope of extinguishing inter-tribal war, suppressing banditry, reopening roads, reviving trade with Iran and Central Asia, and securing Afghanistan for Western-financed pipeline projects that could provide Afghanistan revenue while transporting natural gas from Turkmenistan to Pakistan and on to India; and (b) to preempt Pushtun revival of the demand for a separate Pushtun state (Pakhtunistan) that had threatened Pakistan's integrity in the northwest tribal belt for many years after Independence, by ensuring the primacy of Pushtun stakes in Afghanistan's future.

The Taliban association emerging from the refugee settlements provided a natural political vehicle for this Pakistani strategy. It depended on the cooperation of the Islamist political parties that sponsored the Taliban in the camps. The task merely involved lightly arming and training Taliban cadres, and negotiating their entry through Quetta to join those Pushtun militia leaders inside Afghanistan who deplored the country's internal disintegration and aspired, however crudely, to pacify, reunify and rebuild Afghanistan. The Pakistani armed intelligence arm, the Inter-Services Intelligence agency (ISI)—which had served as the main American and Saudi conduit for training, financial support, and transferring arms to the Afghan mujahideen—became the overseers and managers of Pakistan's assistance to the Taliban. This ISI role was secretive, but it was no rogue operation—as some in Pakistan and the United States may now wish to believe. Rather, it was the policy of Pakistan's elected governments from 1993, including that of the Harvard- and Oxford-educated Benazir Bhutto, Pakistan's first female prime minister.

The Taliban gained a local foothold around Kandahar in 1994 and then rapidly spread within southern and eastern Afghanistan, seizing Kabul and asserting a claim to govern Afghanistan in 1996, with all but a northeastern tenth of the country falling under their sway by 1998. Some financial support for the Taliban came from

Saudi Arabia and other Gulf states. The Taliban regime was formally recognized by Saudi Arabia, Pakistan, and United Arab Emirates as the government of Afghanistan. Other governments and the United Nations either continued to recognize the first mujahideen (Rabbani) government even after it fled Kabul, or declined to recognize the Taliban regime, hoping that diplomacy and United Nations relief could patch together a workable, coalition government more representative of the country as a whole.

Almost imperceptible to Westerners at the start, the Taliban project at first was not considered objectionable in Washington. The Taliban became anathema only later, after word of its brutality spread. Having seized power in Kabul, the Taliban's inhumane governing practices undercut its once positive reputation for disarming warlord factions and bringing peace in one locality after another. From Kabul, the new regime imposed uniquely harsh judicial procedures and tried to force the surviving remnants of Afghanistan's battered urban society to give up music and entertainment. On pain of beating or even execution, men were forced to grow beards and wear traditional clothes, and women to leave jobs and whenever outdoors to wear the head-to-toe covering known as *burqas*. Western revulsion was aroused by media reports of the Taliban's draconian interpretation of Islamic law, confinement of women, suppression of female education, arbitrary arrests, mutilation or execution as punishments, and intolerance of non-Muslim religious minorities.

However a great deal the Taliban was eventually despised in the West, it was not the offspring of, nor originally associated with, al-Qaeda. Osama bin Laden apparently left Sudan in 1996 and moved back to Afghanistan some time in 1997. Thereafter, al-Qaeda gradually extended influence over the Taliban by spending its own resources to win the favour of senior Taliban leaders. Al-Qaeda also provided armed support and guidance to Taliban fighters who were fighting the Northern Alliance forces and other autonomous factions elsewhere in the country. The United States focused only on the significance of the Taliban's grant of sanctuary to al-Qaeda after its bombing of U.S. Embassies in East Africa in 1998.

Toward the end of its tenure, the Clinton administration put considerable pressure on Pakistan to arrange communication with Taliban officials, hoping to persuade them to expel Osama bin Laden and his associates. But the Taliban's counter demand was that it be recognized as Afghanistan's de jure government. This price the United States was unwilling to pay. How deeply the Taliban depended on al-Qaeda for armed operations against the Northern Alliance was not apparent to ordinary observers until after 9/11. What was clear, however, was that Pakistan had a major stake in the Taliban's claim to govern Afghanistan, was opposed to the Northern Alliance, and could not disengage from those positions in Afghanistan, short of a world-shaking crisis. September 11 brought just that crisis.

This analysis indicates that Pakistan's stakes in the Taliban were not based on a ordinary religion or on matters or Islamic principle, per se. Pakistan was interested in geopolitical objectives, not in the religious aims of the Taliban or its parochial justification of a strict Islamic discipline. Pakistan hoped to foster order through a client regime in a war-torn country on its borders. In doing so, it aimed to promote the revival of trade, to link Central Asian energy resources with the subcontinent, and to extinguish any Pushtun impulse to tear part of Pakistan away as a separate Pushtun state.

Exploiting reservoirs of Afghan Islamic fervor was useful to Pakistan (as well as to the United States) against the Soviet forces in Afghanistan, and useful again to Pakistan in helping the Taliban come to power, but the Taliban movement's Islamic fundamentalist orientation was never for Pakistan's government an end in itself. Only a smattering of individual Pakistanis and fundamentalist groups—mainly Pushtun tribes and Islamic political parties with roots in the Pushtun tribal regions—identified with the Taliban cause emotionally or ideologically. For the Pakistani authorities, the Taliban's religious appeal was only a tool.

Far more basic for Pakistan's government, and painful to abandon, was the aim of Pushtun dominance within Afghanistan as a means of resolving the civil war and opening the way to the trans-Afghanistan energy project. In achieving this aim, to cut off the Taliban even after George W. Bush threw down the gauntlet was tantamount to sacrificing Pushtun interests in Afghan politics and undermining Pakistan's interests in Afghanistan's stability and its own security. Pakistan's view of the power of the Northern Alliance, perhaps mistakenly, was that it jeopardized stability in Afghanistan. Thus, when Pakistani chief Pervez Musharraf turned against the Taliban under U.S. pressure, the decision was acutely difficult. Because Pakistan's strategy toward Afghanistan—and its own security on its western borders—was based on a successful Taliban campaign for power, it required accepting a fundamentally different calculation of Pakistan's national interests.

The new calculation was that Pakistan could not afford to be stigmatized by the West as a terrorist state. Once the Taliban refused to dissociate itself from al-Qaeda, Islamabad recognized that the United States would regard the Taliban as a de facto "terrorist" regime, and a legitimate object of armed attack. For Pakistan to be associated with the Taliban political cause after that would not only put Pakistan on a slippery slope toward international ostracism but could be used, potentially, to justify armed attack on Pakistan itself. Indeed, it was exactly this sensitivity that India latched onto when it initiated a armed confrontation with Pakistan after the attack on parliament in December 2001. But before we examine that crisis, the dramatic progress of the U.S. war in Afghanistan and the potential effects on the Kashmir side of Pakistan's Afghanistan-related entanglement need separate discussion.

## ARMED MOVEMENT AGAINST THE TALIBAN AND AL-QAEDA

Pakistan had to make a decision very quickly whether it would support the U.S. armed effort in Afghanistan. Senior Pakistani officials announced on September 15, *within four days* of the 9/11 terrorist attacks on the United States, that they had agreed to give "full support" to U.S. efforts to combat international terrorism. President Musharraf 's address in Urdu to the nation three days later informed his people that the United States had demanded armed overflight rights, logistical support, and intelligence cooperation against three targets—Osama bin Laden, the Taliban, and international terror-ism. Musharraf noted that the United

States had won United Nations support and confided to the nation that neighbouring India had offered its armed facilities to the United States in the hopes of isolating Pakistan and getting it declared a terrorist state. Musharraf made it clear to his countrymen that Pakistan had to assist the United States; otherwise four vital interests of Pakistan would be in jeopardy—its sovereignty, its economy, its strategic (nuclear and missile) assets, and its cause in Kashmir. Musharraf and his advisors apparently drew the line, however, at inserting Pakistani armed forces into Afghanistan.

Despite concerns about a violent domestic backlash from political parties and groups that had links with the Taliban as well as the threat of al-Qaeda or Taliban attacks across the border, Pakistan thus committed itself almost overnight to give the United States valuable flight corridors over its territory and access to stage U.S. search and rescue forces at facilities near Karachi in the south and closer to Afghanistan at the Pakistani armed airfield near Jacobabad. Pakistani forces also provided backstopping for U.S. operations against al-Qaeda and the Taliban later, by attempting to seal the mountainous borders so as to prevent hostile units fleeing across the border into Pakistan. Pakistani intelligence and security forces also cooperated with covert U.S. forces in efforts to hunt down those al-Qaeda and Taliban elements that succeeded in entering Pakistan to take refuge, or to slip out of the country.

*Operation Enduring Freedom* against al-Qaeda and Taliban forces in Afghanistan began with air strikes on October 7, 2001. Saudi Arabia had vetoed U.S. use of amenities on its soil for the attack and Iran denied access through its airspace. This put a much greater burden on U.S. aircraft carriers and other naval forces that assembled in the Arabian Sea, on bombers that had been flown to Diego Garcia and some that flew all the way from the United States, and on the prodigious use of aircraft refueling capabilities. But to the surprise of most observers, Russian President Putin gave his blessing to the U.S. counterterrorist effort and the leaders of three post-Soviet Central Asian states neighbouring Afghanistan—Uzbekistan, Tajikistan, and Kyrgizstan—provided the United States air access and staging facilities near Afghanistan in the north and west. Use of these facilities greatly eased U.S. cooperation with the Afghan Northern Alliance and the Uzbek elements that had reestablished a presence under General Rashid Dostum and that would retake Mazar-i-Sharif.

As a result, not merely was the United States able to use its own infiltrated ground spotters and air strikes to destroy exposed Taliban armed assets and installations—there were relatively few big targets— but it was also able to use airborne firepower to break down the front lines of the Taliban forces opposite the Northern Alliance, enabling the alliance and the other anti-Taliban forces that reemerged to advance, taking Mazar-i-Sharif, Kabul, Herat and Konduz in succession. Mazar-i-Sharif fell on November 9. Kabul was retaken on November 12, and Herat fell the same day. Konduz, where a combined force of about twenty thousand al-Qaeda and Taliban forces put up a fierce resistance, fell on November 24.

A thousand U.S. marines were airlifted on November 26 into a remote landing strip (dubbed Camp Rhino) fifteen miles southeast of Kandahar to provide protection for a buildup of helicopters, armored personnel carriers, and the entry of additional special operations units.

This also provided the United States with a staging area inside Afghanistan to pursue operations in the Pushtun areas to the north and east, including near the border with Pakistan. Coupled with well-targeted air raids, the ground presence of U.S. combat forces helped break the main, residual Taliban resistance in the south, stimulated defections, and forced the hard core to disperse into hiding. Kandahar fell on December 7.

Aided by the Rome political process of negotiating a new Afghan government, Hamid Karzai's leadership had begun by this time to make significant headway among Pushtun elements in the south and east that could absorb defectors and accommodate the Northern Alliance in forming a new government in Kabul. The U.S.-assisted Afghan meetings in Rome helped negotiate agreed steps to constitute a new, representative government in stages—and made the level of international commitment to rehabilitating Afghanistan clearer.

Special combat operations shifted once Kandahar had fallen to the White Mountains, near Khost, adjoining Pakistan, where al-Qaeda and Taliban forces had taken refuge in fortified and well-provisioned mountain caves and bunkers. The Tora Bora operations heavily bombed the cave complexes and ground units then cleared most of them on the ground by early January 2002. Several hundred al-Qaeda and Taliban prisoners were taken, with many shipped to Guantanamo Bay in Cuba for interrogation. A significant number of the al-Qaeda Arabs at Tora Bora evidently slipped through into Pakistan, however. In March, U.S. and allied forces gathered in Operation Anaconda to attack a well-dug-in al-Qaeda/Taliban force of about 1,500 fighters in the Shah-e-Kot Mountains south of Gardez in northeastern Afghanistan. Anaconda produced the largest number of U.S. casualties in a single Afghan operation, but apparently took a heavy toll on the enemy, killing an estimated four hundred to eight hundred opponents. Again, some of the fighters melted away into Pakistan, although in this case Pakistani forces intercepted and fought small units, capturing and turning over a number of al-Qaeda members to the United States for interrogation.

In roughly six months U.S. and allied armed intervention, coupled with the residual anti-Taliban forces in Afghanistan, had radically transformed the situation. Momentum increasingly favored the formation of a new Afghan government—although it was clear that such a government would be hard put to establish order throughout the country and develop the capacity, even with international assistance, to conduct a far-reaching economic and social rehabilitation program. Pockets of Taliban and al-Qaeda resistance remained, with a capacity to harass the emerging Karzai government and foment perceptions of disorder, but by summer 2002, these isolated elements no longer held the capacity to counter-attack the U.S. and allied presence in any major way.

During that armed campaign, the radical Islamic backlash that the Musharraf government had feared would erupt within Pakistan launched a handful of demonstrations but then largely subsided during the remainder of 2001. Considerable anti-American feeling and anger with Musharraf's decisions percolated below the surface but potentially massive, violent agitation was contained. Meanwhile, the level of violence in Kashmir rose to a degree. Then on December 13, 2001, halfway through the armed campaign, terrorists struck the Indian parliament and precipitated a full Indian armed mobilization against Pakistan.

## PAKISTAN'S GAINS FROM REHABILITATED U.S. NOTICE

The United States had been moving away from the sanctions policy toward both India and Pakistan that it had imposed after each country's nuclear tests in May 1998 and used this opportunity to drop many of the provisions affecting financial and non-sensitive material assistance temporarily. The United States also approved a financial aid package for Pakistan that permitted the rescheduling of its international indebtedness, lifting a cloud from its economy. But the most important gain for Pakistan was the sudden U.S. need for Pakistan's armed and intelligence support, a reflection of Pakistan's geopolitical importance in pursuing the initial stages of the war against terrorism in Afghanistan—giving Pakistan an unexpected opportunity to get back into the good graces of Washington.

During most of the 1990s, the Clinton administration had courted India assiduously, even before the ascent of the Bharatiya Janata Party (BJP) and the shock of the nuclear tests in early 1998, and continued to seek an improved relationship despite the nuclear shocks. Pakistan's covert armed operations across the line of control (LOC) in Kashmir near Kargil in May 2001 precipitated a mini-war with India that could have escalated. President Clinton's use of his good offices to persuade Pakistani Prime Minister Nawaz Sharif to end this conflict and withdraw Pakistani paraarmed forces behind the LOC measurably improved Delhi's disposition toward the United States. Much the same trend toward a closer U.S.-India relationship continued in the Bush administration. The increasing tilt toward India and away from Pakistan was in sharp contrast to the special relationship Pakistan had had with Washington during the Cold War years. But the 9/11 crisis showed, at least momentarily, that India's armed and intelligence value to the United States in launching the war on terrorism in Afghanistan was less than that of Pakistan's, once it was clear that Pakistan's cooperation was readily available.

In calculation to reviving Pakistan's importance, the U.S. armed presence within Pakistan, albeit limited and restricted largely to southern Pakistan, could have been construed to have an implicit deterrent value against direct Indian aggression on Pakistan, at least while the tempo of operations in Afghanistan remained high and Pakistan's active cooperation in pursuit of al-Qaeda and Taliban elements who fled into Pakistan was needed. This calculated judgment may have eased Pakistan's initial decisions to shift some armed capability away from the east, facing India, to seal the borders and provide a form of backstopping of U.S. and allied operations against al-Qaeda and Taliban forces, raising barriers to cross-border infiltration.

It became clear later, however, that this unspoken deterrence was not comprehensive or robust. It did not dissuade India from mounting a sustained conventional armed confrontation in December, and the United States moved rather slowly in 2002—staying far quieter about the risk of nuclear war in the subcontinent than its previous policies would have implied—before it began to press India to unwind the confrontation in June and July. Nevertheless, the operations in Afghanistan gave Pakistan opportunities to put its relationship with Washington on a more productive footing, and to compete for Washington's attention after years of losing ground. If momentum is sustained in repairing this relationship, it could pay very significant dividends to Pakistan over time. It is too early to tell at this juncture whether this will be the case.

Judging by the reaction of its media and attentive public, Indians were greatly outraged by the attention Pakistan got from the United States after Musharraf signaled his support to Bush and U.S. armed operations in Afghanistan began. This belied the fact that U.S. efforts to build a broader relationship with India not only stayed in high gear but intensified, drawing satisfaction from India's strong rhetorical support of, and offer of its facilities for use in, the war against terrorism. India's disarmingly positive reception of Bush's decision to withdraw the United States from the Anti-Ballistic Missile (ABM) Treaty, coincidentally announced on December 13, 2001, was received by the Bush administration as an unexpected boon. Thus, while the war against terrorism brought Pakistan back to the foreground, it did nothing to diminish India's growing influence in Washington, although this would not have been apparent to an outsider watching the intense indignation and recrimination portrayed in the Indian press and television.

## HOW PROGRESSIVES GOT AFGHANISTAN WRONG

Against the sunny predictions of the cruise missile left, Afghanistan is in ruins. Western bombings in Herat, Farah, and Kunduz have led to mass civilian death, while nighttime house raids murder more intimately in Ghazi Khan and Khatabeh.

The casualty figures should shame the war's supporters. Bob Dreyfuss and Nick Turse of the *Nation* calculate that even by conservative counts, the deaths of 6,481 civilians were directly attributable to ISAF and the Afghan government with which it is allied. Thousands more have been killed by insurgents, fighting a war of the West's making.

Nor has this blood soaked path led to a promising post-Taliban future. Afghanistan has the worst rate of infant mortality in the world. Half of Afghan children suffer irreversible harm from malnutrition. The UN's 2013 Human Development Index ranks Afghanistan 175 out of 186 countries. Thomas Ruttig of Afghanistan Analysis Network writes that "economic activity in general [is] falling," unemployment and crime are rising, and that 60 percent of children are malnourished. Just 27 percent of the population has access to safe drinking water.

The record of Hamid Karzai's government is blighted by torture, corruption,warlords, and a fraudulent 2009 election. Nor has freedom and safety for Afghanistan's ever-instrumentalized women come about.

In March of 2013, the ISAF-backed Karzai endorsed a statement that refers to women as "secondary," bars violence against women only for "un-Islamic" reasons, and advocates gender segregation in schools, workplaces, and public spaces. In 2012 the burn unit of an Afghan hospital admitted a record number of women who tried to set themselves on fire. And Suraya Pakzad, who runs women's shelters in the country, has described cases of women being publicly stoned while ISAF-trained Afghan troops looked on.

Moreover, the war's hideous violence has benefited the ultra-misogynistic Taliban. A November 2013 study conducted by a team of scholars from Yale and Princeton finds that among Afghans "Harm inflicted by the International Security Assistance Force (ISAF) is met with reduced support for ISAF and increased support for the Taliban, but Taliban-inflicted harm does not translate into greater ISAF support."

All of these outcomes are perfectly predictable and were in fact anticipated by many. As the United States prepares to withdraw most of its forces from Afghanistan, it is worth looking back at the debates many had during the lead-up to and early phases of that war.

While it is easy to say in hindsight that such writers as Tariq Ali and Marjorie Cohn were correct to oppose the intervention and that others like Michael Bérubé, Michael Kazin, Todd Gitlin and Michael Walzer were wrong to endorse it, an examination of how the latter group got it wrong is necessary. Clarifying the analytic errors made by the imperialist "left" at the time are important because some have since taken similar approaches to Iraq and more recently to Libya and Syria.

"Progressive" boosterism for the Afghan war had several calling cards. Chief among them was how authors touted their credentials in opposing past cases of US aggression, in some cases professed concern for the Palestinians, and bragged of a left-of-center track record on social and economic issues.

However, the left-imperialists believed that differences in the tactics and ideological orientation of the US' enemies in Afghanistan were major reasons that the Afghan war was legitimate whereas the ventures in Vietnam and Nicaragua were not. Cruise missile leftists ignored that while the context of US military action had changed, no moment of rupture had taken place within the American state that directs that military.

By contrast, leftists who opposed the war in Afghanistan did so because they understood that the character of US power and its allied states is such that wars against the smaller and poorer nations are exercises in accumulation and imperialism by their very nature.

The cruise-missile leftists also made sure to attack those who were not so eager to drop cluster bombs on Afghan villagers. For example, Chomsky accurately pointed to a September 16, 2001 report that the US government "demanded" that Pakistan end "truck convoys that provide much of the food and other supplies to Afghanistan's civilian population." Chomsky used Burns' report to decisively show that the US was taking actions that it knew would harm Afghan civilians, and that it was therefore unreasonable to believe the war was going to liberate Afghans or even attempt to do so.

In response to this, Bérubé raged that Chomsky was exhibiting "a repellent mix of hysteria and hauteur," without even attempting to refute the argument.

Progressive warmongers frequently accused anti-imperialists of claiming in a simplistic way that the US is incapable of helping the world's oppressed. Yet in the same breath such cruise missile leftists would demand simplistic, unequivocal declarations of the US' moral superiority.

Gitlin wrote that the anti-imperialists were "Like jingoists who consider any effort to understand terrorists immoral, on the grounds that to understand is to endorse, [because these leftist] hard-liners disdain complexity." For Gitlin, the problem is that anti-imperialism is a "cartoon view of the world [where] there is nothing worse than American power — not the woman-enslaving Taliban, not an unrepentant Al Qaeda committed to killing civilians as they please."

According to Gitlin's one-dimensional view, there was no room for considerations such as the degree to which bombing and occupying Afghanistan and propping up a warlord regime with its own rather patriarchal tendencies might have adverse effects on the people of that country, particularly Afghan women. To

Gitlin, it was necessary to overlook complications such as the fact that ISAF's (ultimately failed) "rescue" of Afghan women would inevitably mean killing, detaining or horribly wounding thousands of their fathers, grandfathers, brothers, community members, and friends—and quite a few Afghan women themselves.

Anti-imperialist arguments against war in Afghanistan can be roughly divided into three categories. The first category of anti-war argument was to point out, asChomsky and Cohn did, that the invasion of Afghanistan violated international law and was also fundamentally unjust.

The second involved identifying the US state as imperialist, and thus pre-occupied with the standard concerns of imperialism: militarized accumulationand geostrategic advantage — goals which tend to harm the peoples of the South.

Arguments of this variety were supported by the third approach, which showed that Western policy in Afghanistan belied the idea that ISAF's actions would better the lives of Afghans. For example, Chomsky pointed to the UN's Food and Agriculture Organization, who advised that the bombing of Afghanistan "had disrupted planting that provides 80 percent of the country's grain supplies." And Arundhati Roy took the same approach when she noted, just before the war began, that "the UN estimates that there are eight million Afghan citizens who need emergency aid. As supplies run out – food and aid agencies have been asked to leave – the BBC reports that one of the worst humanitarian disasters of recent times has begun to unfold."

By contrast, much of the "progressive" defense of the war in Afghanistan, and the War on Terror more generally, was based on vacuous excoriations of the Left for its failure to "live up to its core values."

Similarly, then-*Dissent* editor Michael Walzer explained that he had "a modest agenda: put decency first." Bérubé dismissed "morally odious" the idea that "the bombing of Afghanistan was the moral equivalent of the 9/11 attacks." Gitlin described Roy as "in the grip of a prejudice invulnerable to moral distinctions" because she compared the corruption and brutality of Bush to that of bin Laden. In place of engagement with details and complexities, what the progressive imperialists offered were arbitrary, content-free, ill-defined concepts being put forth by tut-tutting, finger-wagging white guys with tenure.

Little has changed. The pro-war progressives have made the same points amid the 2011 NATO bombing of Libya and leading up to the military campaign that the US nearly undertook in Syria in 2013 and may attempt again in the future.

For example, in the spring of 2012 Bérubé was denouncing anti-imperialists who opposed NATO's war in Libya. He boasts that the intervention prevented a massacre — even though NATO and the forces whose victory they enabled actually carried out multiple massacres. In so doing, Bérubé resurrects Walzer's question of whether a "decent left" was possible, though Bérubé thinks the phrasing could be tweaked:

The question, rather, should have been whether there can be a rigorously internationalist left in the U.S., a left that will promote and support the freedom of speech, the freedom to worship, the freedom from want, and the freedom from fear—even on those rare and valuable occasions when doing so puts one in the position of supporting U.S. policies.

Set aside that in Libya NATO did no such thing. Bérubé blithely assumes, as pro-war progressives had in Afghanistan, that NATO states act in pursuit of the freedom of oppressed peoples. It is holding idealist beliefs such as these despite all evidence to the contrary that causes Bérubé to celebrate in Libya, as he had in Afghanistan, an empire shedding of the blood of dark-skinned people.

On Syria, *Dissent* editor Michael Kazin was upset by the tenor of Dreyfuss's opposition to Western intervention. Though Kazin is equivocal about the merits of bombing Syria, he thinks it reasonable "to want to punish the Syrian government for violating a ban on [sarin gas] the first weapon which nearly every nation agreed, back in the 1920s, never to use again."

As with Bérubé's misdiagnosis of the Libyan war, there's no need to dwell on Kazin's easy acceptance of the claim that it was

Bashar al-Assad's government who used sarin gas in August 2013 despite significant evidence to the contrary.

Kazin's basic error is to principally focus on the nature of Assad's regime while ignoring the character of the institutions that determine policy within Western states and overlooking how that could undermine the chances that their bombing of Syria will create a just peace in that country.

Furthermore, Kazin took exception to leftists who he felt opposed bombing Syria in overly strident terms, on the grounds that this allegedly "dishonors the vision of a left which, at its best, has always adhered, in essence, to the motto of the late, great New York City daily PM: 'We are against people who push other people around, just for the fun of pushing, whether they flourish in this country or abroad.'"

Presumably the civilians who would die in a US-led bombing campaign, and in the likely escalation of the Syrian war, might feel "push[ed] around" by the cruise missiles falling on them but Kazin could not see that.

An opposition to those who "push other people around" is the vaguest of vague abstractions, belied most of all by its inattention to the biggest bully on the block: the American ruling class. Indeed, while it may be a fine principle on which to supervise recess, it completely overlooks the myriad complexities and contingencies that characterize any war and most certainly the one in Syria.

In the debates over the West's imperialist aggression against Afghanistan, the assessments made by the radical Left proved correct primarily because they derived from observable phenomena.

And among the most significant lessons to draw from progressive support for the war in Afghanistan is one that progressives had to no excuse not to know by 2001: while there is often a shortage of immediate results-yielding ways to support people in the Global South dealing with problems of inequality and human rights, one surefire way to not be of use is to rally support for imperial armies to invade, bomb, militarily occupy, jail en masse, torture, and kill the people in question.

## EXPANSION OF PAKISTAN'S ANTI-TERRORISM REGIME

The purpose of this paper is to examine the policies of Pakistan relevant to its goal of combating terrorism during the past five years. Regardless of how one defines "terrorism," Pakistan is a particularly appropriate case study when one approaches policies of "anti-terrorism." First, the political history of Pakistan is rife with policies designed to combat terrorism in its various guises. Clearly, the Ayub Khan regime was no stranger to the use of policies to justify the suppression of domestic opposition as it PRODA'ed and EBDO'ed its way through periods of guided democracy. One should also not forget Z.A. Bhutto's contribution to the craft. His Suppression of Terrorist Activities Ordinance, 1975 held the field in the Sindh and Punjab until its repeal in 1997 and remained the law in the North West Frontier Province (NWFP) and Baluchistan until August 2001. Zia ul-Haq was not averse to the use of the extra-judicial device to counter "threats to the state," and the democratic tag team of Benazir Bhutto and Nawaz Sharif transformed the use of the ad hoc special court into an art form to combat each other and each other's political supporters from 1989–97.

Second, Pakistan has had its share—perhaps more than its split— of domestic violence. The ethnonational violence that eventually occasioned the horrors of the Bangladesh civil war is a case in point. But, one should not forget the Baloch nationalist movement (*really* "civil war"), nor the Movement for the Restoration of Democracy (MRD) disturbances, nor the bloody Muhajir Qaumi Mahaz (MQM)- Sindhi riots. Each of these conflicts raised issues similar to those raised during the past five years—the state was challenged by violent opposition; civil order was threatened; the state needed latitude to respond; departures from "normal" legal practice were justifiable, if not required. Despite these earlier events, however, the post-1997 policies of Nawaz Sharif mark a qualitative departure in the nature of Pakistan's policies. Nawaz Sharif was the first Pakistani decision maker to craft an "anti-terrorism" strategy. Heretofore, successive Pakistani decision makers had adopted policies designed to target political opponents or to address ethnonational conflict. Such policies, at times, departed from the norm—they were justified as "necessary" or as meeting "emergencies"—and, at times, the targets of such policies were labeled "terrorists." But, such decision makers did not create an ideology that justified such departures from the norm, they did not create permanent institutions that dealt with "terrorism," and they did not construct an "anti-terrorism regime."

## Construct the Regime

On 18 January 1997 Mehram Ali, a foot soldier of the Shia militant organization Tehrik Nifaz Fiqh-i-Jafaria (TNFJ), planted a remote-controlled pipe bomb in the grounds of the district court complex in Lahore. He detonated the bomb. When the debris settled the bodies of twenty-three victims were found, including those of Maulana Zia-ur-Rehman Farooqi and Maulana Azam Tariq, both members, the latter the chairman, of the Sipah-i-Sahaba Pakistan (SSP), a militant Sunni organization.

The latter victims had been brought to the Additional Sessions judge's office from the Kot Lakhpat jail where they were serving sentences related to their earlier anti-Shia crimes. Fifty-five others were also injured in the blast. Mehram Ali was caught at the scene but his trial before the Sessions court dragged on. The case generated considerable press coverage and provided the context, perhaps pretext, for the government's introduction of the Anti-Terrorism Act of 1997, which came into effect on 20 August. The Mehram Ali case was transferred to the newly constituted special Anti-Terrorism Court (ATC) in late August, where Ali was awarded a death sentence, convicted for twenty-three counts of murder, and various other sentences related to the bombing. He filed an appeal before the newly constituted Anti-Terrorism Appellate (ATA) Tribunal, also in Lahore. The ATA upheld his conviction. The petitioner then filed a writ petition before the Lahore High Court claiming, among other things, that the formation of the special courts violated provisions of the constitution. The Lahore High Court claimed jurisdiction to hear the appeal, but held that the conviction should still stand. Mehram Ali then filed an appeal to the Supreme Court of Pakistan. The Anti-Terrorism Act of 1997 was the brainchild of the Nawaz Sharif government, which had been returned to power in February 1997 following a landslide victory that left Sharif 's party, the Pakistan Muslim League, with an overwhelming majority in the national assembly. The motives for the introduction of the Anti-Terrorism Act were mixed. Clearly, Pakistan had suffered from very significant communal and sectarian violence for the past several years, and the regular criminal justice system had not been able to curb such violence. In this context, the ATCs, with their "promise" of speedy justice, unencumbered by the procedural niceties of the regular court system, would serve as a deterrent to would-be terrorists. Also, Nawaz Sharif and his political allies may have seen merit in establishing a parallel judicial system in which the numerous ongoing trials of his political enemies (especially prominent officials of the Pakistan People's Party [PPP]) could be transferred for speedy disposal. In any case, the Anti-Terrorism Act was a bold departure from the normal legal system. First, the 1997 act broadly defined "terrorism" to include:

> Whoever, to strike terror in the people, or any section of the people, or to alienate any section of the people or to adversely affect harmony among different sections of the people, does any act or thing by using bombs, dynamite or other explosive or inflammable substances, or firearms, or other lethal weapons or poisons or noxious gases or chemicals or other substances of a hazardous nature in such a manner as to cause, or to be likely to cause the death of, or injury to, any person or persons, or damage to, or destruction of, property or disruption of any supplies or services essential to the life of the community or displays firearms, or threatens with the use of force public servants in order to prevent them from discharging their lawful duties commits a terrorist act.

Crimes included within the purview of the act were: a) murder; b) the malicious insult of the religious beliefs of any class; c) the use of derogatory remarks in respect of the holy personages; d) kidnapping; e) and various statutes relating to "robbery and dacoity." Clearly, terrorism as defined by the act was in the "eyes of the prosecutor," that is, the terms of the act could be interpreted to include virtually any violent act, or encouragement of the commission of a violent act. Second, the act created special "anti-terrorism" courts. Such courts would be established by the government in their discretion and would be headed by a judge of a Sessions court, or an additional Sessions judge, or a district magistrate, or a deputy district magistrate, or an advocate with ten or more years of experience appointed by the government. Such judges would have no specific tenure of office, serving at the discretion of the government. Strict time constraints would govern the procedures of such particular courts—the prosecution would be given seven days to complete the investigation and the court would be given seven days to try the case. The recalling of witnesses would be prohibited and no adjournments, beyond two days, would be countenanced. Those accused of crimes could be tried in absentia if adequate notice concerning the dates of the trial were published in the press. Appeals against conviction and acquittal of such courts would lie *only* with special ATA Tribunals, also constituted at the discretion of the government. Such tribunals would have seven days from receipt of the appeal, which would have to be filed within three days of conviction to render a decision. The decision of the Appellate Tribunal would be final; no further appeal could be entertained. Such special courts would also have the power to have cases pending before other courts (regular courts—Sessions courts, magistrate courts) transferred to its jurisdiction, without the necessity of recalling witnesses.

As stated above, Mehram Ali's case was transferred from a Sessions judge to a special Anti-Terrorism court wherein he was convicted and awarded a death sentence; he appealed to the relevant ATA Tribunal where his conviction was upheld; he then appealed to the Lahore High Court, which claimed standing to hear the appeal despite the terms of the Anti-Terrorism Act, but still upheld the conviction; and then finally he filed an appeal before the Supreme Court. In its decision, *Mehram Ali versus Federation of Pakistan,* the court upheld Mehram Ali's conviction and he was later executed, but the court declared the bulk of the 1997 Anti-Terrorism Act to be unconstitutional.

Although the court found nothing inherently unconstitutional in the establishment of special courts for specific and pressing needs of the government, such courts would nonetheless be subject to the rules and procedures of the existing constitutionally established judicial system. That is, (1) judges of such courts would have a fixed and established tenure of service; (2) such special courts would be subject to the same or similar procedural rules as regular courts, including rules of evidence, etc.; and (3) the decisions of such special courts would be subject to appeal before the relevant constitutionally mandated regular courts. Namely, appeal against the decisions of the special courts would lie with the respective High Courts and ultimately with the Supreme Court. As Ajmal Mian, then Chief Justice of the Supreme Court found, the supervision and control over the subordinate judiciary (including the special courts) vests with the High Courts. Moreover, no parallel legal system can be constructed that bypasses the operation of the existing regular courts. Despite this finding the Supreme Court evinced sympathy for the government's avowed intent to speed justice. In a concurring opinion Justice Irshad Hasan Khan stated:

> [The] speedy resolution of civil and criminal cases is an significant constitutional goal, as envisaged by the principles of policy enshrined in the constitution. It is therefore, not undesirable to create Special Courts for operation with speed but expeditious disposition of cases of terrorist activities/heinous offenses have to be subject to constitution and law.

In light of this finding, the Nawaz Sharif government had no recourse but to amend the Anti-Terrorism Act and incorporate the changes ordered by the Supreme Court. Accordingly, on 24 October 1998 the Anti-Terrorism (Amendment) Ordinance, 1998 was issued. The new act met all of the objections raised in the *Mehram Ali* case. Therefore, Special Anti-Terrorism courts remained in place but the judges of such courts were granted tenure of office (two years, later extended to two and one-half years); the special Appellate Tribunals were disbanded, appeals against the decisions of the Anti-Terrorism courts would henceforth be to the respective High Courts; and restrictions were placed on the earlier act's provisions regarding trial in absentia to accord with regular legal procedures.

Unfortunately, civil order in Pakistan, particularly in Sindh province, continued to unravel. On 17 October 1998, Hakim

Muhammad Said, one of Karachi's most well-known citizens, a former governor of Sindh and founder of the Hamdard Foundation (*Hamdard Islamicus)* and Hamdard University, was murdered. Under increasing pressure from within his own political circle—and most likely from the military—to do something to curb such lawlessness and violence, Nawaz Sharif chose to impose Article 232 and declare a state of emergency (Governor's Rule) in Sindh Province. The purpose of the order, as expressed in the order itself, was to empower the governor to take all necessary actions "to create a peaceful environment in which ordinary citizens can conduct their day-to-day affairs in accordance with their constitutional rights and entitlement within the province."

Such laudable ends, however, led to an invitation to the armed, acting in its capacity of "aid to civil power," to take over law and order duties in Sindh Province. The result was the introduction of a form of martial law that was imposed on the province as a whole, but most enthusiastically implemented in Karachi. Perhaps understandably the armed, asked to assume functions beyond its normal duties, desired a free hand in its mission. Standing in its way were the civilian courts, with their procedures and processes and their alleged corruption. The remedy, they insisted, was the creation of armed tribunals. Nawaz Sharif complied.

The result, the Pakistan Armed Forces (Acting in Aid of Civil Power) Ordinance, 1998, is a remarkable document. Promulgated on 20 November 1998, the ordinance, which had application only to Sindh Province, extended broad judicial powers to the armed. The ordinance granted armed officers at the rank of Brigadier and above the right to "convene as many courts as may be deemed necessary to try offenders." Such courts could try civilians. Appeals against conviction by such courts would lie only with such appellate tribunals as the armed authorities deemed necessary to establish. Moreover, cases pending before other courts (regular courts and ATCs) could be transferred to such newly established armed courts. The courts would have jurisdiction to award sentences, including the death penalty, for specified crimes. The ordinance also created a "new crime" punishable with a penalty of up to seven years of rigorous imprisonment—the crime of "civil commotion."

"Civil commotion" means creation of internal disturbances in violation of law or intended to violate law, commencement or continuation of illegal strikes, go-slows, lock-outs, vehicle snatching/lifting, damage to or destruction of State or private property, random firing to create panic, charging bhatha [protection money/extortion], acts of criminal trespass, distributing, publishing or pasting of a handbill or making graffiti or wall-chalking intended to create unrest or fear or create a threat to the security of law and order.... On 30 January 1999, the authority of the ordinance was extended to the whole of Pakistan. Also, the ordinance was amended so that accused "absconders" from justice could be tried in absentia by any armed court established in Pakistan. Despite the government's claims that this ordinance was temporary and necessary given the breakdown of law and order, there was considerable public opposition to the establishment of the armed courts. Political opponents of Nawaz Sharif were particularly hostile to the implementation of the ordinance as it gave his government almost unlimited power to harass and imprison opponents. The invention of the crime of "civil commotion," particularly subject to implementation by armed courts, was very troublesome—many of the activities defined as "crimes" could also be interpreted as "normal" political behaviour. Numerous constitutional petitions were filed before the superior courts challenging the validity of the ordinance— the Supreme Court consolidated such petitions and heard the petitioners. The result was the landmark decision—*Liaquat Hussain versus Federation of Pakistan* issued on 22 February 1999.

The *Liaquat Hussain* decision is one of the most unequivocal, if not harsh, decisions ever rendered by the Supreme Court of Pakistan. It wholly repudiates the impugned ordinance, declaring the Pakistan Armed Forces (Aid to Civil) Act "unconstitutional, without legal authority, and with no legal effect." Furthermore, the court, as per the unanimous decision of the nine-member full Bench, rejected the government's argument that the act was designed to be temporary in duration and/or limited only to Sindh Province. Indeed, it uses the evidence of the aforementioned 30 January amendment to the act to prove the government's bad faith. The court also rejected the government's contention that the ordinance was expedient, and defensible under the so-called "doctrine of necessity."

It may be stated that it seems to be correct that after taking over of the executive power by the Governor in Sindh, commission of crimes has been reduced including the acts of terrorism.... Be that as it may ... if the establishment of the Armed Courts is not warranted by the constitution, simpliciter the fact that their establishment had contributed to some extent in controlling the law and order situation or the factum of delay in disposal of the criminal cases by the Courts existing under the general laws or under the special laws ... would justify this Court to uphold their validity. In my humble view, if the establishment of the Armed Courts under the impugned Ordinance is violative [sic] of the constitution, we cannot sustain the same on the above grounds or on the ground of expediency.... The Doctrine of Necessity cannot be invoked if its effect is to violate any provision of the constitution, particularly keeping in view Article 6 thereof which provides that "Any person who abrogates or attempts or conspires to abrogate, subverts or attempts or conspires to subvert the constitution by use of force or show of force or by other unconstitutional means shall be guilty of high treason."

The court also found the ordinance to be unconstitutional in that: a) civilians cannot be tried by armed courts; b) the special courts cannot perform parallel functions to those assigned to regular courts; and c) the armed's powers with regard to "aid to civil authority" do not extend to the creation of courts or the exercise of judicial functions.

The court, and particularly the lengthy concurring opinion of Justice Irshad Hasan Khan, was sympathetic with the dilemma facing the government caused by the breakdown of law and order. But, the remedy was in following the advice of the *Mehram Ali* decision. The court also ordered as a procedural amendment to the *Mehram* procedure that cases be assigned to special courts one at a time until the case is decided—that is, that the ATCs should not have a docket of pending cases.

Given the forcefulness of the Supreme Court's verdict, Nawaz Sharif capitulated. On 27 April 1999, the Armed Forces (Acting in Aid of Civil Power) was repealed—however, "civil commotion" was made a crime under the Anti-Terrorism Act. On 27 August the Sharif government made its last revision of the anti-terrorism regime when it further amended the Anti-Terrorism Act to allow for the establishment of ATCs in any province of Pakistan.

On 12 October Nawaz Sharif was removed from power by means of a armed coup—General Parvez Musharraf as a result inheriting the anti-terrorism regime from his predecessor.

# 5

# Afghanistan, Islamic Militancy, and the Nexus with Kashmir

One was that Islamic extremists could destabilize Pakistan domestically, making it hard to govern. The other was that Pakistan's influence with India over the Kashmir question (Pakistan's leaders believed this had been revived by the insurgency that began in Kashmir in 1988–89) would now be neutralized. Pakistan's fifty-year-old claims to that disputed territory might be lost irretrievably. It remains a fundamental tenet of Pakistani politics that no government that makes deep concessions on the future of Kashmir, let alone surrenders it to India altogether, can survive.

These two threats were closely intertwined in the aftermath of 9/11. Musharraf had to face the dilemma that Islamic militancy would be aroused at home by the assault on the Taliban, and extremism could overturn the moderate core and national goals of Pakistan itself. Yet Islamic militancy operating within Kashmir itself, led in part by Kashmiri Muslims, was also viewed as a crucial source of pressure on India to negotiate Kashmir's future. Moreover, Islamic militancy was increasingly being seen abroad as the core of "international terrorism," and this could stigmatize all efforts to free Kashmiris, including native Kashmiri insurgents, as forms of terrorism.

Fundamentalist Islamic political parties and groups emerged in British India long before India and Pakistan became independent and have always been a troublesome undercurrent in Pakistan's modern politics, much as Hindu extremist groups have been in

India. Islamic extremist tendencies during Pakistan's early years were restrained or diffused by the conduct of elections and the moderate outlook on Islam that was prevalent in the subcontinent, as well as by the usual bread-and-butter issues of all politics. Islamic fundamentalist parties collectively have won relatively few seats in Pakistan's past national and provincial elections.

Nonetheless, the potency of Islamic fundamentalist parties and the violent propensities of their armed militia formations have increased over time in Pakistan. Contributing factors or stimuli came from the armed seizure of power from Zulfiqar Ali Bhutto by General Zia ul-Haq in 1977, the shock effects on the wider region of the Islamic revolution in Iran in 1979, and the mobilization of mujahideen groups to carry the Afghan war against the Soviets in the 1980s. In the period since the Soviet withdrawal, the smoldering civil war in Afghanistan, a secular slowdown in the Pakistani economy, stagnation of the public school system, and the initially spontaneous emergence of a liberation struggle in Indian-held Kashmir have given the Pakistani Islamicist organizations—and not just Islamic extremist groups— additional footholds.

A common theme that has emerged among analysts in the wake of these developments is that a nexus has emerged between extremist Islamic groups and their allegedly terrorist operations in Afghanistan, Pakistan, and Kashmir—creating a so-called Kalashnikov culture.

While there may be a kernel of truth here, it is also a gross oversimplification to ascribe the aims of these groups and the political linkages that may exist among some of them to the singular design, common inspiration, and coherent direction of Pakistani armed and security organizations, notably the ISI. Where official ties with these groups may exist to use them externally, the internal objectives are to play them off against each other and prevent their uniting against the state.

Islamic religious fundamentalism, Islamic political radicalism, and Islamic armed militancy are distinct conceptually, and their organized forms seldom if ever exist under a single roof. There is no homogeneous Islamic fundamentalism, but rather a variety of schools of thought, many cultural variants of each, and even more varieties of styles of Islamic life and behaviour—readily visible when moving from one Muslim society or community to the next. "Terrorism" as a generic phenomenon—targeted killing of innocents—is as antithetical to Islamic tenets as it is to the mainstream of any world religion, or to the norms of modern civilization. Political violence frequently has a political context without which it is not properly understood. By understanding political violence in any particular instance, one need not condone it or justify it, or hesitate to pursue means to stop or eradicate it. But neither is it productive automatically to equate "terrorism" with freedom struggles against invaders and occupiers, revolutionary actions against perceived tyranny or oppression, or the use of force in response to force over a historical dispute—whether differences of religion are involved or not.

That said, several Pakistani fundamentalist following groups have not only willingly joined the Afghan wars and the Kashmir insur-gency—against "foreign occupiers" as they see it—but have, like the *ayatollah* and *pasdaran* movements against the secular regime of the Shah of Iran—developed revolutionary aspirations vis-à-vis the liberal constitution and representative governing institutions of Pakistan. Their goals are to replace the existing political order with their own concepts of Islamic society.

Naturally, the real content of their visions of Islamic society varies from group to group, by school of thought and by organizational proclivity. In most cases the vision of an Islamic order is traditional and based on the *shari'a,* but their styles of interpretation of Islamic law and tradition vary. One of Pakistan's three most prominent Islamicist parties, the Jamaat-i-Islami (JI), actually has a modernist idea of Islamic revival that accommodates genuine learning and even natural science, and thus has strong appeal in certain intellectual, professional, and middle class circles. But the JI counterparts in Afghanistan and Kashmir do not necessarily subscribe to the same program or ideas, or draw from the same social base, as does the JI in Pakistan. While the government of Pakistan actively supported the role of these groups in Afghanistan, their efforts in Kashmir are best understood as an extension of their efforts to build platforms for the takeover of political power within Pakistan itself.

Moreover, one should understand the revolutionary aspirations of these Islamic parties not in terms of how many votes or seats they can win in national elections but rather in terms of how they build bastions of local influence, incrementally. This is achieved by the largest and arguably most aggressive of these Pakistani Islamist organizations, the Jamiat Ulema Islam (JUI)—which split many years ago into two branches led by Maulana Fazlur Rahman and Maulana Sami-ul-Haq, respectively. The two JUI organizations use intimidation and infiltration of authority, the building of mosques, development of welfare institutions, publication of local language newspapers and magazines, recruitment of supporters, targeting and acquisition of disputed land and property, and accumulation of other resources, at the local levels to aggrandize power and influence in society. JUI leaders pursue these goals in a decentralized way—in districts, towns, and major cities. The armed militias not only provide protection to the leaders and their political activities but also serve as agents in putting the squeeze on vulnerable local property owners and influentials.

Some of these organizations also ruthlessly exploit the sectarian divisions of Islamic society, especially Sunni versus Shia, confusing their ultimate objectives with near-term and situational objectives. The leaders of these organizations are often quite entrepreneurial, and some of the most successful also receive funds from Islamic groups in Saudi Arabia or other Gulf states. In their defensive and essentially introspective response within Pakistan, Shia leaders and organizations have also received financial help from Iran. The Pakistan-based extremist groups that have been most active in the fighting in Afghanistan, as well as those that have joined the insurgency in Kashmir, are generally Sunni by sectarian affiliation.

Views differ on whether the activities in Kashmir of the Pakistani militants were also actively sponsored by the Pakistan government, or provided official assistance by some cabal of bureaucratic and armed officials behind the scenes. But there seems little doubt that successive political and armed governments turned a blind eye to the infiltration of these groups into Kashmir to join the insurgency in the early 1990s. It is also possible that even if the militant formations were privately recruited and trained, they found tacit encouragement in Islamabad's official political and armed circles. Mujahideen training of Pakistani recruits, and perhaps some combat experiences with groups in Afghanistan, were readily transferable to Kashmir. The influx of light arms and ammunition to support the guerrilla war against the Soviets left stockpiles that could be put to other uses.

The insurgency in Kashmir began spontaneously in late 1989, led by native Kashmiri militant groups that recruited fighters from a younger generation of Muslim Kashmiris who were frustrated with Indian political interference in state elections and government. It was some time, therefore, before groups in Pakistan began to react in an organized way, with the infiltration and support of militants from Pakistani sources broadly welcomed by most politically active Kashmiris in the Vale of Kashmir, especially in the initial years.

In the development of resistance objectives and tactics, several of the Pakistani militant groups developed reputations for taking greater risk and using more aggressive tactics against Indian security forces than did their Kashmiri counterparts, but a majority of these groups shunned wanton terrorism—avoiding direct attacks on civilians and ordinary Kashmiri property. The Jammu and Kashmir Liberation Front (JKLF), based essentially in Kashmiris in both Pakistan- and Indian-held parts of Kashmir, for instance, began with a militant approach to Indian security installations (avoiding violence on civilians, and never deliberately terrorist) but changed course later to adopt exclusively political methods.

A handful of Pakistan-origin extremist groups, however, did cross the line during the 1990s to terrorist actions, pure and simple, including capture and execution of foreign tourists, as well as other attacks on civilians and civilian infrastructure. Pakistani-origin groups reportedly associated with such activities in the early 1990s included al-Badr (sponsored by the Pakistani JI) and Harkat-ul-Ansar, later renamed Harkat-ul-Mujahideen. The Harkat-ul-Ansar was the earliest of these militant Pakistani or Kashmiri organizations to be put on the list of terrorist organizations by the U.S. Department of State. The sponsor of the Harkats was the Sami-ul-Haq branch of the JUI in Pakistan; this branch of the

JUI is believed to have had closer Afghanistan ties than any of the other Pakistani Islamic parties and is suspected of having early contacts with Osama bin Laden, dating back to the late 1980s during the Afghan war against the Soviets.

In the late 1990s, the Lashkar-e-Toiba (sometimes written Lashkar-i-Tayyaba), sponsored by the politically invisible but Wahabi-dedicated Ahl-e-Hadith, and the Jaish-e-Muhammed, a more recent extremist offshoot of the Sami-ul-Haq branch of the JUI, became active in Kashmir. India pointed to the Jaish-e-Muhammed and the Lashkar-e-Toiba as the source of the attack on parliament in New Delhi on December 13, 2001, claimed that the attackers were Pakistanis, and accused Pakistan of sponsoring their attack. The State Department also added these organizations to its official list of terrorist organizations in December 2001. India began a full-scale armed mobilization of seven hundred thousand troops opposite Pakistan—along the entire border and in the Arabian Sea—and made a series of demands, including total cessation of Pakistani-origin infiltration and "terrorism" in Kashmir.

## THE AHL-I-HADITH IN PAKISTAN AND THE RISE OF THE LASHKAR

Since the Lashkar has its headquarters in Pakistan and most of its fighters in Kashmir are Pakistani nationals, the role of the Lashkar in Kashmir must be seen in the context of the growing salience within Pakistan itself of the Ahl-i Hadith, to which it owes allegiance. Following the creation of Pakistan in 1947, the Ahl-i Hadith began making gradual progress in the country, establishing mosques and *madrasas* of its own. It had to face with stiff resistance from traditional Sufis, for its opposition to Sufism and *taqlid*. It tended to have a more visible presence in urban areas, its strict scripturalist literalism appealing to groups such as urban traders who were not tied down to local Sufi shrines.

Although the Ahl-i Hadith still has a limited following in Pakistan, from the 1980s onwards it was able to make considerable inroads in Pakistani society. A number of factors have combined to make for this. Firstly, the growing appeal of scripturalist Islam as a result of the rapid expansion in the number of *madrasa*s or

Islamic seminaries in the country in recent decades, many of which are sponsored by the Saudis and preach a conservative yet militant form of Islam that has a close resemblance with that of the Ahl-i Hadith. Secondly, the active sponsorship and patronising of such *madrasa*s by the Pakistani state, under and after General Zia-ul Haq (d. 1988). Thirdly, the Afghan *jihad*against the Soviets, which saw a great expansion of resources for groups such as the Ahl-i Hadith, with massive amounts of aid, in the form of money and arms, pouring in from Saudi Arabia and other Arab countries. Many Ahl-i Hadith and other Sunni *madrasa*s emerged at this time as training grounds for militants active in the Afghan *jihad*. After expelling the Soviets from Kabul, these *mujahid*s turned their attention to fresh pastures, Kashmir being one of them. Thus, from being a relatively minor group in Pakistan's Islamic landscape, the Ahl-i Hadith grew, by the end of the 1980s, into a major force, with scores of *madraṣa*s all over the country, particularly in the Punjab and the North-West Frontier Province, and several newspapers and journals articulating its vision of an Islamic revolution.

Along with other Islamist groups, the Ahl-i Hadith immersed itself in the *jihad* in Afghanistan. In 1986 it set up the Markaz Da'wat wa'l Irshad, based in a sprawling 160-acre campus at Muridke, a town some 30 kilometres from Lahore, to train *mujahidin* to fight the Soviets. As the Markaz's activities rapidly grew, it was decided to divide its work into two separate but related sections: the educational and the *jihad*ist. Thus, in 1993, the Markaz established its separate '*jihadic* and warfare' wing, the Lashkar. The Lashkar later set up four training centres in Pakistan and Afghanistan, where, 'thousands of *mujahidin* from all over the world are being trained'. Markaz authorities claim that the militants produced at these centres have played a leading role in armed struggles, first in Afghanistan, and then in countries as far afield as Bosnia, Chechenya, Kosovo, the southern Philippines, Kashmir and 'in other areas where Muslims are fighting for freedom'. All Muslims, it believes, are members of one global community. Oppression of Muslims anywhere makes it incumbent on Muslims everywhere to assist them, if necessarily through active engagement in violent conflict with their non-Muslim opponents. As the Lashkar case so strikingly illustrates, one of the characteristic features of some contemporary Islamist movements is precisely this global agenda, a marked contrast with the local or national scope and ambitions of Islamist movements in the past.

According to one report, in recent years the spread of the Markaz/Lashkar in Pakistan has been 'phenomenal', and today it has some five hundred offices all over the country, most of them in Punjab, which operate as recruitment centres for would-be *mujahidin*. At its Muridke headquarters, the Markaz runs an Islamic school and university, most of whose students are local Pakistanis, with some from both Pakistan-administered Kashmir and Kashmiris from the Indian-ruled part of the state, and several Afghans and Arabs. Established in 1994, several hundred students have already graduated from the school. Scores of smaller schools run on the same lines have been set up in various other parts of Pakistan, and, by mid-2001, their number was said to be almost 130, with some 15,000 students and 800 teachers on their rolls. Young boys of the age of eight are taken in and are given a 12-year training, which includes the standard Islamic disciples, taught from an Ahl-i Hadith perspective, English, Arabic, and Science, as well as the handling of weapons and techniques of armed combat. A strict military atmosphere is enforced. Students must wear military uniforms, abide by military discipline and 'properly assimilate the commandments of their theologians and military instructors that their future profession-as *mujahidin*-will be in great demand in the Muslim world on the threshold of the new millennium'. Students from different countries and ethnic groups live together, and every effort is made to discourage ethnic differences. They must wear the same clothes, speak the same language (Urdu, Arabic). Names that might suggest local, clan, tribal or caste origins must be effaced. The only identity that should matter to them is of being Muslim, ethnic differences being seen as working to divide and weaken the worldwide Muslim *ummah*.

At its four training centres, would-be *mujahidin* are given rigorous military training. This is of two kinds. Firstly, a short twenty-one day course, the *daura-i 'ama* ('general course'). Secondly, a three-month intensive course, the *daura-i khasa* ('special course'), geared to guerrilla warfare, in which trainees learn how to handle small arms as well as survival and ambush techniques. These courses, it is claimed, 'change the course of life' of the trainees completely', and a sign of this is said to be that they 'no longer shave' and 'wear their *shalwars*(baggy trousers) above their ankles, as enjoined by the Prophet Muhammad (peace be upon him)'. They are fired with a passionate zeal in what is said to be a 'holy' cause, willing to sacrifice their lives and attain 'martyrdom' for it. Families whose sons die in battles with the Indian forces are said to celebrate and rejoice their deaths, rather than mourn, for they are confident of their securing a place for themselves in heaven. This has particularly crucial implications for how Kashmiri Lashkar activists see themselves. If, traditionally, Kashmiri Muslims were depicted as 'cowards', 'passive' or 'mild', and lax as far as religious observances were concerned, at least compared to their Pathan and Punjabi Muslim neighbours, they are now sought to be made 'true', 'brave' and 'fearless' Muslims, fired by the zeal of would-be 'martyrs' for the faith.

## THE IDEOLOGY OF THE LASHKAR

Like other Islamist groups, the Markaz/Lashkar sees Islam as a perfect, all-embracing system (*nizam*). Islam is said to govern all aspects of personal as well as collective life, in the form of the *shari'ah*. For the establishing of an Islamic system, an Islamic state is necessary, which will impose the *shar'iah* as the law of the land. This is seen as 'the solution to all our problems'. If such a state were to be set up and all Muslims were to live strictly according to 'the laws that Allah has laid down', then, it is believed, 'they would be able to control the whole world and exercise their supremacy'. Since the laws have already been laid down by God, there is no room for human beings to exercise their judgement in creating fresh legislation. Hence, democracy, in the sense of a system where people make their own laws, is condemned as completely un-Islamic. Since Islam is seen as the very antithesis of nationalism, it demands the establishment of one universal Islamic state, ruled by a single *khalifah*. Thus, the present division of the Muslims into many nation-states must be overcome. Since 'the *ummah* is one', it follows from this that 'the system of *khilafah* does not recognise the physical borders or the independence, of one Muslim country from another'. Hence, 'the state is one, the army is one, the flag is one, the budget is one, etc.'.

The struggle for the establishment of the Islamic state can take various forms, peaceful as well as violent. Islam, the Lashkar admits, is 'a religion of peace and harmony', and seeks to 'eliminate mischief and disorder, and to provide peace, not only to Muslims but also to the entire humanity'. However, Muslims are commanded to take to armed struggle, or *jihad,* to defend their co-religionists suffering from the oppression of others. Such a situation is said to prevail over much of the world today. While *jihad* in defence of Islam and of Muslims labouring under oppression is presented as a liberation struggle, it is also seen as a means for Islam to 'prevail on this earth', for Islam is seen as the only true religion. Armed *jihad* must continue 'until Islam, as a way of life, dominates the whole world and until Allah's law is enforced everywhere in the world'. Since Islam is meant for all peoples, the Islamic State must spearhead a movement to spread the Islamic 'ideology' all over the world. In the course of this struggle, it is 'expected' that it will encounter 'conflict' with other states and their ideologies. The conflict can be resolved through peaceful diplomacy, but, if that fails, then the only course left open for the Muslims is armed*jihad*. In this sense, the Markaz/Lashkar believes, *jihad* is 'the foreign policy' of the Islamic State. This does not, however, mean that force can be used to coerce others into accepting Islam. Rather, *jihad* is seen as providing them with the 'security that comes from the application of Islam', while leaving them free to follow their own religion or to become Muslims.

The subject of armed *jihad* runs right through the writings and pronouncements of the Markaz/Lashkar and is, in fact, the most prominent theme in its discourse. Indeed, its understanding of Islam maybe seen as determined almost wholly by this preoccupation, so much so that its reading of Islam seems to be a product of its own political project. Being born as a result of a war (in Afghanistan), fighting for a holy cause has become the very raison d'être of the Lashkar, and its subsequent development has been almost entirely determined by this concern. The contours of its ideological framework are constructed in such a way that the theme of armed *jihad* appears as the central element of its project. In the writings and speeches of Markaz spokesmen *jihad* appears as violent conflict (*qittal*) waged against 'unbelievers' who are said to be responsible for the oppression of the Muslims. Indeed, it is projected as the one of the most central tenets of Islam, although it has traditionally not been included as one of the 'five pillars' of the faith. Thus, it is claimed that 'There is so much emphasis on this subject that some commentators and scholars of the Qur'an have remarked that the topic of the Qur'an is *jihad*'. Further, a Markaz statement declares, 'There is consensus of opinion among researchers of the Qur'an that no other action has been explained in such great detail as *jihad*'.

The global *jihadist* programme of the Markaz presents itself as a 'liberationist' project, basing itself on widespread feelings of discontent and suffering of sections of Muslims who see themselves as being persecuted by Western-oriented elites in their own countries, as well as by the 'West' more generally. The greatest problem of the Muslims, says Hafiz Muhammad Sa8eed, head of the Markaz, is their 'subjugation to the West'. Thus, the Markaz is reported to have gone so far as to call for a *jihad* against the USA. 'All Muslims', the Markaz believes, are oppressed today, by such 'enemies' as the Hindus, the Jews or Christians. 'Wherever you look, you will find that non-believers are everywhere trying to enslave Muslims and destroy them', it argues. Hence, Muslims must form a 'solid bloc' to defend themselves from these 'enemies', and if all peaceful means fail they must resort to armed *jihad* for their liberation. This Muslim bloc must be led by both Pakistan and Saudi Arabia, and have its headquarters at Mecca. It must aim at forming a pan-Islamic union based on strong trade, education and defence links, including a joint military command. *Mujahidin* from various Muslim countries would be trained to undertake *jihad* against unbelievers if peaceful means to put an end to oppression of Muslims fail. However, the Markaz insists, *jihad* is to be directed only at military and not civilian targets. It is contrasted with other forms of war that are pursued for purely worldly concerns, and is described as 'the act of supreme sacrifice to preserve human rights bestowed by Allah'. *Jihad* is thus a means for challenging 'oppression' and of establishing the rule of Islam.

*Jihad* is seen as the secret of Muslim power in the past when much of the known world was under Muslim rule, and it is argued that when Muslims 'abandoned *jihad* and other injunctions they began to degenerate'. In Markaz/Lashkar discourse, *jihad* is projected as a religious duty binding on *all* Muslims today. Thus, it is claimed that the prevailing global situation warrants *all* Muslims to be involved in some way or the other in *jihad* against non-Muslim 'oppressors'. In this grand enterprise there are different roles for different people to play. Those who are ordered by the *khalifah* to fight must do so, while others may be required to assist the *mujahidin* by supplying them food, arms and other supplies, providing medical assistance, looking after their families in their absence or even simply by exhorting others to participate in the war. Thus, *every* Muslim, man or woman, must be mobilised to assist in the struggle in some form or the other, and if any Muslim has 'never intended to fight against the disbelievers', his or her faith 'is not without traces of hypocrisy'. Those believers who have the capacity to participate or assist in the *jihad* but do not do so are said to 'be living a sinful life'. On the other hand, Muslims are promised that they would receive great rewards, both in this world and in the Hereafter, if they were to actively struggle in the path of *jihad*. Not only would they be guaranteed a place in Heaven, but they would also 'be honoured in this world', for *jihad* is also 'the way that solves financial and political problems'.

## THE JIHAD IN KASHMIR AND INDIA

The Markaz sees its active involvement in the armed struggle in Kashmir as only one stage of a wider, indeed global, *jihad* against the forces of disbelief, stopping at nothing short of aiming at the conquest of the entire world. As Qari 'Abdul Wahid, former *amir* of the Lashkar in Indian-administered Kashmir, puts it, 'We will uphold the flag of freedom and Islam through *jihad* not only in

Kashmir but in *the whole world*'.Likewise, Nazir Ahmed, in-charge of the public relations department of the Markaz, declares that through the *jihad* that the *mujahidin* have launched, 'Islam will be dominant all over the world, *Inshallah* (God willing)'. This war is seen as a solution to all the ills and oppression afflicting all Muslims, and it is claimed that 'if we want to live with honour and dignity, then we have to return back to *jihad*'. Through *jihad*, it is believed, 'Islam will be supreme throughout the world'. The *mujahidin* are promised that with the launching of the global *jihad* against all the 'unbelieving oppressors' of the world, 'The day is just round the corner when Islam will prevail in this earth, *Insha Allah*'.

In Markaz/Lashkar discourse, the conflict in Kashmir is seen not as a territorial dispute between India and Pakistan, but as nothing less than a war between two different and mutually opposed ideologies: Islam, on the one hand, and disbelief [*kufr*], on the other. This is portrayed as only one chapter in a long a struggle between the two that is said to have characterised the history of Hindu-Muslim relations for the last 1400 years ever since the advent of the Prophet Muhammad. The Prophet is claimed on the basis of a *hadith* to have singled out India as a special target for *jihad*. 'Whosoever will take part in *jihad* against India', Markaz leader Muhammad Ibrahim Salaf claims that the Prophet had declared, 'Allah will set him free from the pyre of hell'.

The Markaz/Lashkar sees the roots of the Kashmir problem as lying in its Muslim rulers having been replaced, first by the Sikhs and then by the Hindu Dogras through British assistance. With India (the 'Hindus') having taken over Kashmir in 1947, a long and protracted reign of bloody terror is said to have been unleashed on the Kashmiri Muslims. This is seen as a direct and logical consequence of the teachings of Hinduism itself, because, it is alleged, 'the Hindus have no compassion in their religion'. Hence, it is the duty of Muslims to wage *jihad* against the 'Hindu oppressors', for 'it is the Hindu who is a terrorist'. All Hindus are tarred with the same brush, described in such essentialist terms as 'terrorists', 'traitors', 'cowards', 'enemies', etc., these powerfully echoing widely shared sentiments among Pathan and Punjabi Muslims of Hindus being 'weak' and 'slavish', having been subjected to 'Muslim' rule for centuries, and of being 'crafty' and 'cunning', probably owing to Hindu near-monopoly of trade and commerce in India. This also builds on Pathan sentiments of 'manly honour', 'chivalry' and 'bravery', which Hindus are supposed to lack, being allegedly 'effeminate' and 'cruel'. Thus, Hafiz Muhammad Sa8eed declares: 'In fact, the Hindu is a mean enemy and the proper way to deal with him is the one adopted by our forefathers who crushed them by force. We need to do the same'. India is a special target for the Markaz's *mujahidin*. According to the *amir* of the Markaz, Hafiz Muhammad Sa'eed, 'The *jihad* is not about Kashmir only. It encompasses all of India'. Thus, the Markaz sees the *jihad* as going far beyond the borders of Kashmir and spreading through all of India. The final goal is to extend Muslim control over what is seen as having once been Muslim land, and, hence, to be brought back under Muslim domination, creating 'the Greater Pakistan by dint of *jihad*'. Thus, at a mammoth congregation of Markaz supporters in November 1999, Hafiz Muhammad Sa'eed declared, 'Today I announce the break-up of India, *Inshallah*. We will not rest until the whole of India is dissolved into Pakistan'. On the same occasion, Amir Hamza, senior Markaz official and editor of its Urdu organ, *ad-Da'wa*, thundered: 'We ought to disintegrate India and even wipe India out'.Those who take part in this anti-Indian *jihad* are promised that 'Allah will save [them] from the pyre of hell', and 'huge palaces in paradise' await those who are killed in fighting the 'disbelieving enemies'.

This project for the disintegration of India, followed by its take-over by Pakistan and the establishing an Islamic state in the entire sub-continent, is sought to be justified by an elaborate set of arguments that use the rhetoric of liberation. Thus, instances of human-sacrifice, untouchability, infanticide, the oppression of the 'low' castes by the Brahmins and the suppression of women in Hinduism are described in great detail, and on this basis it is sought to be shown that such a religion as Hinduism should not 'be allowed to flourish'. In Markaz literature, the mass slaughter of Muslims by Hindu chauvinist groups, often in league with the Indian state and its agencies, and the growing wave of attacks on other marginalised groups in India such as the 'low' caste Dalits, Shudras and Christians, are presented in stark colours, and the point forcefully made that such a country 'where non-Hindus are not allowed to exist' should break-up. The Markaz/Lashkar poses as a 'champion' of not just the oppressed Muslims of Kashmir or India but even of the 'low' caste Shudras and Dalits. It sees itself as having a divinely appointed mission of saving the Shudras from Brahminical tyranny. Thus, it says, 'It is incumbent upon us to save the Shudras of India from the clutches of Brahmins', and insists that 'the Brahmin Authority' must be 'ransack'. Although it claims that its *jihad* is aimed only against 'the tyrannical government and the army' and that 'nowhere do the *mujahidin* target non-Muslim or innocent people', there are reports that speak of Lashkar fighters being involved in the killing of several Hindu villagers in Jammu, Kashmir and in neighbouring Himachal Pradesh.

## THE LASHKAR'S INVOLVEMENT IN KASHMIR

### *Roots of Islamism in Kashmir*

The emergence of the Lashkar as a powerful military force in Kashmir must be seen in the context of the emergence of an Islamist constituency in the region, a process that can be traced back to the early years of the twentieth century. A major development in Kashmir at this time was the establishment of the first branch of the Ahl-i Hadith in Srinagar, in 1925, by Sayyed Hussain Shah Batku, a Kashmiri student of the Madrasa Miyan Sahib in Delhi, a seminary set up by one of the pioneers of the Ahl-i Hadith in India, Maulvi Nazir Hussain. On his return to Kashmir after completing his education, Batku began directed his attention at attacking what he saw as 'un-Islamic' and 'Hinduistic' practices and beliefs associated with the popular Sufism of the Kashmiri Muslims. Batku is said to have 'raised a storm of controversy' for his critique of customary practices which he condemned as 'un-Islamic', such as visiting Sufi shrines, imploring Sufi saints for interceding with God, keeping fasts on particular days dedicated to various saints and reciting litanies (*aurad*) in the mosques. This is said to have seriously 'aggrieved the leading theologians of Srinagar'. The leading Hanafi *ulama* of Kashmir are said to have issued several *fatawa* against him, branding him as 'an apostate and an infidel' and as the *dajjal* (Anti-Christ), subjecting him to a 'social boycott'.

Among the other notable pioneers of the Ahl-i Hadith in Kashmir were Maulana Anwar Shah Shopiani (d.1969), Maulana Ghulam Nabi Mubaraki (1902-80) and Sabzar Shah. Anwar Shah was a close disciple of Batku, and played a major role in spreading the message of the Ahl-i Hadith in Srinagar and Shopian. He also undertook missionary tours to outlying regions of the state, including Bhadarwah (Doda) and Ladakh. Like Anwar Shah, Maulana Mubaraki was a trained *'alim*, a prolific writer and a powerful orator. He edited two Ahl-i Hadith journals, *Tauhid* and *Muslim*, and wrote extensively against the Ahmadis, the Shi'as, the Arya Samajists and the Christian missionaries, all of whom he saw as bent on the extirpation of Islam from Kashmir. He served as the president of the Ahl-i Hadith *jama'at* in Kashmir for several years, as well as the Imam of the Ahl-i Hadith Jamia mosque in Srinagar. Unlike Anwar Shah and Mubarakpuri, Sabzar Shah was not a trained 8*alim*, although he is said to have 'grasped the fundamentals of Islam and wedded himself to the cause of the Ahl-i Hadith'. In order to convey the message of the Ahl-i Hadith beyond the relatively narrow circle of middle-class Kashmiris, to which it had been largely restricted, he would roam the streets of Srinagar in the garb of a peddler selling soaps, combs, pins, bangles and toys. To his customers, mostly women and children, he would invariably speak about the 'strict monotheism' of the Ahl-i Hadith and would fiercely denounce 'shrine worship and other polytheistic practices'. For this, it is said, he was beaten on numerous occasions, but, it is said, he refused to relent.

In the face of the great opposition, the Ahl-i Hadith managed to make a small, yet significant number of converts, mainly in the towns of Srinagar, Islamabad (Anantnag) and Shopian. In 1923, in order to co-ordinate the efforts of individual activists, and to 'face the determined challenge posed by the *mullas* of Kashmir', a central organisation, the Anjuman Ahl-i Hadith Jammu and Kashmir, was established in Srinagar, with one Haji Muhammad

Shahdad as its president. The establishment of the organisation 'came as a thunderbolt' to the traditional Hanafi *'ulama* and Sufis of Kashmir, who are said to have now 'declared a virtual war' on the Ahl-i Hadith. Several Ahl-i Hadith activists were physically attacked; a social boycott was instituted against them; they were turned out of their localities; and, being branded as apostates, they were refused entry into the mosques, following which they had to set up their own separate places of worship. Leading Hanafi 8*ulama* issued *fatawa* declaring them to be non-Muslim renegades.

Despite the zeal of its activists, the Ahl-i Hadith singularly failed to develop a mass following in Kashmir. Several factors may be adduced for this. Firstly, its stern opposition to the 'blind imitation' of the schools of jurisprudence brought upon it the wrath of the traditional Hanafi *'ulama,* who exercised a significant influence in Kashmir. Secondly, its hostility to Sufism, which it branded as an innovation not sanctioned by the practice of the Prophet, could hardly win the hearts of many Kashmiris, given the strong influence of popular Sufism in the region. For their trenchant criticism of popular practices associated with the shrines and cults of the Sufis, the followers of the Ahl-i Hadith were branded by the Kashmiri *'ulama* as *kafirs* (unbelievers) and *munkar-i auliya* ('deniers of the friends of God'), this greatly limiting their appeal to the Kashmiri Muslims. Thus, The Mirwai'z of the Khanqah-i Mu'alla, one of Kashmir's most important Sufi shrines, denounced the Ahl-i Hadith as the *dajjal* (Anti-Christ). One Hanafi *'alim* issued a *fatwa* declaring that no Muslim should marry a follower of the Ahl-i Hadith, and nor could the corpse of an Ahl-i Hadith follower be buried in a Muslim graveyard. Other *'ulama* declared it impermissible (*haram*) for Hanafi Muslims to pray along with Ahl-i Hadith followers. For their part, Ahl-i Hadith Imams condemned Kashmiri Hanafi mosques as 'little better than temples', because of the practice therein of reciting litanies (*aurad*) aloud before the congregational prayers

The Ahl-i Hadith's advocacy of a stern, legalistic understanding of Islam brooked no compromise with deeply rooted local cultural traditions, many of which it did not hesitate to brand as 'Hindu' or 'un-Islamic'. This naturally limited its appeal among many

Kashmiris. In addition, the Ahl-i Hadith focussed most of its efforts in the towns of Kashmir, almost completely neglecting the countryside, where most Kashmiri Muslims lived. It confined itself, by and large, to stirring religious controversy and preaching, not providing any significant social services which might have made for a larger following. Further, internal differences contributed to the weakening of the movement. In 1940, it split into two rival groups on the issue *of qabl-i zawal*, or on whether the Friday congregational prayers could be offered between 11 am and 12 noon.

Writing in 1997, Wani noted that the Ahl-i Hadith has not been able to 'take deep roots in the [Kashmir] valley'. Rather, it remains a largely elitist phenomenon, with its core support base among a limited section of the urban lower middle and middle classes, roughly the same core support-base of competing groups such as the secular nationalist JKLF and the Islamist Jama'at-i Islami. Although Ahl-i Hadith thus failed to establish a mass base for itself in Kashmir, it did provide fertile soil for the emergence of other Muslim reformist trends from the 1930s onwards, inspired by its efforts at purging the popular Kashmir Muslim religious tradition of elements that were deemed to be 'un-Islamic'. These trends, in turn, played a significant role in preparing the ground for radical Islamist groups, including the Lashkar. Of particular importance in this regard was the emergence of the Jama'at-i Islami. Established in 1941 by Sayyed Abul 'Ala Maududi, and organised as an independent organisation and political party in Kashmir in 1952, the Jama'at-i Islami is now a major force to contend with in the region. Like the Ahl-i Hadith, the Jama'at-i Islami sought to combat 'un-Islamic' practices, but, unlike it, it abstained from directly attacking the Sufi tradition, and refrained from branding other Muslims as apostates or deviant. In contrast to the Ahl-i Hadith, the Jama'at was not opposed to Sufism as such but only to those practices and beliefs associated with popular Sufism, which it saw as 'un-Islamic'. Its advocacy of an Islam based on the model of the Prophet's Companions and its opposition to what was seen as local 'un-Islamic' customs, such as prostration at the graves of saints, beseeching them for help, keeping fasts or holding feasts on special days dedicated to them, made for a growing appeal to a class of educated, particularly urban, Kashmir Muslims who were influenced by Muslim reformists currents from outside. Unlike the Ahl-i Hadith, which devoted most of its energies simply to preaching and entering into controversies with its Muslim opponents, the Jama'at gave great stress to modern education, setting up scores of schools where secular as well as religious subjects were taught. Its social services, combined with its resolute opposition to Indian rule, won it considerable support among many Kashmiri Muslims, disillusioned with the politics of the ruling National Conference for what they saw as 8selling out9 the interests of the Kashmiris to India. For many young Muslims belonging to this class, the Jama'at's understanding of a socially engaged Islam was seen as an attractive alternative to popular Sufism, that was branded as 'other-worldly', 'superstitious', 'corrupt', and, above all, 'un-Islamic'. It is primarily among this constituency that the Ahl-i Hadith's vision of Islam, which the Lashkar represents, derives its greatest support in Kashmir today. Owing to their shared commitment to a radical understanding of Islam, the Lashkar seems to have been able to win over the support of several Kashmiris associated with or sympathetic to the Jama'at-i Islami, thus making for a broader appeal for the Ahl-i Hadith than it previously enjoyed.

## The Lashkar in Kashmir

As in the case of the other Pakistan-based militant groups now active in Kashmir, the Lashkar's direct participation in the Kashmir conflict dates back to the end of the Afghan war in 1992, in which an estimated 1600 of its militants are said to have participated. After the Soviet withdrawal from Afghanistan, the Lashkar shifted its attention to Kashmir to 'help the oppressed and innocent Kashmiris who were undergoing Indian aggression for the past fifty years'. In this, it was assisted by the Jama'at-i Islami of Pakistan and the Inter-Services Intelligence (ISI), the powerful Pakistani secret service agency, both key players in the Afghan *jihad*. Raman, an Indian political analyst, writes that from 1992 onwards, the Pakistani authorities began sponsoring militant Islamist outfits, including the Lashkar, to undertake what it called a *jihad* in

Kashmir, instead of channelling such aid directly, in order to escape being branded as a 'terrorist state'. Raman calls this the 'privatisation of jihad', and remarks that the patronage given to these groups must be seen as a reflection of the growing fear of mass support of the JKLF and its advocacy of an independent Kashmir, which went fundamentally against Pakistan's own perceived interests. The Islamists were seen as a far more reliable ally, for all of them are fiercely opposed to nationalism, and, therefore, insist that Kashmir must join Muslim Pakistan, this being seen as but the prelude to a grand unity of all Muslims. With various militant Islamist groups, many of them Pakistan-based and led by Pakistanis, now being liberally assisted by the Pakistani state, assistance to the JKLF began drying up. Presumably, the Indian authorities must have seen this new situation to their advantage, as it meant a serious division in Kashmiri Muslim ranks.

The Lashkar is said to have first entered Kashmir in 1990, sending in a number of its trained activists, most of who were Pakistani nationals. It then 'upgraded' its *jihad* there in 1993, when its militants attacked an Indian army base in Poonch. In 1994, following the laying down of arms by the JKLF, the Lashkar began sending large numbers of its fighters into Kashmir, most of them from outside Kashmir, mainly Pakistanis, Kashmiris from Pakistan-controlled Kashmir and Afghans. 1996 witnessed a major shift in the Lashkar's Kashmir strategy, with greater attention being paid to the border districts of Jammu, particularly Rajouri and Poonch, areas dominated by non-Kashmiri Muslims such as the cattle-grazing Gujjars and Bakkarwals, ethnically related to the Punjabi Muslims, as well as Doda. Reports suggest that some of the mass killings of Hindu villagers in these areas have been its handiwork, with the aim of engineering an exodus of the Hindu population of these areas so as to make its task easier. By mid-2001, the Lashkar claimed, it had killed 14369 Indian soldiers in Kashmir, losing in the process 1016 of its own men.

In mid-1999 India and Pakistan almost came to war after Pakistan-based militants, believed to have been backed by the Pakistani army, occupied certain strategic heights in the Kargil sector in the Ladakh region in the remote northern part of Kashmir. The four principal militant groups taking part in this operation, all Islamist and manned mainly by non-Kashmiris, were the Harkat ul-Mujahidin, the Tehrik-i Jihad, al-Badr and the Lashkar. These groups together formed a joint military command to co-ordinate their military operations against the Indian army. The Lashkar contingent consisted, among others, of several students from its college at Muridke, led by one 'Abdur Rahman 'Abid, a graduate of Madinah University. The Lashkar force was joined by some two hundred militants from the Nuristan province of Afghanistan, the first time that such a large number of Afghan fighters had entered Kashmir in recent years.

The Pakistani attempt to enter Kashmir through Kargil, however, failed, and under pressure from the West, the then Pakistani Prime Minister, Nawaz Sharif, appealed to the militants to withdraw from the heights that they had captured. The militants reluctantly obeyed what they saw as Sharif's capitulation to the USA, but announced what they called 'the second stage' of the Kashmir *jihad*-taking the battle against the Indian army right inside the Kashmir valley itself, in order, as Zaki ur-Rahman Lakhvi, the *amir* of the Lashkar, put it, 'to avenge' the atrocities unleashed by the Indian army on the Kashmiri Muslims. According to the *amir* of the Markaz, Hafiz Muhammad Sa'eed, in this second phase 'the *jihad* would spread all across Kashmir. It would spread to every peak, every forest and every path'. As part of this new strategy, the Lashkar came up with a new means of attack suicide bombers, which it named as 'Ibn Taimiya Fida'i ('Faithful') Missions', in memory of the medieval Arab Islamic scholar who crusaded against what he saw as un-Islamic practices, and to whom the Ahl-i-Hadith owes much of its inspiration. The successful attack by a *fida'i* mission on the Indian army headquarters in Srinagar in November 1999, in which several Indian soldiers were killed, came as a great boost to the morale of the Lashkar fighters, smarting under their forced withdrawal some months earlier from the Kargil heights. In the wake of the attack, Hafiz Muhammad Sa'eed declared before an audience of an estimated three hundred thousand people in Muridke in November 1999 that his fighters could now 'strike anywhere in India', threatening even to target the Indian Prime Minister's office if India did not stop its aggression against the Kashmiri Muslims and vacate Kashmir. The *jihad*, declared the Hafiz, was not now limited simply to freeing Kashmir from Indian control. Rather, he stressed, it was aimed at 'liberating' India itself.He revealed that the Lashkar was now planning to extend its activities beyond the borders of Kashmir deep inside India. Some 50,000 Pakistani youth are said to have responded to this appeal to join the grand anti-India crusade. That this was no empty boasting was made clear in a Lashkar attack on an Indian army post at the Red Fort, the very heart of Delhi, in December, 2000, in which several Indian soldiers are said to have been killed.

## THE LIMITS OF *JIHAD*: ITS IMPLICATIONS FOR KASHMIR, INDIA AND PAKISTAN

The development of the Ahl-i Hadith in Kashmir, from being a marginal group, fiercely opposed to by many Kashmiri Muslims, to emerging, in the form of the Lashkar, as the most formidable element in the on-going armed struggle in the region, poses crucial questions regarding the actual level of support for the Ahl-i Hadith's own vision of Islam in Kashmir. Given the limited support for the Ahl-i Hadith in Kashmir prior to the outbreak of the armed struggle in 1989, it appears that its emergence as a major actor in the region owes largely to the role of the Lashkar in taking on the Indian army. The support for the Lashkar in Kashmir, limited though it might be, must, then, be seen as essentially a result of its stern opposition to Indian rule rather than as representing any considerable acceptance of its theological vision. In assessing the Kashmiri Muslim response to the Lashkar9s involvement in the region, a clear distinction needs to be made between how many Kashmiri Muslims would probably see the Lashkar's military strikes against Indian soldiers and army installations, on the one hand, and how far they might accept its understanding of Islam and its own ultimate agenda, on the other. Many Kashmiris, and not necessarily all supporters of a 'Wahhabi' sort of Islam, might well support the Lashkar in its willingness to take engage the Indian army. On the other hand, the consistent opposition of the Lashkar to any negotiated settlement of the Kashmir issue, insisting that the only solution of the question is carrying on with the *jihad* till the region finally merges with Pakistan, certainly limits its potential support base. The fact that the Lashkar is almost entirely in the hands of Pakistanis and Kashmiris from Pakistan-controlled Kashmir and that it refuses to recognise the possibility of an independent Kashmir, means that it has a very limited appeal to those Kashmiris who support an independent, sovereign state, which, however, neither India nor Pakistan seem willing to accede.

A further obstacle in the path of the Lashkar in Kashmir is its own understanding of Islam, rigid, regimented and vehemently opposed as it is to Sufism. 'Sufism', the Lashkar insists, 'has been designed with no other purpose than to dampen the spirit of *jihad'*.Since *jihad* is seen as integral to Islam, Sufism is regarded as 'un-Islamic'. The Lashkar's vehement opposition to Sufism, in line with the Ahl-i Hadith position on the matter, seems at striking odds with Kashmir tradition, where Sufism is still deeply rooted. The history of the spread of Islam in Kashmir is virtually synonymous with the missionary efforts of various Sufi orders, most notably the Kubrawi, the Suhrawardi, the Qadri, the Naqshbandi and the Rishi. Till today, Sufism remains the dominant form of Islamic expression in Kashmir, and the vehement opposition to it from Islamist groups that see it as 'un-Islamic' has registered little success. Indeed, defenders of the cults centred round the Sufi saints have not hesitated to brand the 'Wahhabis' as 'un-Islamic' and 'enemies of the faith' in turn. Till such time as Sufism remains dominant in the region, and continues to play a central role in the definition of Kashmiri identity, there seems little hope for groups such as the Lashkar to see their understanding of Islam win popular acceptance for their vision of Islam. The Lashkar is even less likely to find warm support among the Shi'as of the region, who form the majority in the Kargil district of Ladakh and are a sizeable minority in the Kashmir Valley, for the Shi'as are seen by the Ahl-i Hadith as non-Muslim 'heretics'.

If the odds seem so heavily weighed against the Lashkar in attempting to win support for its own vision of Islam among the Kashmiri Muslims, it can still continue to play a major role in escalating the conflict in the region, making it even more difficult to resolve the issue. The Lashkar insists that dialogue with the 'disbelievers' is prohibited in Islam, and that hence the only way ahead is through armed *jihad*.This intransigence has serious implications for all three parties to the Kashmir dispute India, Pakistan as well as the people of Kashmir. While carrying on with the armed strikes in order to inflict maximum damage to India might suit the short-term interests of the Pakistani establishment, it might, as some commentators have warned, have major consequences for Pakistan's own future, the full implications of which do not seem to have been appreciated by the managers of Pakistan's Kashmir policy. It is quite possible that the growing strength of groups like the Lashkar might mean that Pakistan, too, could soon be engulfed in civil war, with armed groups seeking to take over the country in the name of establishing an Islamic order.

The Lashkar, for its part, insists that it will not stop with its *jihad* in Kashmir, but, rather, regards it as but the beginning of a greater struggle to establish an Islamic state in all of South Asia, including both India as well as Pakistan. It has repeatedly condemned what it sees as 'un-Islamic' forces within Pakistan, demanding that there should be a 'total enforcement of Allah's *shari'ah'* in the country. The Pakistani ruling elite are accused of 'disbelief', for taking the name of Islam, while at the same time refusing to establish an Islamic system in the country. There is every fear that if the Pakistani state were to enter into some sort of agreement with India on Kashmir, armed Islamist groups active in Kashmir today might turn their attention inwards, and seek to carry on with their agenda at home through armed struggle. Hafiz Muhammad Sa'eed, the *amir* of the Markaz, himself hints at the possibility, cautioning that, 'As soon as we start to fight the disbelievers, we are sure to stop fighting among ourselves. But if we persist in keeping from *jihad* against the enemy, we are bound to go on fighting among ourselves'. Pakistani political scientist Eqbal Ahmad, sensing the very real threat of militant Islamist groups, many of them active in Kashmir today, plunging Pakistan into a bloody civil war, warns his countrymen, 'The chickens of *jihad*s once sponsored by imperialism and the [Pakistani] state have been coming home to roost. Afghanistan threatens to become a metaphor for the future'.Ahmad's appeal seems to have fallen on deaf ears, for the Pakistani establishment seems oblivious to the consequences of its continued patronage of groups such as the Lashkar, that today have become so powerful as to be, in the words of Minhas, a Pakistani analyst, quite 'unmanageable'.

The implications of the Lashkar's determination to carry on with what it calls a *jihad* against India poses serious questions for India, too, faced as it is with the growing threat of Hindu militancy, targetted primarily against the country's large Muslim population. As mentioned earlier, the Lashkar views its involvement in Kashmir as merely a prelude to a grand war against India, aiming at nothing less than the merger of India into a 'Greater Pakistan'. It sees itself as crusading on behalf of India's Muslims, who are said to be labouring under great oppression at the hands of militant Hindu organizations and the Indian government. Leading Markaz spokesmen have appealed for Indian Muslim leaders to launch an armed struggle against India. Not many Indian Muslims would, however, seem to be receptive to the appeals of the Lashkar to launch a *jihad* against the Hindus. With a Hindu right-wing government in power in India, and the growing challenge of Hindutva fascism, voices calling for peace and dialogue with the Hindus seem to prevail over those insisting on confrontation and conflict.

## THE CRISIS IN AFGHANISTAN AND THE LASHKAR IN KASHMIR

The American reprisals against the Taliban following the 11 September, 2001 attacks on the World Trade Centre and the Pentagon, were fiercely opposed by Islamist groups, including the Lashkar. In the wake of the attacks, the Lashkar is said to have despatched several of its armed volunteers to Afghanistan, to supplement the 600 Lashkar special guards who had earlier been specially appointed as personal security for Osama bin Laden. The Lashkar viewed the American assault on Afghanistan as the launching of a new 'crusade' by the 'Christian' West against the Muslim world. One of the principal aims of the attacks, it claimed, was to destroy Pakistan's nuclear capabilities. The head of the

Markaz warned Pakistani President General Pervez Musharraf not to co-operate with America, and issued a thinly veiled threat, calling for defiance of the government if it continued to toe the American line. The head of the *fatwa* section of the Markaz, Mufti 8Abdur Rahman, issued a *fatwa* claiming it a binding duty on all Muslims to help their Afghan co-religionists. If Pakistan's rulers supported America, he laid down, this would be treated as a gross violation of Islam, and they would be considered as 'rebels and traitors of Allah and His prophet'. If a group of Muslims is attacked by 'unbelievers', the *fatwa* said, 'the entire Muslim community must help it, even through war'. In the ongoing 'war between Islam and disbelief', as it described it, it declared, 'it has become obligatory for all the Muslim states in the interest of the dignity of Islam and the Muslims to forge unity in their own ranks and send their armies to support*jihad* and the *mujahidin'*.

Under pressure from the Americans, Musharraf was forced to take action against some militant groups based in Pakistan and active in Afghanistan, including the Lashkar. Several leading Lashkar activists, including the head of the organisation, Hafiz Muhammad Sa'eed, were arrested, only to be soon released. Careful not to embarrass Musharraf, and to win his support for its continued involvement in Kashmir, the Markaz reorganised itself in December 2001, setting up two separate wings. The first, christened as the Jama'at ud-Da''wa, was to focus on *tabligh* or Islamic missionary activism and on 'political and reformist activities'. The other, which would retain the name of the Lashkar-i Tayyeba, would devote itself to *jihad*, which would remain confined to Kashmir alone. In other words, *jihad*ist activities of the Lashkar in other parts of the world were to be stopped, and the resources of the organisations directed to Kashmir. In the face of charges that the mainly Punjabi Pakistani Lashkar activists in Kashmir had taken over the movement and had, in the process, marginalized the Kashmiris, a new central committee of the Lashkar was set up in late December 2001, which consisted entirely of Kashmiris, from both Pakistani-and Indian-administered parts of the state, and headed by a little-known Kashmiri Islamic scholar, 'Abdul Wahid. This promoting of Kashmiris within the central apparatus of the organisation was also intended to rebut charges of the militant movement in Kashmir being an externally inspired and directed one, and not an indigenous 'liberation' struggle. Significantly, alongside this, the radical anti-American rhetoric was toned down in the Markaz's official website, probably under pressure from Musharraf. However, despite Musharraf's insistence that Pakistan was taking all possible steps to prevent the entry of militants into Kashmir from its territory, Lashkar activists continue to cross over into Kashmir and their military engagements with the Indian armed forces show no sign of letting up.

The continuation of the armed conflict in Kashmir has resulted in untold sufferings for the Kashmiris, and has also diverted scarce resources from desperately needed development work to an unprecedented arms build-up in the region. An entire generation has grown up in Kashmir for whom killings are a daily affair. It is increasingly becoming clear to many, including the Kashmiris themselves, that the only possible long-term, viable solution to the vexed Kashmir issue is through a negotiated agreement between India, Pakistan and the people of Kashmir that satisfies all parties to the dispute. Armed conflict can only mean a further tragic loss of life and continued destruction. Given this, it appears that if groups such as the Lashkar refuse to read the signs of the times they might be threatened with further marginalisation. Already muffled voices within Kashmir's pro-Pakistan Jama'at-i Islami, in addition to pro-independence Kashmiri nationalist groups, have been calling for peaceful dialogue, and it seems, one hopes, a matter of time before other Islamist groups would begin to veer round to seeking a resolution of the dispute through peaceful means.

In this context, the refusal of certain Islamist groups in Pakistan and Kashmir, such as the Lashkar, on the one hand, and militant Hindu groups in India, on the other, to consider a negotiated settlement of the dispute, based on the aspirations of the Kashmiris themselves, is the greatest hurdle in the path of establishing peace in the region. With any move towards peaceful negotiation of the dispute ruled out on the grounds that entering into agreements with 'disbelievers' is forbidden in Islam, the Lashkar insists that the *jihad*must continue till its logical culmination the break-up of

India and its absorption into a 'Greater Pakistan'. While this seems an obviously vain and dangerous hope, it is a vision, one must recognise, that inspires thousands of Lashkar activists, leading them on to even sacrificing their lives, to kill or to be killed.

The Lashkar has been able to carve for itself a presence as a major actor in the Kashmir conflict less because of the appeal of its ideology than owing to its engagement with Indian armed forces in the region. The Islamisation of the conflict has had crucial implications for the way in which numerous Kashmiris have come to see themselves. The image, long internalised, of Kashmiris as 'passive' 'cowards' has been forcefully challenged by gun-wielding militants. The tolerant, rich and vibrant Kashmiri Sufi tradition has come under great strain, as new forms of understanding Islam have emerged, stressing conflict, armed *jihad* and martyrdom. If Kashmir was one of the few parts of South Asia that were spared the frenzy of Hindu-Muslim violence in 1947, it owed, in large measure, to the deeply embedded Sufi traditions of the Kashmiris. Today, with traditional Sufism being under threat from competing understandings of Islam, and with unrelenting assaults on Muslims in India at the hands of Hindu chauvinist groups, Kashmir's indigenous religious resources of conflict-management and inter-community dialogue seem powerless to pose any major challenge to the politics of religious hatred. In the meanwhile, the toll of innocents, sacrificial victims at the altar of communal strife, continues to mount.

## PAKISTAN'S UNHOLY ALLIANCE THE MILITANTS

The heavily guarded, high-walled concrete structure right in the heart of Islamabad has no signboard. But everyone in the capital knows that the sprawling compound surrounded by barbed wire houses the Directorate for Inter-Services Intelligence (ISI). The spy agency has been the country's big brother. It is powerful, ubiquitous and has functioned with so much autonomy from the central government that it has almost become a state within a state. It is not only responsible for intelligence gathering, but also acts as a determinant of Pakistan's foreign policy and a vehicle for its implementation. For every civilian and military government, control of the ISI was seen as crucial to maintaining a firm grip on power. The agency had been so powerful for so long that it played by its own rules. Its various heads had contrasting profiles, but emerged among the most powerful figures in the country's establishment. For years they ran semi-independent operations in Afghanistan and Kashmir and helped to form and topple civilian governments.

For more than two decades the ISI had sponsored Islamic militancy to carry out its secret wars. It was a crucial partner in the CIA's biggest covert operation ever, one that forced the Soviet Union to pull out of Afghanistan and served as a catalyst to the disintegration of the communist superpower. In Afghanistan, as well as Kashmir, the agency discovered the effectiveness of covert warfare as a method of bleeding a stronger adversary, while maintaining the element of plausible deniability. The ISI falls directly within Pakistan's military chain of command and had also served as an instrument for promoting the military's domestic political agenda and the guardian of its self-professed 'ideological frontiers' of the country. Almost all ISI officers are regular military personnel, who are rotated in and out for a fixed tenure. However, there have been some exceptions. The export of jihad sponsored by the ISI had its blowback. It had allowed the Islamists a huge space for their activities. State patronage, in the form of an 'unholy alliance' between the military and the mullahs, resulted in an unprecedented rise of radical Islam. The ISI had helped to create much of the Islamic militancy and religious extremism that Musharraf was confronted with. That unholy alliance had been a major factor in the country's drift to Islamic fundamentalism. Founded in 1948 by a British army officer, Major-General R. Cawthome, then Deputy Chief of Army Staff in Pakistan, the agency was initially charged with performing all intelligence tasks at home and abroad. Its scope of operation extended to all areas related to national security. Until the 1960s, the ISI largely remained an obscure organization that confined itself to playing its specified role. But in the mid 1970s its scope was expanded to domestic politics. Ironically, it was a civilian leader, Zulfikar Ali Bhutto who created the ISI's internal wing which played a critical role in the ousting of his government a few years later. It was to cast its heavy shadow over the country's politics in later years.

A charismatic and populist leader, Bhutto took over a humiliated military and a brutally truncated Pakistan in search of a new identity, following the Indian-supported secession of East Pakistan (now Bangladesh), in 1971. The country had been dismembered by civil war and Indian military action. It was no longer the country created by Mohammed Ali Jinnah. The Pakistan that emerged from the ashes of defeat required a different geopolitical orientation. A revolt by young Turks in the army in the aftermath of a humiliating defeat in the war had forced the military ruler, General Yahya Khan, 3 to hand over power to Bhutto. His legitimacy was rooted in the country's first democratically held elections in 1970. Bhutto's socialist Pakistan People's Party had swept the fateful polls in the western wing of then-united Pakistan, trouncing the right-wing Islamic parties.

The scion of a feudal family of Sindh and a former foreign minister, Bhutto was seen as the savior of the new Pakistan. He successfully negotiated with India the release of 90,000 troops taken prisoner by Indian forces. He had come to power with the largest support base of any Pakistani leader since the inception of the country in 1947.

But he failed to sustain the confidence of the nation. Bhutto was ideally placed to put into practice the objective of social democracy and develop secular ideas and institutions. But it did not happen. Bhutto's strategy was to bring the disparate elements of this divided society together through a kind of Islamic nationalism, which was then supposed to create the cohesion and stability necessary for socialist economic reforms, but unfortunately all Bhutto succeeded in doing was to rehabilitate religious extremism. Under pressure from the religious parties whose cooperation they were courting, Bhutto's government increased the religious content in school syllabuses and, succumbing to pressure from Saudi Arabia as well as to the demands of religious parties, declared the Ahmedis, an Islamic sect, to be non-Muslim. This apparently minor action had long-term implications for the country as it fuelled Islamic zealotry and sharpened the sectarian divide. Bhutto's attempt to co-opt religious elements merely emboldened them, and eventually the clergy joined hands with their traditional ally, the military, to plot the overthrow of his government. Bhutto's attempt to establish an authoritarian rule led him to rely more and more on the coercive apparatus of the state and the intelligence agencies.

Bhutto did little to strengthen democratic institutions and to make the process of democratic reform irreversible. Instead, his entire effort was aimed at promoting a personalized rule. He did not trust anyone. Given his overwhelming paranoia and insecurity, Bhutto geared up the ISI to keep surveillance not only on his opponents, but also on his own party men and cabinet ministers. The agency kept dossiers on politicians, bureaucrats, judges and anyone else considered important. The collapse of democratic institutions and the Constitution's loss of sanctity created a vacuum of authority that provided a favourable condition for the Bonapartist generals. Bhutto's use of the army to crush the uprising in Pakistan's western province of Balochistan provided an opportunity to the military to reassert itself in the country's politics. Bhutto's politics of expediency and attempts to appease the country's religious lobby allowed the Islamists, who were routed in the 1971 elections, to revive themselves. A nationwide agitation, led by right wing Islamic parties in the aftermath of the controversial elections in 1977, shook his government. In a desperate attempt to appease the Islamists, Bhutto prohibited the sale and use of alcoholic beverages, banned gambling and closed down nightclubs. But the die had already been cast.

Bhutto had handpicked General Zia ul-Haq, a lesser-known officer, for the post of army chief in 1976 over the heads of half a dozen senior officers, believing he did not have any personal ambitions. General Zia was a devout Muslim and Bhutto thought he would never betray his trust. Once elevated to the top position, the General did not take much time to develop secret contacts with hardline religious groups and conspired with them to overthrow his benefactor. On 5 July 1977, a bloodless military coup brought an end to Bhutto's six-and-a-half-year civilian rule. There was a complete convergence of interests between the Islamists and the military leadership which had ousted the Bhutto government. Several accounts of Bhutto's last days in power revealed that Major-General Ghulam Jilani, Bhutto's handpicked chief of the ISI, played a key role in the coup plan. Two years later, in April 1979, Bhutto was hanged after a dubious trial on charges of murdering a political rival. A secularist, elected with an overwhelming mandate in 1970, Bhutto probably had the best chance of any leader of taking on the Islamists and winning. His inglorious demise can only fill Pakistan's current leader, attempting a similar task, with foreboding.

Bhutto's usurper, General Zia, came from a humble lowermiddle-class background. His father, a religious man, held a clerical government post during British rule in India. Despite his poverty, he provided his son with a decent education. Zia was educated at Delhi's most prestigious St Stephen's College before getting a commission in the Royal Indian Army in 1942. He was a captain at the time of the creation of Pakistan in 1947. He was a hard-working officer, but lacked brilliance. Many of his colleagues believed he was lucky to be promoted beyond Colonel. From a young age, Zia was actively involved with the popular religious movement, Tablighi Jamaat, 6 one of the most influential grassroots Islamic movements in the South Asian subcontinent, which had hardline traditionalist views on the role of Islam in modern society.

A short man with a thick moustache, Zia bore a strong resemblance to the British comedian, Terry-Thomas. But he was by no means a fool. He was shrewd enough to know how to make his way up. He convinced Bhutto of his absolute loyalty and more importantly of his incapacity to be otherwise. Zia was not only an authoritarian; he also aspired to turn Pakistan into an ideological state ruled by strict Islamic sharia laws. He was an unpopular and controversial leader, whose survival in power largely owed to the external factors that emerged after the invasion by Soviet forces of Pakistan's northern neighbour, Afghanistan, in 1979. Pakistan became a frontline state and a bulwark in the West's war against communism.

General Zia brought in his close confidant, Lt.-General Akhter Abdur Rehman, to head the ISI in 1979, as the spy agency became a crucial cog in the resistance against the Soviet forces. Its tentacles started to spread far and wide. An artillery officer, General Rehman 'had a cold, reserved personality, almost inscrutable, always secretive, with no intimates except his family.' His officers remembered him as a hard man to serve due to his brusque manner and reputation as a strict disciplinarian. 'That made him an ideal man for the job,' said Brigadier Mohammed Yousuf, a former ISI officer who served under him. General Rehman ran the organization until 1987. He was not a radical Islamist, but a staunch Muslim nationalist. Under General Rehman, the ISI, in partnership with the CIA, conducted the biggest covert operation in modern history. The two organizations had secretly collaborated for years, yet General Zia was not prepared to give a free hand to the CIA. He laid down strict rules to ensure that the ISI would maintain control over contacts with Afghan mujahidin groups. No CIA operatives would be allowed to cross the border into Afghanistan. Distribution of weapons to the Afghan commanders would be handled only by the ISI. All training of mujahidin would be the sole responsibility of the ISI. While the CIA supplied money and weapons, it was the ISI that moved them into Afghanistan. The Americans relied almost entirely on the Pakistani service to allocate weapons to the mujahidin groups. The framework provided the Pakistani spy agency with almost total control over the covert operation inside Afghanistan. The decade-long secret war raised the organization's profile and gave it huge clout. With the active help of the CIA and Saudi Arabia, the ISI turned the Afghan resistance into Islam's holy war.

The decade-long conflict in Afghanistan gave the Islamic extremists a rallying point and a training field. Young Muslims around the world flocked to Afghanistan to fight against a foreign invader. Some 35,000 holy warriors joined the Afghan war from 1979 to 1989. The largest number came from the Middle East. Some were Saudis, among whom was a young man called Osama bin Laden.

The 23-year-old son of a wealthy construction magnate said he arrived in Peshawar for the first time in 1980. He was a very shy person who had no experience of war and, as a fresh graduate from the King Abdul Aziz University, bin Laden had left the luxury of his home to help the mujahidin fighting jihad in Afghanistan. It was the beginning of his long association with Afghan and Pakistani Islamic radicals. By 1984 he was spending most of his time in Peshawar, sometimes with Abdullah Azzam, a Palestinian Islamic scholar and an ideologue who inspired the rush of foreign Muslims to fight in Afghanistan. It was also during this period that he developed links with the ISI, which had become the main conduit for arms and training for the Islamic warriors. The Afghan war placed enormous resources at the agency's disposal. Weapons provided by the CIA were channelled to Afghan fighters through the ISI. By the mid 1980s, every dollar given by the CIA was matched by another from Saudi Arabia. The funds, running into several million dollars a year, were transferred by the CIA to the ISI's special accounts in Pakistan. The backing of the CIA and the funnelling of massive amounts of US military aid helped the ISI develop into 'a parallel structure wielding enormous power over all aspects of government.' It became all-pervasive and there was an unprecedented expansion in the surveillance of political opponents.

Even those in the army were not spared. According to a former senior intelligence officer, part of the ISI's function was to keep a careful watch on the generals and ensure their loyalty to the regime. In the words of Brigadier Yousaf, 'So powerful had the ISI become that apprehension, even fear, of what the ISI could do, was real.' The Afghan war provided the agency with the public profile that it did not have before. Former ISI officials point out that the general expansion the agency underwent as a consequence of its Afghan role had a bearing on its overall functioning. While its role in supervising a successful covert operation in Afghanistan won the ISI international acclaim, at home it was a dreaded name.

The Afghan resistance was projected as part of the global jihad against communism. The ISI's training of guerrillas was integrated with the teaching of Islam. The prominent theme was that Islam was a complete socio-political ideology under threat from atheistic communists. The Afghan war produced a new radical Islamic movement. Besides the holy warriors from Islamic countries, thousands more joined madrasas set up with funding from Saudi Arabia and some other Muslim countries. More than 100,000 foreign Muslim radicals were directly influenced by the Afghan jihad. The military's involvement in the politics of religion, however, had started long before the Afghan jihad. General Zia not only ushered Pakistan into its longest period of military rule, but also tried to turn the country into an ideological state. He extended the army's role in domestic politics much further than defined by earlier military rulers. Previously, the military was seen as the ultimate guarantor of the country's territorial integrity and internal security. But Zia expanded its role as the defender of Pakistan's ideological frontiers as well.

Addressing army officers, Zia argued that, as Pakistan was created on the basis of the two-nation theory and Islamic ideology, it was the duty of the 'soldiers of Islam to safeguard its security, integrity and sovereignty at all costs, both from internal turmoil and external aggression'. He claimed the state was created exclusively to provide its people with the opportunity to follow 'the Islamic way of life.' Preservation of the country's Islamic character was seen to be as important as the security of the country's geographical frontiers. Zia's military rule differed by its very serious attempt to create an ideological basis for all areas of activities of the state and society. General Zia cleverly used Islam to consolidate his power and legitimize his military rule. The Islamization process became the most important feature of his eleven- year rule and its raison d'e^tre. For General Zia, Pakistan was an Islamic ideological state and therefore politics could not be separated from religion. He believed that he had a divine obligation to establish an Islamic society ruled in accordance with the Qur'an and sharia. Afraid to face a free electorate and having no mandate to govern, the General turned to Allah. He introduced a rigid interpretation of Islamic sharia, thus empowering the clergy. The move to Islamize the state found ready allies among the religious parties, many of which already had close ties with the military. The Jamaat-i-Islami and other Islamic groups were co-opted by the government. For the first time in Pakistan's history, the Islamists occupied important government positions. Being in power helped

Jamaat-i-Islami, the most influential and organized mainstream religious party, penetrate state institutions. Thousands of party activists and sympathizers were given jobs in the judiciary, the civil service and educational institutions. These appointments strengthened the hold of the Islamists on crucial state apparatuses for many years to come.

The process of the Islamization of the state and society took place on two levels. Firstly, changes were instituted in the legal system. Sharia courts were established to try cases under Islamic laws. For the first time, the government assumed the role of the collector of religious taxes. Secondly, Islamization was promoted through the print media, radio, television and mosques. Through a series of religious decrees, the government moved to Islamize the civil service, the armed forces and the education system. School textbooks were overhauled to ensure their ideological purity. Books deemed un-Islamic were removed from syllabuses and university libraries. It was made compulsory for civil servants to pray five times a day. Confidential reports of government officials included a section in which the staff were given marks for regularly attending prayers and for having a good knowledge of Islam. General Zia's move to Islamize the army carried the most critical implications. Pakistan's army, carved out of the British Indian army, inherited British traditions and remained a secular organization until General Zia tried to give it a new Islamic orientation. Islam was incorporated into the army's organizational fabric. For the first time Islamic teachings were introduced into the Pakistan Military Academy.

Islamic training and philosophy were made a part of the curriculum at the Command and Staff College. A Directorate of Religious Instruction was instituted to educate the officer corps on Islam. Islamic education also became a part of the promotion exams. The officers were required to read The Quranic Concept of War, a book written by a serving officer, Brigadier S. K. Malik. The officers were taught to be not just professional soldiers, but also soldiers of Islam.

In his foreword to the book, General Zia wrote: 'The professional soldier in a Muslim army, pursuing the goals of a Muslim State, cannot become "professional" if in all his activities he does not take on "the colour of Allah".' To gain promotion an officer was required to be a devout Muslim. Scores of highly professional and secular officers were sidelined for not meeting the criterion of a 'good Muslim'. As a consequence of this policy, many conservative officers reached the senior command level. Radical Islamist ideology permeated the army with the free flow of religious political literature in the armed forces training institutions. Friday prayers at regimental mosques, a matter of individual choice in the past, became obligatory. Mullahs belonging to the Deobandi sect were appointed to work among the troops.

They were supposed to be the bridge for officers between the westernized profession and the faith. Units were required to take noncombatant mullahs with them to the front line. Soldiers were encouraged to attend 'Tablighi' gatherings. The purpose was to indoctrinate cadets and young officers with an obscurantist interpretation of Islam. Many of those cadets later rose to positions of power and took control of sensitive institutions, including the ISI. The change in the social composition of the officer corps also led to the ideological reorientation of Pakistan's army in the 1980s. The army officer corps, till the 1970s, was elitist in character and composition.

But the trend changed. In the past, members of the upper class or the rural aristocracy had largely dominated the army ranks; now the new officers mostly came from the lower and middle social strata. The rank and file of junior officers since the 1970s had come, not from prosperous central Punjab, but from the impoverished and relatively backward northern districts where a fundamentalist religious ethos prevailed. Unlike their predecessors, the new officers did not come from elite English-language schools, but were the product of modest state-run educational institutions. The spirit of liberalism, common in the 'old' army, was practically unknown to them. They were products of a social class that, by its very nature, was conservative and easily influenced by Islamic fundamentalism. They were distinctively less westernized.

Their narrow nationalist orientation and education, professional training and culture made them very receptive to the influence of Islamic groups, particularly to the Jamaat-i-Islami (JI), which freely carried out propaganda work among the officers and circulated Islamic literature. Most importantly, the JI's propaganda among vast numbers of troops was officially sanctioned by commanding officers on the battalion level and above. That led to the evolution of a long-lasting alliance between the military and the mosque. The main objective of the JI was to penetrate the army and use it to seize state power. The practice introduced by General Zia of sending combat officers to universities in Pakistan, in which the JI often had pervasive influence, facilitated the party's objective. The influence of the JI was particularly visible among officers from rural and semi-urban backgrounds. They had a high level of religious intolerance and held extremist views regarding 'external enemies' and the threat to Islam.

The number of officers sporting beards for religious reasons had visibly risen. These young officers constituted the main base for General Zia's regime. According to a retired general, 25 to 30 per cent of the officers had Islamic fundamentalist leanings. Many of them regularly attended 'Tablighi' groups that propagated the faith. They would take time off to join missionary bands preaching a return to purist Islamic values and recruiting other Muslim men to join them.

Thousands of soldiers and army officers would join the annual gathering of the TJ at Raiwind on the outskirts of Lahore. More than one million faithful from across the country and abroad attend this Muslim congregation, the largest after the Haj in Mecca. Even the liberals adopted the philosophy on issues like jihad and support for militancy in Kashmir. The humiliating military defeat by the Indian army in the 1971 war, coupled with the disintegration of the country, also had a very deep impact on the psyche of army officers. Many young officers turned to religion for solace and became born-again Muslims. Given this situation, it was not surprising that radical Islamic officers made unsuccessful coup attempts in the mid 1980s. They wanted to bring about an Islamic revolution and establish a theocratic state. The fact that the attempts were crushed and the rebel officers were charged with treason indicated that, notwithstanding its Islamization, the state was not prepared to tolerate a theocratic rule.

The situation in Afghanistan provided inspiration to a whole generation of Pakistani Islamic radicals who considered it their religious duty to fight the oppression of Muslims anywhere in the world. It gave a new dimension to the idea of jihad, which till then had only been employed by the Pakistani state in the context of mobilizing the population against the arch rival – India. The Afghan war saw the privatization of the concept of jihad. Militant groups emerged from the ranks of traditional religious movements, who took the path of an armed struggle for the cause of Islam. The ISI's active role in the Afghan jihad brought Pakistani army officers into direct contact with the radical Islamists.

The handling of jihad also indoctrinated the military and intelligence officers. At least two former ISI chiefs – General Hamid Gul and General Javed Nasir – remained actively involved with Islamic radical movements. Both promoted pan-Islamism and strove for an Islamic revolution that would free Pakistan from perceived western, and particularly American, cultural and political influences. General Gul, who liked to call himself a 'Muslim visionary', succeeded General Rehman in 1987 when the Afghan resistance had entered its most critical juncture.

The most charismatic of the ISI chiefs, he openly aligned himself with the hardline Afghan mujahidin leader, Gulbuddin Hekmatyar, and right-wing Pakistani Islamic parties. He would later take credit for dismantling the Soviet Union. General Gul had worked closely with the CIA, but turned anti-American after the Geneva Accord in 1987, which paved the way for the withdrawal of Soviet forces from Afghanistan. The Accord was signed by the Pakistani civilian government led by Prime Minister Mohammed Khan Junejo against the wishes of President Zia, who believed it deprived the Afghan mujahidin of the opportunity to take over Kabul. Resentment among the military and ISI officers deepened in 1990, just one year after the Soviets pulled out of Afghanistan and the US administration imposed sanctions on Pakistan for its nuclear programme. The CIA ended its support for the Afghan rebels and its links with the ISI went cold. It was a sudden end to the strong link between the two agencies. The military leadership accused the United States of dumping Pakistan after the collapse of the Soviet Union. Long before the Afghan war was over, General Gul had started organizing a new jihad front in Kashmir. 'It is the years of our work that has realized the armed uprising against the Indian forces in Kashmir,' he told me in early 1990 when he was commanding the country's elite armoured corps.

The death of General Zia ul-Haq in a mysterious air crash in August 1988 brought an end to Pakistan's longest-serving military government. It left the generals with the choice of either imposing martial law again or holding elections and transferring power to a democratically elected civilian government. They went for the second option, realizing that a perpetuation of military rule might provoke public resistance and exacerbate the turmoil in an already highly polarised society. However, the generals were not prepared to pull out completely and leave the political field solely to the politicians, particularly to the daughter of Zulfikar Ali Bhutto, Benazir Bhutto, who now led the Pakistan People's Party, which was certain to sweep the polls. To contain Benazir, the military cobbled together the Islamic Democratic Alliance (IDA), uniting all the right-wing parties under the leadership of Nawaz Sharif. General Aslam Beg, then Chief of Army Staff, and General Gul justified the move by saying it was necessary for the viable functioning of a democratic system.

The main objective, however, was to ensure the military's continued role in the new system, overseen by the generals. By creating a counterbalance in the form of the IDA, the generals constrained the new government of a political party that had led the resistance against military hegemony for ten years. The military-sponsored alliance comprised a mix of traditional power brokers, religious parties and politicians who had emerged on the scene during the 1980s under military patronage. General Zia's regime, needing a measure of legitimacy and a social base of support, had co-opted segments of Punjab's dominant socio-economic strata: influential landlords, industrialists and emerging commercial groups. The new leadership of the Pakistan Muslim League thus largely consisted of politicians who owed their political rise to the military's backing. The other important components of the alliance were the right-wing Islamic groups, including the Jamaat-i-Islami, which had been involved in the Afghan jihad against the Soviet forces and the separatist war in Indian-controlled Kashmir.

While the IDA, which carried General Zia's legacy, could not achieve any significant electoral gains in the 1988 elections in the three smaller provinces, it did relatively well in Punjab and prevented the PPP from winning an absolute majority in the National Assembly. The military reluctantly handed over power to Benazir at the centre, but prevented her party from forming the government in Punjab, the biggest and most important of Pakistan's four provinces, which was being ruled by Nawaz Sharif. Political manipulation by the ISI helped Sharif retain power in the province with the support of independent members. Benazir Bhutto's assumption of power, touted at the time as the dawn of a new democratic era, was in fact a transition from direct to indirect military rule. The formal restoration of civilian rule in 1988 did not reduce the ISI's clout. A return to the barracks did not mean that the military's structure of control and manipulation had been dismantled. The ISI still kept a close watch on civilian rulers. The strains in civil and military relationships remained the biggest obstacle to democracy taking root in Pakistan.

The Chief of Army Staff remained the power behind the scenes in alliance with the new President, Ghulam Ishaq Khan, who held sweeping powers under the Eighth Amendment in the constitution introduced by General Zia. For the army, the new political situation offered power without responsibility. The military continued to oversee Pakistan's policies on Afghanistan and India, managing relations with the USA and controlling the country's nuclear weapons programme. The army high command's decision to rest content with dominance, rather than direct intervention, was based on a careful calculation of the advantages and disadvantages of playing arbiter in Pakistan's highly polarized and conflict-ridden political scene. A hamstrung Benazir Bhutto found herself directly clashing with the army when she removed General Gul from the ISI. The General, who was the architect of the IDA, had never reconciled himself to even restricted civilian rule. Benazir was never trusted by the establishment and many generals made it a point not to salute her. It was in February 1990 when I met General

Gul in Multan, where he was posted as the commander of Pakistan's main strike corps, after being sacked from the ISI. It was the period when the army had just concluded a major war exercise called 'Zarb-i-Momin'. The General accused Prime Minister Benazir of trying to make peace with India and questioned her patriotism. 'By conducting the exercise we have blocked her designs to undermine Pakistan's defence,' he said.

It was apparent that the generals were looking for an opportune moment to remove Benazir from power. The clash came to a head when the Prime Minister tried to retire the Chairman of the Joint Chiefs of Staff Committee, Admiral Iftikhar Ahmed Sarohi, and gave a year's extension in service to Lt.-General Alam Jan Mehsud, a senior general believed to be close to her government.

The army top brass saw this as blatant interference in the army's internal affairs. Eventually, on 6 August 1990, President Ghulam Ishaq Khan dismissed her government on charges of corruption and dissolved the National Assembly. President Khan, a former top bureaucrat, was the central pillar of General Zia's military rule and represented his legacy. Benazir's party met a humiliating defeat in the following elections, losing the government even in her home province and political stronghold, Sindh.

The military leadership did not want to take any chances that time. To ensure the IDA's electoral victory, the ISI financed the election campaign of many top Alliance leaders. The list, which was published in national newspapers, contained the names of some leading politicians, including Nawaz Sharif.

Most of them later held important posts in the new government. In 1988, the long-simmering political discontent in Kashmir exploded into a popular uprising against Indian control. Thousands of young Kashmiris crossed over to the Pakistani side of the Line of Control to receive guerrilla training as the Indian authorities tried to crush the insurgency by brute force. Essentially an indigenous rebellion, it soon turned into an armed struggle against Indian forces. Thousands of Kashmiri youths joined the separatist struggle, which was initially led by the independent nationalist organization, Jammu and Kashmir Liberation Front (JKLF)

The ISI used the extensive intelligence and militant network that it had built up during the Afghan war to support a new jihad against the Indian forces in Kashmir. In Afghanistan in the 1980s, jihadist cadres came from the ranks of motivated Islamists across the Muslim world who were prepared to die for the cause, as well as kill the 'communists'. The spirit saw its continuation in Kashmir, which became one of the world's hottest 'Islamic jihad' spots. The ISI's involvement increased further in the early 1990s when, in an attempt to sideline the JKLF, it started supporting the pro-Pakistani Hezb-ul Mujahideen. The move divided the Kashmiri struggle and led to internecine battles. The mid 1990s saw the increasing role of Pakistani-based militant groups. That was when Harkat-ul-Mujahideen (HuM), Lashkar-e-Taiba (LeT) and later Jaish-e-Mohammed (JeM) emerged as the main guerrilla forces in the disputed state. Those hardline Islamic groups changed the complexion of the struggle.

# 6

# Post-Taliban Nation-Building Efforts

With Afghanistan devastated after more than 20 years of warfare, the 2001 fall of the Taliban regime raised questions about the extent of a U.S. and international commitment to Afghanistan. Taking the view that leaving the Afghanistan-Pakistan theater after the 1989 Soviet pullout had led Afghanistan degenerate into chaos, the decision was made by the Bush Administration to try to rebuild try to build a relatively strong central government and to assist Afghanistan's economy, in order to prevent a return of the Taliban, Al Qaeda, and other militants to Afghanistan.

The effort, which many outside experts described as "nation-building,"was supported by major international institutions and U.S. partners in several post-Taliban international meetings. The task has proved slower and more difficult than anticipated, in part because of the devastation that years of war wrought on governing institutions, on the education system, and on the already limited infrastructure. Some observers believe the international community had unrealistic expectations of what could be achieved in a relatively short time frame—particularly in establishing competent, non-corrupt governance and a vibrant democracy.

The Obama Administration's two "Afghanistan strategy reviews," the results of which were announced on March 27, 2009, and on December 1, 2009, narrowed official U.S. goals to preventing terrorism safe haven in Afghanistan and Pakistan. However, the elements of Obama Administration strategy in many ways enhance the nation-building strategy put in place by the Bush Administration. Reforming Afghan governance was emphasized both at the international January 28, 2010, "London Conference" and the July 20, 2010, "Kabul Conference."

## POST-TALIBAN POLITICAL TRANSITION

The 2001 ouster of the Taliban government paved the way for the success of a long-stalled U.N. effort to form a broad-based Afghan government and for the international community to help Afghanistan build legitimate governing institutions. In the formation of the first post-Taliban transition government, the United Nations was viewed as a credible mediator by all sides largely because of its role in ending the Soviet occupation. During the 1990s, a succession of U.N. mediators adopted many of former King Zahir Shah's proposals for a government to be selected by a traditional assembly, or *loya jirga*. However, U.N.-mediated cease-fires between warring factions did not hold. Non-U.N. initiatives made little progress, particularly the "Six Plus Two" multilateral contact group, which began meeting in 1997 (the United States, Russia, and the six states bordering Afghanistan: Iran, China, Pakistan, Turkmenistan, Uzbekistan, and Tajikistan). Other failed efforts included a "Geneva group" (Italy, Germany, Iran, and the United States) formed in 2000; an Organization of Islamic Conference (OIC) contact group; and prominent Afghan exile efforts, including discussion groups launched by Hamid Karzai and his clan, former *mujahedin* commander Abd al-Haq, and Zahir Shah ("Rome process").

### *Bonn Agreement*

Immediately after the September 11 attacks, former U.N. mediator Lakhdar Brahimi was brought back (he had resigned in frustration in October 1999). U.N. Security Council Resolution 1378 (November 14, 2001) called for a "central" role for the United Nations in establishing a transitional administration and inviting member states to send peacekeeping forces to promote stability and aid delivery. After the fall of Kabul in November 2001, the United Nations invited major Afghan factions, most prominently the Northern Alliance and that of the former King—but not the

Taliban—to an international conference in Bonn, Germany. On December 5, 2001, the factions signed the "Bonn Agreement." It was endorsed by U.N. Security Council Resolution 1385 (December 6, 2001). The agreement was reportedly forged with substantial Iranian diplomatic help because Iran had supported the military efforts of the Northern Alliance faction and had leverage to persuade temporary caretaker Rabbani and the Northern Alliance to cede the top leadership to Hamid Karzai as leader of an interim administration. Other provisions of the agreement:

- authorized an international peace keeping force to maintain security in Kabul, and Northern Alliance forces were directed to withdraw from the capital. Security Council Resolution 1386 (December 20, 2001, and renewed yearly thereafter) gave formal Security Council authorization for the international peacekeeping force (International Security Assistance Force, ISAF);
- referred to the need to cooperate with the international community on counter narcotics, crime, and terrorism; and
- applied the constitution of 1964 until a permanent constitution could be drafted.

### *Permanent Constitution*

A June 2002 "emergency" *loya jirga* put a representative imprimatur on the transition; it was attended by 1,550 delegates (including about 200 women). Subsequently, a 35-member constitutional commission drafted the constitution, unveiling it in November 2003. It was debated by 502 delegates, selected in U.N.-run caucuses, at a "*constitutional loya jirga* (CLJ)" during December 13, 2003–January 4, 2004. The CLJ, chaired by Sibghatullah Mojadeddi (mentioned above) ended with approval of the constitution with only minor changes. It set up a presidential system, with an elected president and a separately elected National Assembly (parliament). The Northern Alliance failed in its effort to set up a prime ministership (in which the elected parliament would select a prime minister and a cabinet) , but the faction did achieve a limitation on presidential powers by assigning major authorities to the parliament, such as the power to veto senior official nominees. The constitution made former King Zahir Shah honorary "Father of the Nation," a title that is not heritable. Zahir Shah died on July 23, 2007.

### First Post-Taliban Elections in 2004

Security conditions precluded the holding of the first post-Taliban elections simultaneously. The first election, for president, was held on October 9, 2004, missing a June constitutional deadline. Turnout was about 80%. On November 3, 2004, Karzai was declared winner (55.4% of the vote) over his 17 challengers on the first round, avoiding a runoff. Parliamentary and provincial council elections were intended for April-May 2005 but were delayed until September 18, 2005. Because of the difficulty in confirming voter registration rolls and determining district boundaries, elections for the 364 district councils, each of which will likely have contentious boundaries because they will inevitably separate tribes and clans, have not been held to date.

### Formation of an Elected National Assembly (Parliament)

The National Assembly (parliament), particularly the elected lower house, has emerged as a relatively vibrant body that creates accountability and has often asserted itself politically. The most notable example has been the 2009-2010 confirmation process for Karzai's cabinet choices, in which many of Karzai's nominees were voted down, and the lower house's subsequent vote against a Karzai election decree to govern the September 18, 2010, National Assembly election. The Assembly's assertiveness shows, in part, that the better educated "independents" are emerging as pivotal members of parliament, although some interpret the activism as a product of emboldened "Northern Alliance" opposition to Karzai and his plan to reconcile with senior Taliban figures.

### Hamid Karzai, President of the Islamic Republic of Afghanistan

Hamid Karzai, born December 24, 1957, was selected to lead Afghanistan at the Bonn Conference because he was a prominent Pashtun leader who had been involved in Taliban-era political talks among exiled Afghans and was viewed as a compromiser rather than a "strongman." However, some observers consider his compromises as Afghanistan's leader a sign of weakness, and criticize him for indulging members of his clan and other allies with appointments. Others view him as overly suspicious of the intentions of the United States and other outside powers, believing they are intent on replacing him or favoring certain groups of Afghans over others.

From Karz village in Qandahar Province, Hamid Karzai has led the powerful Popolzai tribe of Durrani Pashtuns since 1999, when his father was assassinated, allegedly by Taliban agents, in Quetta, Pakistan. Karzai's grandfather was head of the consultative National Council during King Zahir Shah's reign. He attended university in India and supported the mujahdin party of Sibghatullah Mojadeddi (still a very close ally) during the ant-Soviet war. He was deputy foreign minister in the mujahidin government of Rabbani during 1992-1995, but he left the government and supported the Taliban as a Pashtun alternative to Rabbani. He broke with the Taliban as its excesses unfolded and forged alliances with other anti-Taliban factions, including the Northern Alliance. Karzai entered Afghanistan after the September 11 attacks to organize Pashtun resistance to the Taliban, supported by U.S. Special Forces. He became central to U.S. efforts after Pashtun commander Abdul Haq entered Afghanistan in October 2001 without U.S. support and was captured and hung by the Taliban. Karzai was slightly injured by an errant U.S. bomb during major combat of Operation Enduring Freedom (late 2001).

His half brother, Ahmad Wali Karzai, is the most powerful political figure in that province, He is key to Karzai's maintenance of support and the cornerstone of his information network in Qandahar but Ahmad Wali has been widely accused of involvement in or tolerating narcotics trafficking. A New York Times article on October 28, 2009, said Ahmad Wali is also a paid informant for the CIA and some of his property has been used by U.S. Special Forces. Ahmad Wali was the apparent target of at least two bombings in Qandahar in 2009. Others of Karzai's several brothers have lived in the United States, including Qayyum Karzai. Qayyum

Karzai won a parliament seat in the September 2005 election but resigned his seat in October 2008 due to health reasons. Qayyum subsequently represented the government in inconclusive talks, held in several Persian Gulf states, to reconcile with Taliban figures close to Mullah Umar. Another brother, Mahmoud Karzai, is a businessman reportedly under U.S. Justice Department investigation of his business interests in Qandahar and Kabul, including auto dealerships, apartment houses, and a stake in Kabul Bank, which nearly collapsed in September 2010. Other Karzai relatives and associates have formed security companies and other contracting firms that have profited extensively from international reconstruction, transportation, and protection funds, including a $2.2 billion U.S. "Host Nation Trucking" contract.

Karzai also relies heavily for advice from tribal and faction leaders from southern Afghanistan, including Sher Mohammad Akhunzadeh, the former governor of Helmand (until 2005), as well as from well-educated professionals such as his current Foreign Minister Zalmay Rasool, his brother-in-law and key Afghanistan National Security Council official Ibrahim Spinzada, and the former foreign minister, now National Security Adviser, Rangeen Spanta.

With heavy protection, Karzai has survived several assassination attempts since taking office, including rocket fire or gunfire at or near his appearances. His wife, Dr. Zenat Karzai, is a gynecologist by profession. They have been married about 11 years and have a son, Mirwais, born in 2008. In December 2009, he spoke publicly about personal turmoil among relatives in Karz village that resulted in the death of an 18-year-old relative in October 2009.

## 2009 PRESIDENTIAL AND PROVINCIAL ELECTIONS

The 2009 presidential and provincial elections were expected to further Afghanistan's democratic development. However, because of the widespread fraud identified by Afghanistan's U.N.-appointed "Elections Complaints Commission" (ECC) in the August 20, 2009, first round of the elections, the process did not produce that result. The election fraud difficulty may have contributed to the substantial parliamentary opposition to many of Karzai's nominees for his post-election cabinet. In each of three rounds of cabinet nominations in 2009 and 2010, many, if not most, of Karzai's nominees were voted down by the National Assembly. The latest round of nominations occurred in late June 2010, after Karzai forced Interior Minister Mohammad Hanif Atmar to resign, ostensibly for failing to prevent insurgent attacks in Kabul itself. Atmar was close to and well respected by U.S. officials. Also resigning on June 6 was National Directorate of Security (NDS, Afghan intelligence) chief Amrollah Saleh, a Tajik and an ally of the United Front leaders. Both were believed to oppose Karzai's efforts to reconcile with senior insurgent leaders.

### *September 18, 2010, Parliamentary Elections*

A key test of Karzai's repeated commitment to reforms were the September 18, 2010, National Assembly elections. That election was held amid significant violence but not sufficient to derail the voting. Final results were expected October 30, 2010 but widespread fraud complaints have delayed finalization of the results.

Some worry that ethnic differences might resurge once the results are announced. Karzai's allies reportedly want to win enough seats (a majority) to ensure that Pashtun conservative Sayyaf, mentioned above, can replace Yunus Qanooni, an Abdullah supporter, as lower house speaker.

## OTHER MAJOR GOVERNANCE ISSUES

Obama Administration policy, as articulated on March 27, 2009, and December 1, 2009, emphasizes expanding and improving Afghan governance as a long-term means of stabilizing Afghanistan. The latter Obama statement specified that there would be "no blank check" for the Afghan government if it does not reduce corruption and deliver services. This emphasis is expressed extensively in the State Department January 2010 document outlining its policy priorities, entitled *Afghanistan and Pakistan Regional Stabilization Strategy.* The corruption has repeatedly been stressed emphasized by international participants at two international meetings in 2010 (London in January and Kabul in July) as well as by U.S. officials, including top commander in

Afghanistan General Petraeus. However, the Obama Administration reportedly has decided to mute its public criticism of Karzai on the grounds that public criticism causes Karzai to become suspicious of U.S. intent and to ally with undemocratic elements in Afghanistan.

"Unity of Effort": U.S. and International Policy Management and U.S. Embassy Kabul, In line with the prioritization of Afghanistan policy, in February 2009, the Administration appointed Ambassador Richard Holbrooke as "Special Representative for Afghanistan and Pakistan" (SRAP), reporting to Secretary of State Clinton. His team at the State Department consists mainly of members detailed from several different agencies; several have long experience on Afghanistan and Pakistan affairs. Karl Eikenberry, who served as commander of U.S. forces in Afghanistan during 2004-2005, is U.S. Ambassador. President Obama has said he, On February 7, 2010, in an effort to improve civilian coordination between the United States, its foreign partners, and the Afghan government, a NATO "Senior Civilian Representative" in Afghanistan, UK Ambassador Mark Sedwill, took office. Ambassador Sedwill works not only with U.S. military officials but with representatives of the embassies of partner countries and with a special U.N. Assistance Mission–Afghanistan.

At U.S. Embassy Kabul, there is a "deputy Ambassador"—senior official Francis Ricciardone. Another Ambassador rank official (William Todd) manages U.S. economic assistance issues. Another Ambassador-rank official, Joseph Mussomeli, handles Embassy management. Ambassador Timothy Carney oversaw U.S. policy for the 2009 elections. Another official of Ambassador rank, Hans Klemm, arrived in June 2010 to coordinate U.S. Embassy rule of law programs

The U.S. Embassy has progressively expanded its personnel and facilities and will expand its facilities further to accommodate some of the additional civilian hires and Foreign Service officers who have been posted to Afghanistan as mentors and advisers to the Afghan government. The tables at the end of this report include U.S. funding for State Department and USAID operations, including Embassy construction and running the "Embassy air wing," a fleet of twin-engine turboprops that ferry U.S. officials and contractors around Afghanistan. In a significant development attempting to signal normalization of certain areas of Afghanistan, in early 2010 the United States formally inaugurated U.S. consulates in Herat and Mazar-e-Sharif. In November 2010, contracts were announced for expansion of the U.S. Embassy ($511 million) and to construct the two consulates ($20 million for each facility).

The Afghan Ambassador to the United States, Sayed Tayib Jawad, served as Ambassador from 2004 until his recall in August 2010. He was recalled because of complaints in Kabul about Western-style parties that were being held at the Afghan embassy in the United States. No replacement has been named, to date. There is some discussion on the Afghan side of appointing a special envoy, possibly Ashraf Ghani, to interact on a global basis with the Afghanistan donor community.

### *U.S. Efforts to Expand and Reform Central Government/ Corruption*

U.S. policy has been to expand governance throughout the country, a policy that is receiving increased U.S. financial and advisory resources under the Obama Administration. However, in part because building the central government has gone slowly and because official corruption is widespread, there has been a U.S. shift, predating the Obama Administration, away from reliance toward promoting local governance. Some argue that, in addition to offering the advantage of bypassing an often corrupt central government, doing so is more compatible with Afghan traditions of local autonomy.

### *Marginalization of Regional Strongmen*

A key to U.S. strategy, particularly during 2002-2006, was to strengthen the central government by helping Karzai curb key regional strongmen and local militias—whom some refer to as "warlords." These actors controlled much of Afghanistan after the Taliban regime disintegrated in late 2001, but there was a decision by the international community to build up an accountable central government rather than leave Afghanistan in the hands of local militias. These forces often arbitrarily administer justice and use their positions to enrich themselves and their supporters.

Karzai has marginalized some of the largest regional leaders, but he is criticized by some human rights groups and international donors for continuing to tolerate or rely on others to keep order in some areas, particularly in non-Pashtun inhabited parts of Afghanistan (the north and west). Karzai's view is that maintaining ties to ethnic and regional faction leaders has prevented the emergence of ethnic conflict that would detract from the overall effort against the Taliban.

### Anti-Corruption Efforts

An accelerating trend in U.S. policy—and emphasized in both major Obama Administration strategy reviews as well as by many in Congress—is to press Karzai to weed out official corruption. U.S. officials believe that rife corruption in the Afghan government is undermining U.S. domestic support for the U.S. mission in Afghanistan, and causing the Afghan population to sour on the Karzai government. U.S. anti-corruption and rule of law efforts are discussed extensively in the "Afghanistan and Pakistan Regional Stabilization Strategy" issued by Ambassador Holbrooke's office in January 2010, referenced above.

In FY2011 legislation, on June 30, 2010, the State and Foreign Operations Subcommittee of House Appropriations Committee marked up its aid bill. The Subcommittee deferred consideration of much of the Administration's Afghanistan request pending a Committee investigation of allegations of governmental corruption and possible diversion of U.S. aid funds by Afghan officials and other elites.

## ENHANCING LOCAL GOVERNANCE

As emphasized in the January 2010 SRAP strategy document cited earlier, there has been a major

- and Afghan push to build up local governing structures, reflecting a shift in emphasis from the 2001-2007 approach of focusing on building up central authority. However, building local governance has suffered from a deficit of trained and respected local government administrators ready or willing to serve, particularly where hostilities are ongoing. This deficiency has hindered

- counter-insurgency efforts in southern Afghanistan.
- policy has sought to use local governance promotion efforts to support U.S. security strategy for Afghanistan. Several districts have received special attention to become "models" of district security and governance are Nawa, in Helmand Province, and Baraki-Barak, in Lowgar Province, both cleared of Taliban militants in 2009. With substantial infusions of U.S. development funds that put sometime insurgents to work on projects (offering $5 per day to perform such tasks as cleaning irrigation canals), these districts are, by several accounts, far more stable and secure than they were in 2009. As part of "Operation Moshtarek" (Operation Together), launched February 13, 2010, to clear the city of Marjah of militants, a district governor (Hajji Zahir) and district administration were selected in advance. Zahir tried to build up his administration after the town was wrested from Taliban control, but governance there was slow to expand. Zahir was replaced in early July 2010. Still, the British civilian representative in Marjah said in October 2010 that central government ministry representation in Marjah is now in place and operating consistently. (Marjah is currently part of Nad Ali district, and is eventually to become its own district, according to Afghan observers.)

## HUMAN RIGHTS AND DEMOCRACY

The Administration and Afghan government claim progress in building a democratic Afghanistan that adheres to international standards of human rights practices. The State Department report on human rights practices for 2009 (released March 11, 2010) said that Afghanistan's human rights record remained "poor," noting in particular that the government or its agents commit arbitrary or unlawful killings. Still, virtually all observers agree that Afghans are freer than they were under the Taliban. The tables at the end of this report contain information on U.S. funding for democracy, governance, rule of law and human rights, and elections support since the fall of the Taliban.

## Narcotics Trafficking/Insurgent Financing

Narcotics trafficking is regarded by some as a core impediment to the U.S. mission in Afghanistan by undermining rule of law and providing funds to the insurgency. However, it is also an area on which there has been progress in recent years. The trafficking generates an estimated $70 million–$100 million per year for the Taliban.

U.S. officials hope that recent progress will be sustained. A UNODC report of September 2010, continued a relatively positive trend in reporting on this issue, noting that all of the 20 provinces (out of 34 provinces in Afghanistan) in the "poppy free" category remain that way. Total production in 2010 is estimated at 3,600 metric tons, a 48% decrease from 2009, although this was due to a crop disease, for the most part.

Obama Administration policy is focusing on promoting legitimate agricultural alternatives to poppy growing and, in conjunction, Ambassador Holbrooke announced in July 2009 that the United States would end its prior focus on eradication of poppy fields. In this view, eradication was driving Afghans into the arms of the Taliban as protectors of their ability to earn a living, even if doing so is from narcotics cultivation. Encouraging alternative livelihoods has always been the preferred emphasis of the Afghan government. The de-emphasis on eradication also put aside the long-standing differences over whether to conduct spraying of fields, particularly by air. That concept was strenuously opposed by Karzai and not implemented. Congress sided with Karzai's view; the FY2008 Consolidated Appropriation (P.L. 110-161) prohibited U.S. counter-narcotics funding from being used for aerial spraying on Afghanistan poppy fields without Afghan concurrence. That provision was reiterated in the FY2010 consolidated appropriation

Other policies promote incentives; Helmand, for example, received about $10 million in Good Performance funding in 2009 for a 33% cut in poppy cultivation that year. According to Afghan cabinet members, the government also is spending funds on a "social safety net" to help wean landless farmers away from poppy cultivation work.

How consistently to use U.S. and NATO forces to combat narcotics is another facet under debate. Some NATO contributors, such as Britain, have focused on interdicting traffickers and raiding drug labs. The U.S. military, in support of the effort after initial reluctance, is flying Afghan and U.S. counter-narcotics agents (Drug Enforcement Agency, DEA) on missions and identifying targets; it also evacuates casualties from counter-drug operations. The Department of Defense is also playing the major role in training and equipping specialized Afghan counter-narcotics police, in developing an Afghan intelligence fusion cell, and training Afghan border police, as well as assisting an Afghan helicopter squadron to move Afghan counter-narcotics forces around the country. To help break up narcotics trafficking networks, the DEA presence in Afghanistan is has expanded from 13 agents in 2008 to over 80 in 2010, with additional agents in Pakistan.

Ambassador Holbrooke has also placed additional focus on the other sources of Taliban funding, including continued donations from wealthy residents of the Persian Gulf. He has established a multinational task force to combat Taliban financing generally, not limited to narcotics, and U.S. officials are emphasizing with Persian Gulf counterparts the need for cooperation.

Narcotics trafficking control was perhaps the one issue on which the Taliban regime satisfied much of the international community. The Taliban enforced a July 2000 ban on poppy cultivation.

### Narcotics-Related Aid Conditionality

The Bush Administration repeatedly named Afghanistan as a major illicit drug producer and drug transit country, but did not include Afghanistan on a smaller list of countries that have "failed demonstrably to make substantial efforts" to adhere to international counter-narcotics agreements and take certain counter-narcotics measures set forth in U.S. law. The Bush Administration exercised waiver provisions to a required certification of full Afghan cooperation that was needed to provide more than congressionally stipulated amounts of U.S. economic assistance to Afghanistan. A similar certification requirement (to provide amounts over $300 million) was contained in the FY2008 appropriation (P.L. 110-161); in the FY2009 regular appropriation, P.L. 111-8 ($200 million ceiling); and the FY2010 appropriation, P.L. 111-117, ($200 million ceiling). The FY2009 supplemental (P.L. 111-32) withheld 10% of State Department narcotics funding (International Narcotics Control and Law Enforcement, INCLE) pending a report that Afghanistan is removing officials involved in narcotics trafficking or gross human rights violations. No funds for Afghanistan have been held up, and the required certifications have been issued by the Administration or apparently are pending.

## Security Policy and Force Capacity Building

The U.S. definition of "success" of the stabilization mission in Afghanistan, articulated since the ouster of the Taliban in late 2001, is to help build up an Afghan government and security force that can defend itself, expand governance, and develop economically. The Obama Administration's policy reviews in 2009 formally narrowed U.S. goals to preventing Al Qaeda from reestablishing a base in Afghanistan. However, the policy and military tools employed by the Obama Administration in most ways continue and even expand a nation-building goal. The December 1, 2009, speech by President Obama stated U.S. goals as: (1) denying Al Qaeda a safe haven [in Afghanistan]; and (2) reversing the Taliban's momentum and denying it the ability to overthrow the government. The statement generally backed the August 30, 2009, recommendations of then-top commander in Afghanistan Gen. Stanley McChrystal's to undertake a fully resourced counter-insurgency mission. The focus of the mission is on 121 districts (out of 364 total districts in Afghanistan) deemed restive and in which support for the Afghan government is lowest. Of those, 80 districts are of the most intense focus, according to Defense Department reports and officials.

The two major U.S. policy reviews in 2009 did not significantly change most of the basic pillars of U.S. and NATO security strategy that have been in place since 2001, although the emphasis of some of these components might have shifted. The main elements include: (1) combat operations and patrols by U.S. forces and a NATO-led International Security Assistance Force (ISAF) to "provide space" for the expansion of Afghan governance, security leadership, and infrastructure and economic development; (2) U.S. and NATO operation of "provincial reconstruction teams" (PRTs) to serve as enclaves to facilitate the strategy; and (3) the equipping, training, and expansion of Afghanistan National Security Forces (ANSF). Some strategy elements that have emerged since 2008, and which are taking precedence as Western public support for the war effort erodes, include establishing local protection forces and backing efforts to reintegrate Taliban fighters and leaders who might want to end armed struggle.

### *Taliban, Al Qaeda, and Related Insurgents and Their Strength*

General McChrystal's August 2009 initial assessment and the Defense Department April 2010 report, security is being challenged by a confluence of related armed groups who are increasingly well equipped and sophisticated in their tactics and operations, particularly by using roadside bombs. However, there is not agreement about the relative strength of insurgents in all of the areas where they operate, or their degree of cooperation with each other. Afghan and U.S. assessments are that there are more than 20,000 total insurgents operating in Afghanistan, up from a few thousand in 2003.

Prior to U.S.-led offensives launched since mid-2009, the Karzai government was estimated by to control about 30% of the country, while insurgents controlled 4% (13 out of 364 districts). Insurgents "influenced" or "operated in" another 30% (Afghan Interior Ministry estimates in August 2009). Tribes and local groups with varying degrees of loyalty to the central government control the remainder. Outside groups, such as aid groups that released their own findings in September 2010, sometimes report higher percentages of insurgent control or influence. U.S. military officers in Kabul told CRS in October 2009 that the Taliban had named "shadow governors" in 33 out of 34 of Afghanistan's provinces, although many provinces in northern Afghanistan were assessed as having minimal Taliban presence.

As far as tactics, U.S. commanders increasingly worry about growing insurgent use of improvised explosive devices (IEDs), including roadside bombs. IED's are the leading cause of U.S. combat deaths, and IED attacks nearly doubled again in frequency in the first four months of 2010, according to the U.N. Secretary General's report of June 16, 2010. In January 2010, President Karzai issued a decree banning importation of fertilizer chemicals (ammonium nitrate) commonly used for the roadside bombs, but the material reportedly still comes into Afghanistan from Pakistan . Contrary to press reports quoting leaked material about the war effort, U.S. commanders have said they have not seen insurgent use of surface-to-air missiles.

There were about 310 U.S. soldiers killed in 2009, nearly double the previous year, and U.S. deaths in June and July 2010 (about 55 each of those months) were at or near the highs of the war effort thus far. Including the U.S. losses, there were about 506 total coalition deaths in Afghanistan in 2009. A UNAMA report issue in August 2010, covering the first half of 2010, noted a 30% increase in Afghan civilian deaths over the same period one year ago. It attributed the increase to insurgent attacks, and said that casualties caused by Afghan or pro-government forces had fallen 30% during the same period.

### *The Taliban ("Quetta Shura Taliban")*

The core of the insurgency remains the Taliban movement centered around Mullah Umar, who led the Taliban regime during 1996-2001. Mullah Umar and many of his top advisers remain at large and are reportedly running their insurgency from their safe haven in Pakistan. They are believed to be in and around the city of Quetta, according to Afghan officials, thus accounting for the term usually applied to Umar and his aides: "Quetta Shura Taliban" (QST).

Some believe that Umar and his inner circle blame their past association with Al Qaeda for their loss of power and want to distance themselves from Al Qaeda. Other experts see continuing close association that is likely to continue were the Taliban movement to return to power.. On September 19, 2009, Umar issued an audiotape criticizing the Afghan elections as fraudulent.

Some believe that the U.S. "surge" in Afghanistan may be causing Umar, or some around him, to mull the concept of a political settlement. Umar's top deputy, Mullah Bradar, was arrested in a reported joint U.S.-Pakistani operation near the city of Karachi in February 2010 — Karzai considered his capture set back Afghan government-Taliban reconciliation talks, which Bradar reportedly supports. It was also reported in March 2010 that Pakistan had briefly detained another member of the Quetta Shura, Mullah Kabir, and arrested Agha Jhan Motasim, a son-in-law of Umar. In recent years, other top Taliban figures, including Mullah Dadullah, his son Mansoor, and Mullah Usmani have been killed or captured. Some observers say that informal settlement ideas floated between the Taliban and the Karzai government may envision Umar being granted exile in Saudi Arabia.

To address losses, Umar reportedly replaced Bradar with a young leader, Mullah Abdul Qayyum Zakir, a U.S. detainee in Guantanamo Bay, Cuba, until 2007. Some reports assert that other aides (most notably Mullah Ghul Agha Akhund) may not recognize Zakir and might themselves be seeking the number two spot in the organization. The Taliban has several official spokespersons still at large, including Qari Yusuf Ahmadi and Zabiullah Mujahid, and it operates a clandestine radio station, "Voice of Shariat" and publishes videos. Two members of the Quetta Shura, Mullah Hassan Rahmani, former Taliban governor of Qandahar, and Mullah Afghan Tayib, another spokesman, are said to have come under some Pakistani pressure.

## AL QAEDA/BIN LADEN WHEREABOUTS

U.S. commanders say that Al Qaeda militants are more facilitators of militant incursions into Afghanistan rather than active fighters in the Afghan insurgency. Director of Central Intelligence Leon Panetta said on June 27, 2010, that Al Qaeda fighters in Afghanistan itself might number

50-100. Small numbers of Al Qaeda members—including Arabs, Uzbeks, and Chechens—have been captured or killed in battles in Afghanistan itself, according to U.S. commanders. Some of these fighters apparently belong to Al Qaeda affiliates such as the Islamic Movement of Uzbekistan (IMU). Some NATO/ISAF officials said in October 2010, however, that some Al Qaeda cells may be moving back into remote areas of Kunar and Nuristan provinces.

Al Qaeda's top leadership has eluded U.S. forces in Afghanistan and other efforts in Pakistan. In December 2001, in the course of the post-September 11 major combat effort, U.S. Special Operations Forces and CIA operatives reportedly narrowed Osama bin Laden's location to the Tora Bora mountains in Nangarhar Province (30 miles west of the Khyber Pass), but the Afghan militia fighters who were the bulk of the fighting force did not prevent his escape. Some U.S. military and intelligence officers (such as Gary Berntsen and Dalton Fury, who have written books on the battle) have questioned the U.S. decision to rely mainly on Afghan forces in this engagement.

Bin Laden and his close ally Ayman al-Zawahiri are presumed to be on the Pakistani side of the border. CNN reported October 18, 2010, that assessments from the U.S.-led coalition now say the two are likely in a settled area near the border with Afghanistan, and not living in a very remote uninhabited area. A U.S. strike reportedly missed Zawahiri by a few hours in the village of Damadola, Pakistan, in January 2006, suggesting that there was intelligence on his movements. From their redoubt, these leaders are widely believed to continue to be looking for ways to attack the U.S. homeland or U.S. allies and continuing to issue audio statements threatening such attacks. On the ninth anniversary of the September 11 attacks on some U.S. observers said it was still significant to try to capture bin Laden if for no other reason than for symbolic value. Press reports in September 2010 said that Al Qaeda's former spokesman, Kuwait-born Sulayman Abu Ghaith, may have been released from house arrest by Iran and allowed to proceed to Pakistan. Other reports in November 2010 said that another Al Qaeda senior operative, Sayf al Adl, who was believed to be in Iran during 2002-2010, may have left Iran and gone to

Pakistan, and reportedly may have been elevated by bin Laden to top Al Qaeda operational commander.

Among other efforts, a strike in late January 2008, in an area near Damadola, killed Abu Laith al-Libi, a reported senior Al Qaeda figure who purportedly masterminded, among other operations, the bombing at Bagram Air Base in February 2007 when Vice President Cheney was visiting. In August 2008, an airstrike was confirmed to have killed Al Qaeda chemical weapons expert Abu Khabab al-Masri, and two senior operatives allegedly involved in the 1998 embassy bombings in Africa reportedly were killed by a Predator strike in January 2009.

These strikes have become more frequent under President Obama, indicating that the Administration sees the tactic as effective in preventing attacks. Unmanned vehicle strikes are also increasingly used on the Afghanistan battlefield itself and against Al Qaeda affiliated militants in such countries as Yemen.

### Hikmatyar Faction

Another "high value target" identified by U.S. commanders is the faction of former *mujahedin* party leader Gulbuddin Hikmatyar (Hizb-e-Islami Gulbuddin, HIG) allied with Al Qaeda and Taliban insurgents. As noted above, Hikmatyar was one of the main U.S.-backed *mujahedin* leaders during the Soviet occupation era. Hikmatyar's faction received extensive U.S. support against the Soviet Union, but is now active against U.S. and Afghan forces in Kunar, Nuristan, Kapisa, and Nangarhar provinces, north and east of Kabul. On February 19, 2003, the U.S. government formally designated Hikmatyar as a "Specially Designated Global Terrorist," under the authority of Executive Order 13224, subjecting it to financial and other U.S. sanctions. It is *not* designated as a "Foreign Terrorist Organization" (FTO).

While U.S. commanders continue to battle Hikmatyar's militia, on March 22, 2010, both the Afghan government and Hikmatyar representatives confirmed they were in talks in Kabul, including meetings with Karzai. Hikmatyar has expressed a willingness to discuss a cease-fire with the Karzai government since 2007, and some of Karzai's key allies in the National Assembly are former members of Hikmatyar's *mujahedin* party. In January 2010, he outlined specific conditions for a possible reconciliation with Karzai, including elections under a neutral caretaker government following a U.S. withdrawal. These conditions are unlikely to be acceptable to Karzai or the international community, although many of them might be modified or dropped.

### *Haqqani Faction*

Another militant faction, cited repeatedly as a major threat, is the "Haqqani Network" led by Jalaludin Haqqani and his eldest son, Siraj (or Sirajjudin). Jalaludin Haqqani, who served as Minister of Tribal Affairs in the Taliban regime of 1996-2001, is believed closer to Al Qaeda than to the ousted Taliban leadership in part because one of his wives is purportedly Arab. The group is active around its key objective, Khost city, capital of Khost Province. The Haqqani network may have been responsible for the January 18, 2010, attacks in Kabul that prompted four hours of gun battles with Afghan police in locations near the presidential palace.

U.S. officials say they are continuing to pressure the Haqqani network with military action in Afghanistan and air strikes on the Pakistani side of the border. Haqqani property inside Pakistan has been repeatedly targeted since September 2008 by U.S. aerial drone strikes. Siraj's brother, Mohammad, was reportedly killed by a U.S. unmanned vehicle strike in late February 2010, although Mohammad was not thought to be a key militant commander. In July 2010, it was reported that Gen. Petraeus, as part of his adjustments to policy as top commander in Afghanistan, wants the Haqqani network to be named as an FTO under the Immigration and Naturalization Act. Secretary of State Clinton said on July 19, 2010, during a visit to Pakistan, that U.S. policy is moving in that direction. Such a move would be intended to signal to Pakistan that it should not see the Haqqani network, as a whole, as part of a reconciled political structure in Afghanistan that would protect Pakistan's interests and work to limit the influence of India. This view was emphasized in a *New York Times* story of June 25, 2010. The Haqqani faction has been thought not amenable to a political settlement, but some reports in November 2010 have said that members of the faction may have participated in exploratory reconciliation meetings with government representatives.

### *Pakistani Groups*

The Taliban of Afghanistan are increasingly linked politically and operationally to Pakistani Taliban militants. These groups might see a Taliban recapture of Afghanistan's government as helpful to the prospects for these groups inside Pakistan or in their Kashmir struggle.

The Pakistani Taliban (Tehrik-e-Taliban Pakistan, TTP) is primarily seeking to challenge the government of Pakistan, but they facilitate the transiting into Afghanistan of Afghan Taliban and support the Afghan Taliban goals of recapturing Afghanistan. The TTP may also be seeking to target the United States, based on a failed bombing in New York in May 2010. The State Department designated the TTP as a Foreign Terrorist Organization (FTO) under the Immigration and Naturalization Act on September 2, 2010, allegedly for having close connections to Al Qaeda.

Another Pakistani group said to be increasingly active inside Afghanistan is Laskhar-e-Tayyiba (LET, or Army of the Righteous). LET is an Islamist militant group that has previously been focused on operations against Indian control of Kashmir.

### *The U.S. Military Effort*

The large majority of U.S. troops in Afghanistan are under NATO/ISAF command. The remainder are part of the post-September 11 anti-terrorism mission Operation Enduring Freedom (OEF). There are also Special Operations Forces in Afghanistan under a separate command. Serving under General Petraeus is Maj. Gen. David Rodriguez, who heads a NATO-approved "Intermediate Joint Command" focused primarily on day-to-day operations and located in a facility adjoining Kabul International Airport. He has been in this position since mid-2009. The ISAF/U.S. Forces-Afghanistan commander reports not only to NATO but, through U.S. channels, to U.S. Central Command (CENTCOM).

Whether under NATO or OEF, many U.S. forces in Afghanistan are in eastern Afghanistan and lead Regional Command East of the NATO/ISAF operation. These U.S. forces belong to Combined Joint Task Force 101 (as of June 2010), which is commanded by Maj. Gen. John Campbell. As of November 2010, the most restive provinces in RC-E are Paktia, Paktika, Khost, Kunar, Nangarhar, and Nuristan.

Helmand, Qandahar, Uruzgan, Zabol, Nimruz, and Dai Kundi provinces constitute "Regional Command South (RC-S)," a command formally transferred to NATO/ISAF responsibility on July 31, 2006. U.S. forces have not led RC-S; the command was rotated among Britain, the Netherlands, and Canada. However, with the Dutch pullout in July 2010 and the growing U.S. troop strength in RC-S prompted a May 23, 2010, NATO decision to bifurcate RC-S, with the United States leading a "southwest" subdivision focused on Helmand and Nimruz. This is an evolution of the growing U.S. involvement in RC-S since 2008.

## Perception of "Victory" in the First Five Post-Taliban Years

During 2001-mid-2006, U.S. forces and Afghan troops fought relatively low levels of insurgent violence. The United States and Afghanistan conducted "Operation Mountain Viper" (August 2003); "Operation Avalanche" (December 2003); "Operation Mountain Storm" (March-July 2004) against Taliban remnants in and around Uruzgan province, home province of Mullah Umar; "Operation Lightning Freedom" (December 2004–February 2005); and "Operation Pil" (Elephant) in Kunar Province in the east (October 2005). By late 2005, U.S. and partner commanders appeared to believe that the combat, coupled with overall political and economic reconstruction, had virtually ended any insurgency. Anticipating further stabilization, NATO/ISAF assumed lead responsibility for security in all of Afghanistan during 2005-2006.

Contrary to U.S. expectations, violence increased significantly in mid-2006, particularly in the east and the south, where ethnic Pashtuns predominate. Reasons for the deterioration include some of those discussed above in the sections on governance: Afghan government corruption; the absence of governance or security forces in many rural areas. Other factors included the safe haven enjoyed by militants in Pakistan; the reticence of some NATO contributors to actively combat insurgents; a popular backlash against civilian casualties caused by NATO and U.S. military operations; and the slow pace of economic development. Many Afghans are said to have turned to the Taliban as a source of impartial and rapid justice, in contrast to the slow and corrupt processes instituted by the central government.

### *Perception of Deterioration and Growing Force Levels in 2007 and 2008*

Since 2006, the key theater of intensified combat has been eastern and southern Afghanistan. The provinces that are particularly restive include Helmand and Qandahar provinces. NATO counter-offensives in 2006 cleared areas of these provinces, but militants regrouped, following such operations as Operation Mountain Lion, Operation Mountain Thrust, and Operation Medusa (August-September 2006, in Panjwai district of Qandahar Province). Later, British forces—who believe in negotiated local solutions—entered into an agreement with tribal elders in the Musa Qala district of Helmand Province, under which they would secure the main town of the district themselves. That strategy failed when the Taliban took over Musa Qala town in February 2007. A NATO offensive in December 2007 retook it.

As a further response, NATO and OEF forces tried to apply a more integrated strategy involving preemptive combat, increased development work, and a more streamlined command structure. Major combat operations in 2007 included U.S. and NATO attempted preemption of an anticipated Taliban "spring offensive" ("Operation Achilles," March 2007) in the Sangin district of Helmand Province, around the Kajaki dam, and Operation Silicon (May 2007), also in Helmand. (In September 2010, Britain turned over security leadership in Sangin to U.S. forces in the near future; combat in the district has accounted for nearly half of Britain's entire casualties in Afghanistan to date. U.S. strategy for the district is said to try to push out the boundaries of secure area of the district; British efforts focused on better securing the district major city.)

Despite the additional resources put into Afghanistan, throughout 2008, growing concern took hold within the Bush

Administration. Pessimism was reflected in such statements as one in September 2008 by Joint Chiefs of Staff chairman Admiral Mike Mullen that "I'm not sure we're winning" in Afghanistan. Several major incidents supported that assessment, including: (1) expanding Taliban operations in provinces where it had not previously been active, particularly Lowgar, Wardak, and Kapisa, close to Kabul; (2) high-profile attacks in Kabul against well-defended targets, such as the January 14, 2008, attack on the Serena Hotel in Kabul and the July 7, 2008, suicide bombing at the Indian Embassy in Kabul, killing more than 50; (3) the April 27, 2008, assassination attempt on Karzai during a military parade celebrating the ouster of the Soviet Union; and (4) a June 12, 2008, Sarposa prison break in Qandahar (several hundred Taliban captives were freed, as part of an emptying of the 1,200 inmates there).

To try to arrest deterioration, the United States and its partners decided to increase force levels. The added forces partly fulfilled a mid-2008 request by Gen. McKiernan for 30,000 additional

U.S. troops (beyond the approximately 35,000 there at the time of the request). However, as the November 2008 U.S. presidential election approached, the decision whether to fulfill the entire request was deferred to the next Administration. U.S. troop levels started 2006 at 30,000; climbed slightly to 32,000 by December 2008; and reached 39,000 by April 2009. Partner forces were increased significantly as well, by about 6,000 during this time, to a total of 39,000 at the end of 2009 (rough parity between U.S. and non-U.S. forces). Many of the U.S. forces deployed in 2008 and 2009 were Marines that deployed to Helmand, large parts of which had fallen out of coalition/Afghan control.

### Obama Administration Strategy Reviews and Further Buildup

In September 2008, the U.S. military and NATO each began strategy reviews. The primary U.S. review was headed by Lt. Gen. Douglas Lute, the Bush Administration's senior adviser on Iraq and Afghanistan (who was kept on under the Obama Administration with responsibility for Afghanistan). Other U.S. reviews were conducted by the Department of Defense, by

CENTCOM, and by the State Department. These reviews were briefed to the incoming Obama Administration. The Obama Administration, which maintained that Afghanistan needed to be given a higher priority than it was during the Bush Administration, integrated the reviews into an overarching 60-day inter-agency "strategy review." It was chaired by South Asia expert Bruce Riedel and co-chaired by Ambassador Holbrooke and Under Secretary of Defense for Policy Michele Flournoy.

### *Policy Announcement and Troop Increase, First Command Change, and McChrystal Assessment*

President Obama announced a "comprehensive" strategy on March 27, 2009. In conjunction, he announced the deployment of an additional 21,000 U.S. forces, of which about 4,000 would be trainers. Shortly after the announcement, the Administration decided that U.S. military leadership in Afghanistan was insufficiently innovative. On May 11, 2009, Secretary of Defense Gates and Joint Chiefs of Staff Chairman Michael Mullen announced that Gen. McKiernan would be replaced by Gen. Stanley McChrystal, considered an innovative commander as head of U.S. special operations from 2003 to 2008. He assumed command on June 15, 2009.

Gen. McChrystal, after assuming command, assessed the security situation and suggested a strategy in a report of August 30, 2009, and presented to NATO on August 31, 2009. The main elements are:

- That the goal of the U.S. military should be to protect the population—and to help the Afghan government take steps to earn the trust of the population—rather than to search out and combat Taliban concentrations. Indicators of success such as ease of road travel and normal life for families are more important than are counts of numbers of enemy fighters killed.
- That there is potential for "mission failure" unless a fully resourced, comprehensive counter-insurgency strategy is pursued and reverses Taliban momentum within 12-18 months.

- About 44,000 additional U.S. combat troops (including trainers) would be needed to have the greatest chance for his strategy's success—beyond those approved by the Obama Administration strategy review in March 2009.

Some of the data supporting McChrystal's assessment and recommendations included Taliban gains in Konduz, Farah, and other areas in the north that previously were peaceful. McChrystal's report took particular note of Taliban gains in and around Qandahar. A high-profile attack there on August 25, 2009, killing about 40 persons.

### Second High-Level Review and Further Force Increase

The McChrystal assessment set off debate within the Administration. In September 2009, the Administration began a second high-level review of U.S. strategy, taking into account the McChrystal recommendations and the marred August 20, 2009, presidential election. Some senior U.S. officials, such as Secretary of Defense Gates, were concerned that adding many more U.S. forces could create among the Afghan people a sense of "occupation" that could prove counter-productive. Some Members of Congress, including Senate Armed Services Committee Chairman Carl Levin, said that the U.S. focus should be on expanding Afghan security forces capabilities before sending additional U.S. forces.

The high-level review included at least nine high-level meetings, chaired by President Obama, and reportedly concluded on November 19, 2009. The President announced his decisions in a speech at West Point military academy on December 1, 2009. The major features of the December 1 statement included the following:

- That 30,000 additional U.S. forces (plus an unspecified number of additional "enablers") would be sent to "reverse the Taliban's momentum" and strengthen the capacity of Afghanistan's security forces and government in order to pave the way for a transition, beginning in July 2011, to Afghan leadership of the stabilization effort. U.S. force levels did reach their current level of about 104,000 on/ about September 4, 2010. (Perhaps reflecting further need,

Gen. Petraeus did request an additional 2,000 NATO/ISAF forces on September 6, 2010, of which 750 are to be trainers for the Afghan national security forces.)

- The July 2011 deadline is the policy element that has caused significant controversy. The pace and scope of the transition is to be determined as a consequence of a major review of the battlefield situation to be completed by December 2010.

### McChrystal Replaced by Petraeus

On June 23, 2010, President Obama accepted the resignation of Gen. McChrystal after summoning him to Washington, DC, to discuss the comments by him and his staff to a reporter for *Rolling Stone* that disparaged virtually all the civilian figures involved in Afghanistan policy. He named Gen. Petraeus as Gen. McChrystal's successor, a move that appeared to reassure President Karzai. In a June 23, 2010, statement in the Rose Garden, President Obama attributed the change purely to the disrespect of civilian authority contained in the *Rolling Stone* comments, and stated that Afghanistan policy would not change. Gen. Petraeus was confirmed by the Senate on June 30, 2010, and assumed command on July 4, 2010.

### Current U.S. Strategy as Implemented by Gen. Petraeus

The major outlines of Obama Administration strategy have taken shape, and a wide range of U.S. officials have said that the December 2010 DOD review, and a White House review around that time as well, are not likely to result in major changes to strategy. Gen. Petraeus has not dramatically altered the McChrystal strategy, but he has increased (nearly tripled) Special Operations Force operations and air strikes on concentrations across the border in Pakistan to try to drive insurgents to reconcile with the Karzai government and cease fighting. In November 2010, Gen.Petraeus reportedly approved the deployment of about 16 M1A1 tanks for use by the Marines in southern Afghanistan in order to put further pressure on militants:

*Key Goals*: (1) disrupt terrorist networks in Afghanistan and Pakistan to degrade their ability to launch international terrorist attacks; (2) promote a more capable, accountable, and effective government in Afghanistan; (3) develop self-reliant Afghan security forces; and (4) involve the international community to actively assist in addressing these objectives. These relatively targeted goals are in line with comments by President Obama that he wants to "finish the job" in Afghanistan during his presidency.

*Strategy Definition*: The overall counter-insurgency strategy is intended to "clear, hold, build, and transition"—to protect the population and allow time for Afghan governance and security forces to take leadership and for infrastructure and economic development to take root.

*Limiting Civilian Casualties*. Part of the strategy is to win support of Afghans by sharply limiting air strikes and some types of raids and combat that cause Afghan civilian casualties and resentment Some refer to the rules as the "Karzai 12," referring to the number of points of these rules of engagement. The NATO International Security Assistance Force (ISAF) and the Karzai government want to prevent any recurrence of incident such as the one that occurred near Herat on August 22, 2008, in which a NATO bomb killed up to 90 civilians, as well as the incident in September 2009 in Konduz in which Germany's contingent called in an airstrike on Taliban fighters who captured two fuel trucks; killing several civilians as well as Taliban fighters. Still, ISAF-caused civilian casualties continue, mainly due to misunderstandings at ISAF checkpoints, and in November 2010 President Karzai publicly called for a reduction of some of the night raids that are causing popular backlash.

*July 2011 Deadline*. The Obama Administration emphasis on transition to Afghan security leadership beginning in July 2011 has been interpreted by some Administration officials—and by some Afghan and regional leaders—as laying the groundwork for winding down U.S. involvement in coming years.

*Resources and Troops*: The Administration and foreign partners asserts that resource "inputs" are, as of October 2010, aligned with mission requirements.

*Pressing the Afghan Government:* The Administration asserts that the Karzai government is being held to account for its performance, although, as noted, no specific penalties have been imposed on the Afghan government for shortfalls.

*Civilian "Uplift"*: A key strategy component is to develop Afghan institutions, particularly at the provincial and local levels. To be effective, the number of U.S. civilian advisors in Afghanistan reached about 1,000 in early 2010 and is about 1,300 as of November 2010. Of these at least 400 serve outside Kabul as part of initiatives such as the 32 "District Support Teams" and the "District Working Groups." That is up from 67 outside Kabul in early 2009.

*Civilian-Military Integration*: There is a commitment to civilian-military integration, as outlined in a DOD-State Department joint campaign plan and Ambassador Holbrooke's January 2010 strategy document, referenced earlier. High-level "Senior Civilian Representatives" have been appointed to help the military formulate strategy for the regional commands where they serve. This is part of a new "Interagency Provincial Affairs" initiative that is less military-focused.

*Reintegration and Reconciliation*: The Administration supports Afghan efforts to provide financial and social incentives to persuade insurgents to lay down their arms and accept the Afghan constitution. The United States was at first skeptical but is now increasingly supporting Karzai's policy of negotiating with senior insurgent leaders.

*Pakistan*: Engagement with Pakistan and enlisting its increased cooperation is pivotal to U.S. policy.

*International Dimension*: New international diplomatic mechanisms have been formed to better coordinate all "stakeholders" in the Afghanistan issue (NATO, Afghanistan's neighbors, other countries in Afghanistan's region, the United Nations, and other donors). Meetings such as the January 28, 2010, meeting in London and the July 20, 2010, Kabul Conference are part of that effort. To date, at least 25 nations have appointed direct counterparts to Holbrooke, including the UAE, Saudi Arabia, and Turkey, which meet periodically as part of a 44-nation (and growing) "International Contact Group" for Afghanistan. It has met nine times, most recently in Rome on October 18, 2010. (Iran attended it for the first time.)

*Partner Contributions*: Increased partner contributions of funding and troops were sought and offered. Currently, there is U.S. effort to encourage partner forces to remain in Afghanistan at least until a planned transition to Afghan leadership by 2014.

*Metrics:* The Administration will continue to measure progress along clear metrics. Many in Congress, pressing for clear metrics to assess progress, inserted into P.L. 111-32 (FY2009 supplemental appropriation) a requirement that the President submit to Congress, 90 days after enactment (by September 23, 2009), metrics by which to assess progress, and a report on that progress every 180 days thereafter. The Administration's approximately 50 metrics were reported at the website of *Foreign Policy* and were submitted. However, the difficulty in formulating useful and clear metrics that would enable Members and officials to assess progress in the war effort was demonstrated by comments by Ambassador Holbrooke on August 12, 2009, saying that on defining success in Afghanistan and Pakistan: "We will know it when we see it." In its September 22, 2009, report on the situation in Afghanistan (A/64/364-S/2009/475), the United Nations developed its own "benchmarks" for progress in Afghan governance and security.

### July 2011 "Deadline" Giving Way to 2014 "Transition"

The Obama Administration emphasis on transition to Afghan security leadership beginning in July 2011 has been perhaps the most widely discussed and debated aspect of policy. Debate over whether to announce such a timeframe is covered extensively in the book "Obama's Wars," by Bob Woodward. The 2011 "deadline" was interpreted by some Administration critics—and by some Afghan and regional leaders—as laying the groundwork for winding down U.S. involvement in coming years. The Administration has said it set the time frame to demonstrate to a war-weary public that U.S. military involvement in Afghanistan is not open-ended. In a press conference on June 24, 2010, President Obama said "we didn't say we'd be switching off the lights and closing the door behind us [in July 2011]. What we said is we'd begin a transition phase in which the Afghan government is taking on more and more responsibility." In an August 31, 2010 statement, the President asserted that the pace and scope of any drawdown in 2011 would be subject to conditions on the ground, as assessed by the DOD assessment to be completed by December 2010. These comments appear to modify the July 18, 2010, Vice President Biden amended earlier remarks by saying that only a few thousand U.S. forces might come out at that time as part of a process of transitioning some Afghan provinces to Afghan lead.

Comments by Ambassador Holbrooke at seminar hosted by the Center for American Progress. August 12, 2009. Commander NATO International Security Assistance Force, Afghanistan, and U.S. Forces, Afghanistan. "Commander's Initial Assessment." August 30, 2009, available at http://media.washingtonpost.com/wp-srv/politics/ documents/Assessment_Redacted_092109.pdf. White House. Remarks by the President In Address to the Nation on the Way Forward in Afghanistan and Pakistan. December 1, 2009; Chandrasekaran, Rajiv. "Differing Views of New Afghanistan Strategy." *Washington Post*, December 26, 2009.

Subsequently, in interviews, Gen. Petraeus has said that he would likely recommend to President Obama that any drawdown be limited. At the same time, with European publics tiring of involvement, in July 2010 agreement reportedly was reached on a joint Afghan-NATO board to decide on locations that might be selected for transition to Afghan lead. These locations, most likely whole provinces and districts to transition, beginning in 2011 and running through 2014, are expected to be ratified at the November 19-20, 2010, NATO summit in Lisbon. According to some U.S. commanders, some provinces in the U.S.-led eastern sector, such as Panjshir or Bamiyan, could be turned over in 2011, with Nangarhar considered a candidate for turnover thereafter. Some U.S. officials say that 2014 is not a date certain for a complete international pullout, but rather for a transition to Afghan lead, with some international forces remaining to train and mentor the Afghans.

## IMPLEMENTATION OF STRATEGY, EARLY RESULTS, AND DOUBTS

Going into the November 19-20 NATO summit in Lisbon, U.S. strategy, as implemented by Gen. Petraeus, may be starting to show results, according to statements by Petraeus and other NATO/ ISAF commanders. The possible signs of momentum appear to reflect the beginnings of a possible turnaround from more pessimistic assessments of an April 2010 Defense Department report, and a September 30, 2010, White House assessments of the situation. In an interview with ABC News on September 14, 2010, Gen. Peraeus said that, "in some areas, we have already reversed the momentum of the Taliban. In others, we still need to do that and we are intent on doing that." His reference to those areas where the insurgency still has momentum include previously quiet provinces where violence has increased, including Baghlan, Konduz, and Faryab provinces. Other U.S. commanders say they are receiving overtures from local insurgent leaders who seek to discuss possible terms for their surrender and reintegration. Other reports say that insurgent factions are running low on supplies and ammunition.

According to Gen. Petraeus in November 2010, operations in 2010 have ended Taliban control in large parts of Helmand and produced major progress in Qandahar province. The progress is creating a contiguous secure corridor for commerce between Helmand and Qandahar. Markets and other signs of normal life have proliferated in Helmand, according to several U.S. commanders in October 2010. In August 2010, he took *NBC News* correspondents to Wardak province as a showcase of stability in a province that, in 2008, was considered largely under Taliban influence. The first of the operations in 2009 that produced some of the relatively positive assessments was Operation Khanjar—intended to expel the Taliban and reestablish Afghan governance in parts of the province. The offensive reportedly ended Taliban control of several districts in Helmand, including Nawa, Now Zad, and Musa Qala.

### Operation Moshtarek in Marjah/Nad Ali

The reports of progress in Helmand represent a turnaround from earlier pessimism about the outcome of "Operation Moshtarek" (Operation Together). It consisted of about 15,000 U.S., foreign partner, and Afghan forces (about 8,000 of the total) that, beginning on February 13, 2010, sought to clear Taliban militants from Marjah city (85,000 population) in Helmand. An Afghan governing structure was identified in advance (so-called "government in a box"), the population had substantial warning, and there were meetings with regional elders just before the offensive began—all of which were an apparent effort to cause militants to flee and to limit civilian losses. The city, for the most part, was declared cleared of militants as of February 26, 2010, but some militants continue to fight in and on the outskirts of Marjah and to assassinate and intimidate Afghans cooperating with U.S. and Afghan forces. Some Afghan officials, such as ministry representatives, are now beginning to serve regularly in the city itself, although town governor Hajji Zahir was fired in July 2010.

As part of the U.S. effort, U.S. forces, primarily Marines, have reportedly been disbursing Commanders Emergency Response Program (CERP-funds controlled by U.S. officers) funds to clear rubble from schools, clean canals, repair markets, rebuild bridges, and compensate families who lost members due to the combat. Afghans who work on these projects in Marjah and in the previously cleared Nawa district are reportedly being paid about $5 per day as part of an effort to provide livelihoods to Afghans who might previously have supported the Taliban for purely financial reasons. Some fear that many of these workers might rejoin insurgent activities when U.S. funding for these "cash for work" programs decline.

### Qandahar Effort

As of November 2010, U.S. military assessments of progress in Qandahar province are dramatic, although no one is certain how permanent are the gains. In early 2010, U.S. commanders had emphasized that the Qandahar effort would focus less on combat and more on conducting consultations and *shuras* with tribal leaders and other notables to enlist their cooperation against Taliban infiltrators. U.S. commanders described the operation as more of a "process," or a slow push into restive districts by setting up Afghan checkpoints to secure the city and districts around it (particularly Arghandab, Zhari, and Panjwai)—and not a classic military offensive. Qandahar's population is far larger (about 2 million in the province), and Qandahar province and city have functioning governments, which Marjah did not. The city hosts numerous businesses and has always remained vibrant, despite some Taliban clandestine activity.

A sense of doubt about the prospects for the operation built in April-August 2010 as Afghan tribal and other residential resistance—expressed at local *shuras* —to any combat to secure Qandahar. However, Gen. Petraeus has increased operations by U.S. Special Operations Forces against key militants near the city that began in April 2010. Subsequently, as U.S. forces have expanded their presence in the province in partnership with Afghan forces in September 2010, Taliban control was ended in some neighborhoods and Afghan checkpoints were established. Further *shuras* have been held to promote Afghan governance. As part of the effort to stabilize Qandahar

U.S. officials are also reportedly trying to strengthen Governor Tooryalai Wesa and balance the flow of U.S. and international funds to the various tribes and clans in the province. An unstated objective is also to weaken the influence of Karzai's brother, Ahmad Wali Karzai, chair of the provincial council.

## SECURITY EXPERIMENTS UNDER WAY

### *"Reintegration" and "Reconciliation" With Insurgents*

The issue of reintegration fighters and reconciling with insurgent leaders is an Afghan-led process but one in which the United States and the international community is increasingly involved. The issue has made some in the international community, and within Afghanistan, concerned for the potential to involve compromises with insurgents and perhaps some backsliding on human rights. Most insurgents are highly conservative Islamists who agreed with the limitations in women's rights that characterized Taliban rule. Many leaders of ethnic minorities are also skeptical of the effort because they fear that it might further Pashtun political strength within Afghanistan, and enhance the influence of Pakistan in Afghan politics. Gen. Petraeus has said that the way conflicts like the one in Afghanistan end is through a political settlement. The United States and the Karzai government agree that any settlement must involve fighters and insurgent leaders: (1) cease fighting, (2) accept the Afghan constitution, and (3) sever any ties to Al Qaeda or other terrorist groups.

### Reintegration/"Peace Jirga"

A January 28, 2010, London conference of international donors backed devoting more emphasis to reintegration of fighters amenable to surrendering. Britain, Japan, and several other countries announced a total of about $160 million in donations to a new fund to support the reintegration process. The United States is to contribute an additional $100 million. Some of the incentives to surrendering insurgents that the international community deemed likely to fund are jobs, amnesty, and protection, and possibly making them part of the security architecture for their communities. These are elements included in a reintegration plan drafted by the Afghan government and presented to the peace *loya jirga* during June 2-4, 2010. In its final declaration, the *peace jirga* backed the plan, but also called for limits in NATO-led raids and further efforts to limit civilian casualties. It also called for the release of some detained insurgents where allegations against them are weak. The day after the *jirga* concluded, Karzai sought to implement that recommendation by calling for a review of the cases of all insurgent detentions. In late June 2010, President Karzai issued a decree to implement the plan, which involves outreach by Afghan local leaders to tribes and others who are in a position to convince insurgents to lay down their arms. The international community gave its support to the effort in the communiqué of the July 20, 2010, Kabul Conference.

Although it reached some substantive conclusions, the peace *jirga* itself received mixed reviews for its inclusiveness or lack thereof. Karzai tried to bring other minority communities along in backing the peace *jirga* and the reintegration process, and to do so he appointed former leader Rabbani to chair the *jirga*. However, "opposition leader" Dr. Abdullah Abdullah, Karzai's rival in the 2009 presidential election, boycotted the *jirga*.

However, despite the international funding for the effort, the Afghan-led reintegration process has moved forward only slowly. Only $200,000 of the donated funds have been spent, as of early September 2010, and only about 100 fighters have surrendered since April 2010. However, press reports in September 2010, citing briefings by Gen. Petraeus for senior U.S. officials, say he anticipates many more surrenders of insurgent fighters between September and the end of 2010. In addition, press reports say that some Taliban fighters sought information on the September 18, 2010, parliamentary election as a possible prelude to joining the political process.

To help the process along from the international perspective, in November 2009, ISAF set up a "force reintegration cell," headed by Britain's Maj. Gen. Richard Barrons, to develop additional programs and policies to accelerate the effort to cause insurgents to change sides. These strategies are similar to what was employed successfully in Anbar Province in Iraq in 2006 and 2007.

The Obama Administration has been separately expanding U.S. efforts to lure lower-level insurgents off the battlefield with job opportunities and infrastructure construction incentives. Another component of the program has been meetings with tribal elders to persuade Taliban and other insurgents in their areas to give up their fight. Some U.S. commanders are reporting some successes with this effort, using Commanders Emergency Response Program (CERP) funds. The National Defense Authorization Act for FY2010 (P.L. 111-84) authorizes the use of CERP funds to win local support, to "reintegrate" Taliban fighters who renounce violence. FY2011 budget language requested by the Administration would authorize U.S. funds to be contributed to the reintegration.

Karzai has consistently advocated talks with Taliban militants who want to consider ending their fight. Noted above is the "Program for Strengthening Peace and Reconciliation" (referred to in Afghanistan by its Pashto acronym "PTS") headed by *Meshrano Jirga* speaker Sibghatullah Mojadeddi and former Vice President Karim Khalili, and overseen by Karzai's National Security Council. The program is credited with persuading 9,000 Taliban figures and commanders to renounce violence and join the political process.

### Reconciliation With Taliban/Insurgent Leaders

A separate Karzai initiative—far more widely debated than reintegration—is to conduct negotiations with senior insurgent leaders. Many in the international community, and within the Obama Administration, had feared that reconciliation has the potential to result in insurgent leaders obtaining senior positions or control over some Afghan territory, and that these figures will retain ties to Al Qaeda and commit abuses similar to those under the Taliban regime. The July 20, 2010, Kabul Conference did not issue unqualified support for high-level reconciliation talks, instead endorsing establishment of an Afghan High Peace Council to build Afghan consensus on the issue. That Council was established on September 5, 2010, and its 68 members met for the first time under the leadership of Tajik leader Rabbani on October 10, 2010. Yet, the direct role of the Council in negotiations is unclear; rather, it might be asked to review and endorse any settlement that is reached.

In an apparent shift, the United States has begun backing the effort more clearly as of October 2010. Earlier, in March 2009, President Obama publicly ruled out negotiations with Mullah Umar and his aides because of their alignment with Al Qaeda. Others still differ on the willingness of senior insurgents to bargain in earnest. CIA director Panetta, in a June 27, 2010 interview cited earlier, and reflecting the reported view of several U.S. intelligence agencies as of late 2010, said he saw no indications that insurgent leaders are contemplating settling with the government.

Senior U.S. commanders have grown more optimistic about reconciliation as contacts between Taliban representatives and the Karzai government appear to have broadened.. Several sets of talks have been reported in October 2010, and some press accounts say that NATO/ISAF forces were in fact facilitation the movement of insurgent representatives to these talks. Representatives of the Quetta Shura Taliban purportedly have participated in talks. Mullah Bradar, who is close to Mullah Umar, may have been engaged in talks with the Afghan government prior to his arrest by Pakistan in February 2010. Karzai reportedly believes that Pakistan arrested Bradar in order to be able to influence the course of any Afghan government-Taliban settlement. Other accounts say that even the Haqqani faction, often viewed as least amenable to settlement, has been represented at some exploratory meetings with Karzai government representatives. However, observers say the discussions to date are about modalities and an agenda for further talks. The Taliban continues to demand that (1) all foreign troops leave Afghanistan; (2) a new "Islamic" constitution be adopted; and (3) Islamic law is imposed. However, those are viewed as opening positions; the Afghan government, for its part, may have softened its position on disallowing any changes to the Afghan constitution as part of a settlement.

The October 2010 reports build on earlier reports of contact. The Taliban as a movement was not invited to the June 2-4, 2010, consultative peace *jirga,* some Taliban sympathizers reportedly were there, and Karzai has said he is open to potential talks to reconcile even high-level leaders such as Mullah Umar. In advance of the peace *jirga,* the Karzai government and representatives of Hikmatyar confirmed peace talks on March 21, 2010, in which Karzai, his brother, Ahmad Wali, and several Northern Alliance figures met with the Hikmatyar representatives. The representatives reportedly presented a 15-point peace plan to Karzai that does not necessarily demand his government step down immediately.

Other talks have taken place over the past few years, although with less apparent momentum than is the case in 2010. Press reports said that Afghan officials (led by Karzai's brother Qayyum) and Taliban members had met each other in Ramadan-related gatherings in Saudi Arabia in September 2008. Another round of talks was held in January 2009 in Saudi Arabia, and there were reports of ongoing contacts in Dubai, UAE. Some of these talks apparently involved Arsala Rahmani, a former Taliban official now in parliament, and the former Taliban Ambassador to Pakistan, Abdul Salam Zaeef, who purportedly is in touch with Umar's inner circle. These same Taliban representatives may have been involved in talks in mid-late 2010 as well.

The consultative peace *jirga,* in its final declaration, supported Karzai's call for the removal of the names of some Taliban figures from U.N. lists of terrorists, lists established pursuant to Resolution 1267 and Resolution 1333 (October 15, 1999, and December 19, 2000, both pre-September 11 sanctions against the Taliban and Al Qaeda) and Resolution 1390 (January 16, 2002). Press reports before the July 20 Kabul Conference said the Afghan government has submitted a list of 50 Taliban figures it wants taken off this list as a confidence-building measure. The Conference called on Afghanistan to engage with the U.N. Security Council to provide evidence to justify such de-listings, and U.N., U.S., and other international officials said they would support considering de-listings on a case-by-case basis. On January 26, 2010, Russia, previously a hold-out against such a process, dropped opposition to removing five Taliban-era figures from these sanctions lists, including Taliban-era foreign minister Wakil Mutawwakil, who ran in 2005 parliamentary elections. Also removed was Abdul Hakim Monib, who has served Karzai as governor of Uruzgan, Abdul Hakim Mujahid, who was Taliban representative in the United States, and three others. Mujahid now serves on the High Peace Council. "Mullah Rocketi," not on the sanctions list, is a former Taliban commander who ran for president in the August 2009 elections.

### Afghan Provincial Protection Program (APPP) and Local Defense Initiative

Until mid-2008, U.S. military commanders opposed assisting local militias anywhere in Afghanistan for fear of creating new rivals to the central government who would arbitrarily administer justice. The urgent security needs in Afghanistan caused reconsideration and Gen Petraeus is seeking to expand these type of local security experiments, based on his similar and successful experiences in Iraq. Press reports in July 2010 say he succeeded, after several of his first meetings with Karzai, in overcoming Karzai's reticence to them. Gen. Petraeus reportedly has guaranteed that any local security organs would be under the administration of the Ministry of Interior.

The newest initiative is the Afghan "Local Police Initiative," in which local security organs would be formed from local recruits who want to defend their communities. It was planned that up to 10,000 volunteers will serve in the initiative, but on October 19, 2010, the Defense Department said it would be expanded to at least 20,000, if possible. The ultimate target level might be 50,000, according to press reports. The Defense Department notified

Congress in September 2010 that it will reprogram about $35 million in Afghan security forces funding to support the initiative.

The Local Police Initiative follows on another program begun in 2008, termed the "Afghan Provincial Protection Program" (APPP, commonly called "AP3") and is funded with DOD (CERP) funds. The APPP got under way in Wardak Province (Jalrez district) in early 2009 and 100 local security personnel "graduated" in May 2009. It has been expanded to 1,200 personnel, in a province with a population of about 500,000. (These personnel are expected to be integrated into the local police initiative). U.S. commanders say that no U.S. weapons are supplied to the militias, but this is an Afghan-led program and the Afghan government is providing weapons (Kalashnikov rifles) to the local groups, possibly using U.S. funds. Participants in the program are given $200 per month.

Before the program was placed on hold, it was to be expanded to Ghazni, Lowgar, and Kapisa provinces and eventually include as many as 8,000 Afghans. Gen. Petraeus showcased Wardak in August 2010 as an example of the success of the APPP and similar efforts. As an indication of divisions among Afghan leaders about the concept, the upper house of the Afghan parliament (*Meshrano Jirga*) passed a resolution in November 2008 opposing the concept. The National Defense Authorization Act (P.L. 111-84) calls for a report within 120 days of enactment (October 28, 2009) on the results of the program.

Another program, the Local Defense Initiative, began in February 2010 in Arghandab district of Qandahar Province. U.S. Special Forces organized about 25 villagers into a neighborhood watch group, which is armed. The program has been credited by U.S. commanders as bringing normal life back to the district. A different militia was allowed to operate in Konduz to help secure the northern approaches to that city. Problems arose when the militia began arbitrarily administering justice, fueling concerns of Karzai and Ambassador Eikenberry about these local security approaches.

The local security experiments to date are not *arbokai,* which are private tribal militias. Still, some believe that the arbokai concept should be revived as a means of securing Afghanistan, as the arbokai did during the reign of Zahir Shah and in prior pre-Communist eras.

### Reversal of Previous Efforts: DDR and DIAG Programs

As noted, the local security programs appear to reverse the 2002-2007 efforts to disarm local sources of armed force. The main program, run by UNAMA, was called the "DDR" program—Disarmament, Demobilization, and Reintegration—and it formally concluded on June 30, 2006. The program got off to a slow start because the Afghan Defense Ministry did not reduce the percentage of Tajiks in senior positions by a July 1, 2003, target date, dampening Pashtun recruitment. In September 2003, Karzai replaced 22 senior Tajiks in the Defense Ministry officials with Pashtuns, Uzbeks, and Hazaras, enabling DDR to proceed. The major donor for the program was Japan, which contributed about $140 million.

The DDR program was initially expected to demobilize 100,000 fighters, although that figure was later reduced. Of those demobilized, 55,800 former fighters have exercised reintegration options provided by the program: starting small businesses, farming, and other options. U.N. officials say at least 25% of these found long-term, sustainable jobs. Some studies criticized the DDR program for failing to prevent a certain amount of rearmament of militiamen or stockpiling of weapons and for the rehiring of some militiamen. Part of the DDR program was the collection and cantonment of militia weapons, but generally only poor-quality weapons were collected. As one example, Fahim, still the main military leader of the Northern Alliance faction, continues to turn heavy weapons over to U.N. and Afghan forces (including four Scud missiles), although the U.N. Assistance Mission in Afghanistan (UNAMA) says that large quantities of weapons remain in the Panjshir Valley.

Despite the earlier demobilization, which affected many of the northern minorities, there are indications that some faction leaders may be seeking to revive disbanded militias. The minorities may fear increased Taliban influence as a result of the Karzai reconciliation efforts, and the minorities want to be sure they could combat any Taliban abuses that might result if the Taliban achieves a share of power.

## DIAG

Since June 11, 2005, the disarmament effort has emphasized another program called "DIAG" — Disbandment of Illegal Armed Groups. It is run by the Afghan Disarmament and Reintegration Commission, headed by Vice President Khalili. Under the DIAG, no payments are available to fighters, and the program depends on persuasion rather than use of force against the illegal groups. DIAG has not been as well funded as was DDR: it has received $11 million in operating funds. As an incentive for compliance, Japan and other donors have made available $35 million for development projects where illegal groups have disbanded. These incentives were intended to accomplish the disarmament of a pool of as many as 150,000 members of 1,800 different "illegal armed groups": militiamen that were not part of recognized local forces (Afghan Military Forces, AMF) and were never on the rolls of the Defense Ministry. These goals were not met by the December 2007 target date in part because armed groups in the south say they need to remain armed against the Taliban, but UNAMA reports that some progress continues to be achieved.

## IRAN'S FOREIGN POLICY IN POST-TALIBAN AFGHANISTAN

Since the collapse of the Taliban regime in 2001, Iran has followed a two-pronged policy in Afghanistan: first, preserve stability and support the Afghan central government, and second, oppose the presence of foreign forces in the country. For Iran, Afghanistan is the focus point of its "Look to the East" grand strategy—which primarily seeks increased energy and economic relations between Iran and eastern countries in the Asia region, especially India, China, and Japan, and is the axis of its goal to establish stability in Southern and Central Asia. That is why, for the past 13 years, Iran has supported so many state-building efforts in post-Taliban Afghanistan.

At the same time, Iran opposes the presence of foreign forces—especially U.S. forces—in Afghanistan, asserting that it is a pretext for spreading extremism in the country and the region at large. Moreover, Iran perceives the presence of U.S. forces as part of

Washington's strategy to strengthen its own strategic position in Central and South Asia, as well as the Persian Gulf, at the expense of Iran's national and security interests. Iran also believes that U.S. policies in Afghanistan will undermine Iran's legitimate demands, including re-establishing close political and economic ties between the Iranian and Afghan governments. Therefore, Iran criticizes the 2012 U.S.–Afghanistan Strategic Partnership Agreement (SPA), which provides the framework for U.S.-Afghan relations after the 2016 drawdown, maintaining that such an agreement is against the traditional neutrality of Afghanistan in South and Central Asia, consequently sowing distrust in regional states' relations. The environment under such an agreement would minimize Iran's role in its political-security backyard.

An active and strong political-security presence across its immediate borders in order to preempt future security challenges has become a constant in Iran's national security strategy. One of the main objectives of Iran's foreign policy in Afghanistan is to increase its relative security in the broader region. Iran views security as an interconnected network that runs all throughout Asia—insecurity in one area is equivalent to insecurity of the whole region, and so instability in Afghanistan could easily metastasize to other countries. As such, Iran's foreign policy in Afghanistan in the post-U.S. exit era will revolve around the two themes of "cooperation" and "rivalry" with other regional and trans-regional players, such as Pakistan and the United States. This trend is likely to persist during the reign of the pragmatic government of Hassan Rouhani, unless nuclear talks between Iran and the P5+1 could yield a comprehensive agreement that would subsequently improve U.S.–Iran relations.

## IRAN'S INTERESTS IN AFGHANISTAN

Geographically, Afghanistan is located in a region called the "Greater Ariana," a wide area running north-south from Tajikistan to the Maldives and east-west from Burma to Iran. Afghanistan serves as an important gateway to this region, and thus plays an important role in Iran's grand strategy of "Look to the East."

Iran uses a developmental approach to foreign policy here, through energy security and economic integration. Due to Western sanctions during the last few years, the orientation of Iran's energy exports and economic integration has shifted toward Asia, subsequently increasing the volume of economic exchanges with Asian countries, especially India and China. Today, increased economic activities with these countries are vital for Iran's economic development. The way toward achieving this goal is to seek political stability in the South Asia region. In this context, establishing security and stability in Afghanistan is of great importance for Iran's geopolitical interests.

In this context, three different issues are important to Iran in Afghanistan. The first is cultural: the two nations share a rich history that saw the spread of classical empires, Islamic conquest, and the rise and fall of many dynasties. Eventually, the third Anglo-Afghan War started in May 1919 and ended in August that same year (the first and second Anglo-Afghan wars took place between 1839–1842 and 1878–1880, respectively), and Afghanistan declared itself a sovereign and independent state; Iran, meanwhile, continued under various dynastic rulers, called Shahs, until the Iranian Revolution in 1979. Today's Afghanistan was part of Iran's greater Khorasan Province, which historically was called Greater Khorasan and referred to a much larger area of the Persian empire. It contained Iranian-origin sects and ethnicities, thereby making it part of the historical and cultural territory of Iran. Khorasan Province in modern-day Iran was the country's largest until September 2004, when it divided into three smaller provinces that are geographic neighbors to a variety of Afghan ethnic groups (i.e. the Tajiks to Khorasan-e Razavi Province, the Pashtuns to Southern Khorasan Province, and the Baluchis to Sistan and Baluchestan Province). Today, the cultural-identity characteristics of the ethnic groups in these regions are somehow combined.

Another point of cultural commonality is the shared Persian language of the two countries. There are two major languages spoken in Afghanistan: Persian, which is also called Dari, is prevalent in the central, northern, and southern parts of Afghanistan as well as in its capital city, Kabul. The other language is Pashtun, which is one of the Eastern Iranian or Arian-originated languages, a group that includes most major current languages of Europe, the

Iranian plateau, and the Indian subcontinent. It is spoken by Pashtun ethnicities living in east and southeast Afghanistan. This language commonality, despite differences between the governments of the two countries, is a strong link. Nevertheless, wider interactions between the two are needed. For instance, the presence of Afghan refugees in Iran necessitates a cooperative environment. Currently, there are 5,000 Afghan university students and 300,000 Afghan primary school students in Iran, and more than 600 Afghan university students have received Iranian scholarships. Furthermore, more than 160,000 Afghans have so far received legal residence permits in Iran through their Afghan passports, enjoying legal rights just like other Iranian citizens.

Iran's second interest in Afghanistan lies in the economic realm. Energy export and Afghanistan's role as the transit route across Asia, from the Persian Gulf region to China, for transportation and communications have been key themes of Iran's developmental and economic strategy. Iran is one of the main energy suppliers of Afghanistan. Based on the agreement signed on December 26, 2011, between Iran's Oil Minister Rostam Ghasemi and Afghanistan's Commerce and Industries Minister Anwar al-Haq Ahadi, Iran will export one million tons of various oil products—including 600,000 to 700,000 tons of diesel; 250,000 to 300,000 tons of gasoline; and 100,000 tons of jet fuel—to Afghanistan annually. The volume of trade transactions between Iran and Afghanistan (as the fourth major trade partner of Iran) in the first 7 months of the Iranian year 1391 (or March-October 2012) has reached $2 billion. Through this, Iran's exports share was $1.6 million.

Additionally, Iran's future energy pipelines could pass through Afghanistan, transferring even more of Iran's energy to Southern and Central Asia. Several plans have so far analyzed how to transfer Iranian energy to other countries using Afghanistan as a conduit. Another proposed pipeline involves transferring Iran's gas to China through Pakistan, which is mostly dependent on stability in Afghanistan. Some experts, however, maintain that the close proximity of the borders between Iran and Afghanistan to the borders between China and Afghanistan will make an Afghan route better than a Pakistani one, in terms of cost and benefit.

Therefore, because of pipeline geopolitics and regional integration, Afghanistan could serve as the main economic and developmental link between Southern and Central Asia. This will, in turn, have numerous advantages for Iran, Afghanistan, and other countries in the region.

Third and finally, from a political-security perspective, Afghanistan is of great significance to Iran's national security. The September 11 terror attacks have connected the security of Afghanistan to the region and to that of the world, making the fight against the al-Qaeda terrorist group a priority of U.S. foreign policy in the region. This development has led to the direct presence of U.S. forces throughout Iran's eastern borders. Although President Obama's administration is committed to withdrawing U.S. forces from Afghanistan by the end of 2016, the signing of the U.S.–Afghanistan SPA still brings about political-security concerns for Iran for several reasons.

First, Iran believes that due to decades of war, instability, and political-ethnic rivalries in Afghanistan, the Afghan state is weak and therefore dependent on U.S. financial and security assistance. This state of affairs will make the country unable to resist U.S. demands in dealing with various issues, such as improving relations between Iran and Afghanistan. In this respect, the presence of U.S. military bases in Afghanistan will turn into a pressure point on Iran. In other words, the SPA will lead to the indirect political-security presence of the United States in the immediate borders of Iran, thus minimizing Iran's political role in its security backyard.

Meanwhile, with such agreements between Afghanistan and the United States, Afghanistan loses its traditional neutrality in the politics of Central and South Asia. This will provide the ground for the formation of unfriendly activities against Iran within Afghanistan's domestic politics and among political factions (like between the Tajiks and the Pashtuns regarding the way they would like to cooperate with the United States in the future), prompting further regional rivalry between different states (like between Iran and Pakistan in how to deal with the political-security presence of the United States in regional issues). Some experts even believe that by granting military bases to U.S. forces, Kabul no longer has the right and/or the capability to make strategic decisions in relations with its neighboring countries, including Iran and Pakistan. In this context, in the second Bonn Conference on December 5, 2011, Iran's Foreign Minister, Ali Akbar Salehi, reiterated Iran's opposition to the signing of U.S.–Afghani agreements and underscored the necessity for foreign forces to completely withdraw from Afghanistan.

## IRAN'S FOREIGN POLICY IN AFGHANISTAN

Ever since the collapse of the Taliban regime in 2001, Iran's foreign policy in Afghanistan has been based on two aims: upholding stability and opposing the presence of foreign forces.

### *Upholding Stability*

Upholding stability and supporting the Afghan central government has always been a constant in Iran's foreign policy. In this respect, Iran has followed a "developmental" approach in Afghanistan's state-building process after the collapse of the Taliban. From Iran's perspective, poverty and poor development have been the main bases for the revival of the Taliban and extremism in the country. For this reason, Iran has always committed itself to reconstruction and development efforts in such fields as financial aid, transportation and energy, trade, social structure, and refugee matters.

Meanwhile, Afghanistan plays an important role in preserving stability in Iran's eastern borders. Instability in Afghanistan (in spreading terrorism, extremism, and drug trafficking) would pose political-security threats to Iran. Indeed, the failed-state situation in Afghanistan during the past decades has been the main reason behind spreading extremism in the region. This in turn has had precarious consequences for Iran's national security and interests. An example is the killing of the Iranian diplomats in Mazar-e Sharif by the Taliban in 1998.

At present, various groups such as al-Qaeda, the Taliban, and extremist Islamist factions, as well as some local small factions, are fighting the Afghan government and foreign forces deployed in the country. Instability also provides the grounds for these groups to organize terrorist operations against Iran. Based on the available evidence, as well as remarks by Iranian authorities, violent groups operate from their bases inside Afghanistan and Pakistan's borders, the Jundallah terrorist group providing just one example. Recently, another terrorist Salafi group named Jaish al-Adl abducted five Iranian border guards, later releasing all but one, whose fate is still unknown. Further, due to the ethnic and tribal connectivity within the borders of Iran and Afghanistan, any instability in Afghanistan may lead to the creation and continuation of ethnic conflicts, thus increasing migration to the Iranian borders and exacerbating the refugee situation.

Another consequence of instability in Afghanistan is the production of drugs and their transit through Iran. Iran lies at the heart of the transit corridor between opium producers in Afghanistan and opium users in Europe. It is, thus, an important challenge for Iran to preserve security in its rugged borders with Afghanistan and Pakistan. Iran has suffered heavy financial costs and human losses as a result of drug trafficking. Based on the latest statistics, some 15,000 Iranians have so far been killed or injured in fights against drugs, and 89 percent of the world's opium as well as 41 percent of its heroin and morphine are found in Iran, which are the highest figures in the world. Additionally, 60 percent of the Afghan narcotics in 2007 passed through Iranian borders, although this figure has dropped to 30 percent in 2010.

The growing link between terrorism and drug issues highlights the significance of this challenge for Iran. The Taliban has always produced and smuggled opium as a financial resource, and other terrorist groups similarly use drugs to fund their activities. Iranian authorities have always emphasized this link. From Iran's perspective, the presence of Western forces in Afghanistan and the fact that they refuse to fight against drugs under the pretext of fighting terrorism is one of the major reasons for the increased drug production in Afghanistan.

## OPPOSING FOREIGN FORCES

Iran is against the presence of foreign forces, especially U.S. forces, in Afghanistan: it sees them as direct threats to Iranian national security. Although it is beneficial to Iran's national security and interests if the Taliban are eliminated from the central government of Afghanistan, the military operations and the continued presence of foreign forces has led to new challenges such as ethnic geopolitical rivalry, spreading Sunni and Salafi extremism, civil and religious wars, and further general instability and insecurity throughout the region.

Iran opposes the presence of foreign forces in Afghanistan for three main reasons. First is the spread of extremism. Iran believes that the presence of foreign forces, especially U.S. forces, in Afghanistan fosters extremism; past experiences show a direct relationship between the two. For example, al-Qaeda and Osama bin Laden came into existence in the 1980s while fighting against the former Soviet Union. The "war on terrorism" in Afghanistan reached its pinnacle during George W. Bush's administration, continued during President Barak Obama's in a new form, and has offered extremist and local belligerent forces, including the Taliban, the needed opportunity to justify their resistance within the framework of a holy war against the presence of foreigners who endanger their ideology and beliefs. This pretext enabled them to mobilize local forces which traditionally oppose the presence of foreign forces in Afghanistan.

In the Afghan war, the victory of Western countries over opposing forces— including terrorists and hostile groups, local warlords, as well as adversary governments in the region—was considered a victory for the international community and a step in upholding so-called global security. This has raised the expectations of the international community for victory in the Afghan War in such a way that the West is anticipating the full-scale defeat of the Taliban in Afghanistan and the eradication of the roots of al-Qaeda terrorism. In fact, the main challenge of the continuation of the war in Afghanistan is the illusion of this idea of victory against extremist groups such as the Taliban. Such conditions give shallow hope to the Afghan public and raise the expectations of the international community that the Taliban can be eliminated from the Afghan political scene, which is a far cry from the political-security realities on the ground. This could bring negative consequences for the country's state-building and development process. But various signs at present indicate that this strategy is gradually failing, especially now that U.S. forces and other Western powers are on the verge of leaving Afghanistan, and especially because of the potential necessity for engaging in dialogue with the Taliban in order to preserve stability in the post-troop withdrawal era.

The second reason why Iran opposes foreign troops in Afghanistan is to contain the U.S. threat. From Iran's perspective, the presence of U.S. troops in the region is in line with U.S. policy to strengthen its strategic position in broader Central and South Asia as well as the Persian Gulf at the expense of Iran's national and security interests. With pragmatic-centrist President Rouhani in office and the possibility of a thaw in Iran–U.S. relations, the traditional sense of threat from the presence of U.S. forces may diminish. But then again, the sense of indirect U.S. political-security influence in Afghanistan may lead Iran to follow its own way of dealing with conventional threats in the country. This would involve establishing close relations with the central government, primarily at the bilateral level, focusing more on construction and development projects in the regions (such as Herat province) that are closer to Iran's borders and thus more significant from a security perspective. The risk would be that Iran's political capacity to build multilateral cooperation in a post-exit era will go ignored. This is why President Rouhani clearly stressed that Iran "is opposed to the presence of any foreign force in the region, the Middle East, the Persian Gulf and particularly the Islamic country of Afghanistan… They should all leave and leave the security of Afghanistan to its own people."

One should note that Iran has an active presence on its eastern borders, and has plans to implement a containment policy against rival foreign forces to preempt future threats in Afghanistan. From Iran's perspective, any power vacuum in the country will lead rival regional and trans-regional actors such as Saudi Arabia and the United States to expand their role—at the expense of Iran's national security and interests. The recently improved Pakistani-Saudi Arabia relationship is considered to come at the expense of

Iran. Some analysts maintain that Saudi Arabia might have persuaded Islamabad to cancel the Iran– Pakistan pipeline project. Or Iran sees political-security cooperation between the United States and Afghanistan as a potential threat, and therefore opposes it under existing circumstances. This is especially true given that the history of cooperation between Iran and the United States in toppling the Taliban placed Iran in the "Axis of Evil" in 2001 and encouraged the policy of regime change.

Third, Iran opposes foreign presence in Afghanistan in order to ensure the country's neutrality. Iran is traditionally against the presence of foreign forces across its own borders in order to preclude neighbors forming political-security agreements with trans-regional actors.

It believes that such a state of affairs will bring about distrust among regional states, consequently weakening regional political-security and economic cooperation. Iran similarly opposed such an agreement between Iraq and the United States after the withdrawal of U.S. forces there. Iran also strongly opposed the installation of NATO's missile defense shield in Turkish territory in 2011, despite the close relations between Iran and Turkey at that time. Thus, supporting Afghanistan's neutrality in the regional equations of South and Central Asia represents a logical and important component of Iran's regional policy.

In this context, Iran perceives the activities of foreign forces in Afghanistan and some of the policies of the Afghan government as a violation of that neutrality. The U.S.–Afghanistan SPA is meant to last for eight years, starting when foreign forces leave (so likely 2016 through 2024). Negotiations for the conclusion of this security agreement began on November 2012 and continued to October 2013 with the visit of U.S. Secretary of State John Kerry. On May 27, 2016, President Obama said that U.S. troops would be reduced to 9,800 by 2016. However, deployment numbers still hinge on signing the SPA, which has not yet occurred. If the two sides reach a final agreement, the number of military bases and foreign troops deployed in the country will be determined, and the way will be paved to establish permanent military bases in Afghanistan.

Iran opposed the conclusion of the strategic agreement between the United States and Afghanistan, and expressed its concern over the ambiguities in the future of U.S. military bases in Afghanistan and the lack of transparency in the security responsibilities of the United States. To highlight one problem, U.S. drones crossing Afghan borders violates Afghan neutrality. (Following the concerns expressed by regional countries, especially Iran, Afghan authorities emphasized that no country is allowed to use Afghan territory against any other country.) The conclusion of this agreement would also weaken ties between Iran and Afghanistan economically, culturally, and politically.

Since the beginning of the Afghan crisis, the U.S. government has defined any expansion of Iran's activities in Afghanistan within the framework of mutual political-security concerns. Such a policy—considering the realities that Iran and Afghanistan share long common borders and cultural-societal commonalities—will negatively impact the nations' natural relations, bringing distrust and consequently instability in the region.

## IRAN AND THE POST-WITHDRAWAL SCENARIOS

After the withdrawal of foreign troops from Afghanistan in 2016, Iran's foreign policy will involve the concepts of "rivalry" and "cooperation" with local players, like the Taliban, as well as regional and trans-regional players, like Pakistan and the United States.

### *Iran and the Taliban*

Iran has always considered the Taliban and their extremist line of thinking to be a threat to Iran's ideology and national interests. For this reason, Tehran never recognized the Taliban during this group's reign from 1996 to its collapse in 2001. The Taliban invaded the Iranian consulate in Mazar-e-Sharif in 1998 and killed eight Iranian diplomats as well as a journalist. It was a grave mistake for the Taliban, one which deeply tarnished its relations with Iran in such a way that, despite the rivalry and conflict of interests between Iran and the United States in the region, Iran helped the United States topple the Taliban regime in Afghanistan in 2001.

Now, after 13 years since the beginning of the Afghan War, the Taliban are somehow returning to the political-security scene of Afghanistan. The central government of Afghanistan and foreign forces believe that, in order to establish stability, they need to achieve reconciliation with the Taliban. This is why the Taliban were invited to take part in international conferences held on the future of peace and stability in Afghanistan, including those held in Paris in June and December 2012. In these circumstances, what should Iran's policy toward the Taliban involve?

Generally, Iran perceives the Taliban as a threat in two ways: first, from an ideological perspective (the Taliban is anti-Iranian and anti-Shiite), and second from a security and national interests perspective (the Taliban is exclusivist, spreads religious extremism, is against the existence of the state system, and doesn't recognize political borders). The Taliban's identity is based on the Pashtun ethnicity and Sunni Salafi mentality, which is contradictory to Persian culture and the Shiite mentality. For this reason, al-Qaeda, as an anti-Iranian movement, grew under the auspices of the Taliban regime.

Due to their ideological and exclusivist nature, the Taliban are not truly willing to negotiate, compromise, and form a coalitional government with the participation of opposing forces. Since they want to hold all power, it is rather unlikely that a coalitional government involving the Taliban could last in Kabul. Even if it were established, this development could trigger a new civil war, this time from the south of Afghanistan to the north between the Pashtuns, Tajiks, and Uzbeks. The previous civil war in the 1990's, led by the Northern Alliance, was launched from the north to the south of Afghanistan. In this context, it seems that the change in U.S. strategy in handling the Afghan crisis through negotiation with the "good Taliban" will also be fruitless.

Yet, although the Taliban are anti-Iranian and anti-Shiite, it seems that for the sake of preserving stability in Afghanistan, Iran would have no problem with a contained Taliban that has a minimalist role in the Afghan central government and poses no threat to Iran's national and security interests. It is rather unlikely that Iran could hold direct negotiations with the Taliban, due to their bitter history in Iranian society. Iran primarily perceives the Taliban as a Salafist violent faction, against human and women's rights, and paying no respect to international norms and human heritage (for example, Iran saw the destruction of the Buddha Statues in Bamiyan by the Taliban as an outrage). This makes any direct dealing with the Taliban by Iranian government rather tricky before the nation.

However, Iran might welcome indirect talks through other regional and trans-regional players such as Pakistan, Turkey, Saudi Arabia, or even the United States or EU countries. Nevertheless, Iran does not favor an Afghan government in which the Taliban might play a key role—such a situation will lead to a conflict of interests and consistent tension between Iran and the Afghan government, while also giving a dominant role to other rival regional players—Pakistan and to some extent Saudi Arabia—in Afghanistan's political-security scene. This development would, in turn, undermine Iran's regional role. Iran therefore maintains that political stability in Afghanistan depends on the advancement of ethnic and identity plurality in the central government's power-sharing system. This will in turn hinder extremist trends in the Afghan government, as various groups are likely to equate their own interests with the interest of neighboring states in cultural, identity, political, and economic relations. Meanwhile, Iran favors the presence of a stable and friendly government in Kabul.

Iran, like other players involved in Afghanistan, has reached the conclusion that upholding stability in contemporary Afghanistan without the participation of the Taliban in power would be infeasible, but what Iran wants is a minimalist participation of this group in Afghanistan's power. Some Western analysts tend to believe that Iran wants the Taliban to be strong enough to remain a thorn for the United States, but not strong enough to become a challenge for Karzai's or his successor's government, or to turn into a dominant power in Afghanistan. But this is an inaccurate understanding, mainly because the foundations of the relations between Iran and the Taliban are based more on the identity-ideological differences rather than power politics.

### Iran and Pakistan

In the context of cooperation and rivalry, after the exit of foreign troops, Iran–Pakistan relations in Afghanistan will center on the two dimensions of advancing influence on the Afghan central government, and on the scale of the Taliban's role.

In the first dimension, Pakistan has serious disputes with the Afghan government. For one, the two countries have disputes over water-sharing: Pakistan is dependent on the several river basins that flow out of Afghanistan to irrigate its territories, which the Afghans claim. Furthermore, the "Durand Line"—a porous Afghan–Pakistani border drawn by the British in 1893 that divides the Pashtuns in half—was never recognized by the Afghan government. The Afghans' claim on the Pashtun part of Pakistan has always challenged the national interests of Pakistan. Therefore, Pakistan usually favors establishing stability in Afghanistan only if the Afghan government is aligned with the policies of Pakistan. For this reason, Pakistan is also against establishing U.S. military bases in Afghanistan as they might weaken Pakistan's traditional influence in Kabul. For the same reason, some groups in the Pakistani government, such as the Inter-Services Intelligence of Pakistan (ISI), are believed to support the Taliban extremist trend and ethnic-religious violence in Afghanistan, hoping to achieve their own objectives. Meanwhile, Pakistan attempts to penetrate into Afghanistan in order to hedge against India, against whom it has relatively little strategic depth. This could help Pakistan, but only if the Afghan government is under the influence of the Pakistani government.

As the most important non-government player in the Afghan political-security scene, the Taliban currently enjoys utmost importance in some of Pakistan's regional policy. It can play a major role in forming a friendly government for Pakistan in Kabul, shifting the regional balance of power, or disturbing stability and security in Pakistan's favor. Therefore, Pakistan exploiting the Taliban as an instrument of power has implications for Iran's national security and interests.

Traditionally, Iran and Pakistan have had close political-security and economic relations, based on peaceful coexistence and mutual respect in preserving their geopolitical interests and establishing stability in South and Central Asia. For instance, Iran has kept good relations with Pakistan's government despite its anger from the activities of terrorist elements believed to be crossing the Pakistani border into southeast Iran. Yet, relations between Pakistan and the Taliban, or any other group acting against Iran's interests, will adversely affect Pakistani–Iranian relations. The Pakistani government's close relations with the Taliban during their rise to power in Afghanistan and after their regime's collapse are testament enough. During the Taliban era, Pakistan had the best relations with Afghanistan. However, when Hamid Karzai was elected to be Afghan president, relations between Afghanistan and Pakistan experienced serious tensions. Karzai's government has always accused Pakistan of interfering in Afghanistan's domestic affairs, as well as supporting the Taliban.

Some political-security objectives of the Taliban and other groups within the Pakistani government, such as the ISI, are similar and complementary to one another. In order to reach these objectives, both seek replacement of the current political system in Afghanistan with a system that is more dependent on Pakistan. This objective would be fulfilled in two ways: through ousting the current political system and then advancing the legitimacy and power of the Taliban in domestic, regional, and international arenas. Since the Taliban were overthrown, Pakistan has always attempted to prove to trans-regional players that the war in Afghanistan is mostly a domestic and ethnic concern.

Indeed, Pakistan's real policy in Afghanistan is rather complicated. On one hand, Pakistan announces that it no longer supports the Taliban and provides logistic facilities to the United States and coalition forces in Afghanistan, introducing itself as an advocate of the objectives of the international community and the United States. On the other, powerful elements in Pakistan's political and security apparatus support extremist and violent groups such as the Haqqani Network, Islamic Party, Afghan Taliban, and Lashkar-e-Taiba, which generally seek instability in Afghanistan. Such a situation will negatively affect the stability and security of Afghanistan as well as the region.

Some analysts maintain that Pakistan should not play a role that contradicts the interests of Afghanistan's central government. Rather, for preserving its stability after the withdrawal of foreign forces in 2016, Pakistan should concentrate on the tribal regions across the borders, which are the hotspots for conflicts. Overall, in terms of preserving Iran's interests, it will be better if Pakistan focuses more on economic development and stability in South Asia, rather than strengthening ideological ties with the Taliban or other extremist and violent groups around the region.

### *Iran and the United States*

Iran and the United States are two major players in Afghanistan with ample common geopolitical interests in establishing stability in the country. Since the very beginning of the U.S. invasion in Afghanistan in 2001, Iran has pursued a policy of cooperation and rivalry with the United States in Afghanistan. On one hand, cooperation with the United States for overthrowing the Taliban was beneficial to both countries; on the other, the presence of U.S. forces across Iran's eastern borders has become a national security challenge for Iran.

Constructive cooperation between Iran and the United States continued through the constructive role played by Tehran in the first Bonn Conference. However, the policies of George W. Bush's administration in opposing Iran—such as branding it as part of the "Axis of Evil"—stymied the continuation of this cooperation. Of course in the following years, U.S. policy has focused on minimizing Iran's political-security and economic role in Afghanistan, a trend that continues to this date. As a result, the two countries have followed differing strategies in achieving their common interests of establishing stability and battling terrorism, drug smuggling, as well as other mutual threats.

Another common ground for the mutual interests of Iran and the United States in Afghanistan is their cooperation for a minimalist participation of the Taliban in the central government. Iran would have no problem with an involved Taliban under the control of the Afghan government. Now, after 13 years of war in Afghanistan, the United States and NATO member-states have somehow decided that the solution to the Afghan crisis lies in possible reconciliation with the Taliban. Considerable efforts have been made in this regard by the Afghan central government and Western players, especially the United States, for paving the way for negotiations with the Taliban.

Some experts believe that not only is cooperation between Iran and the United States in Afghanistan the best way to demoralize the Taliban, by involving all major regional players in this process, but it can also play an important role in building trust between Iran and the United States in their nuclear talks. Indeed, in past suggested packages, Iran has proposed its close cooperation with the West in solving Afghanistan's crisis. In contrast, other experts believe that Iran and the United States have potential short-term cooperation only on the tribal regions between Afghanistan and Pakistan, since these regions are still a safe haven for Taliban rebels and thus remain a strategic threat. In Obama's strategy, this tribal belt has been rated as the most dangerous border place in the world.

## A WINDOW OF U.S.-IRAN OPPORTUNITY IN AFGHANISTAN?

Establishing security and stability and advancing regional cooperation to settle the Afghanistan crisis have been two main goals of Iran's foreign policy in the country. Iran has a strategic interest in a stable Afghanistan—one ruled by a competent central government that is not under the continued threat of extremist Salfi groups such as the Taliban, groups that could spark another civil war and continued instability. The current instability in Afghanistan gives a pretext to foreign forces to prolong their stay in the country; this is the real motivation for extremist groups to continue in Afghanistan's political-societal scene. Such a situation will weaken Iran's endeavors to establish close and comprehensive political and economic relations with the Afghan government. It will also increase the flow of drugs and refugees across its borders, the result of which would bring further economic pressures on the country. Looking at the larger picture, then, Iran's goals in Afghanistan are very similar to those of the Western countries, especially the United States.

But despite these convergences, the fact of the matter is that the role of regional actors directly correlates to how each actor would like to preserve their interests, as well as the degree of their presence in Afghanistan's issues in the future. In this context, the only way to sustainable peace and stability in Afghanistan is when the West accepts the legitimacy of increased regional cooperation, especially Iran's involvement. This is vital to manage the conflict in post-exit era.

In this regard, given the past conflicting relations between Iran and the United States, especially on the nuclear standoff, Iran has followed its own containment strategy in dealing with the challenges stemming from the Afghanistan crisis. Therefore, expecting close cooperation between the two countries in Afghanistan in the near future would prove rather unrealistic. Although the election of pragmatic Hassan Rouhani has raised the hope for increased regional cooperation between the two nations, as long as U.S. strategy introduces Iran as the main source of threat for the region's security, Iran is unlikely to offer its full cooperation or capacity in solving U.S. problems in Afghanistan and in the region at large.

This situation will, however, change a bit after the withdrawal of forces. Withdrawal will remove Iran's direct sense of threat from the United States, providing the grounds for backing the normal equations of power and politics in Afghanistan in which Iran can play its appropriate role. In this respect, Hossein Sheikholeslam—advisor of the Speaker of Iran's Parliament in International Affairs and former Deputy Foreign Minister— notes that "[i]f foreign security forces completely withdraw from Afghanistan, Iran will be ready to talk with the United States on Afghanistan's developments in the presence of Afghan authorities." He also added, "Iran is ready to give assurance to the Americans that it will not replace the United States in Afghanistan after their exit in 2014. The same assurance that Iran gave the United States in the direct talks over the withdrawal of the U.S. forces from Iraq." Indeed, the exit of U.S. troops from Iraq in 2011 somehow removed the sense of U.S. threat from Iraq's scene. In turn, Iran has become more relaxed and secure, thereby developing increased conventional state-to-state relations.

Some other experts of regional issues tend to believe that cooperation between Iran and the United States in resolving the Afghan crisis can occur in the context of a "grand bargain" between the two countries. Yet again, it is rather unlikely that a grand deal between Iran and the United States will evolve around a regional issue such as Afghanistan's crisis. The aims and expectations of the two sides in entering into such issues are mainly based on increasing their respective roles, thus in conflict with one another. Regional issues can only realistically act as a trigger to initiate strategic talks.

The nature of U.S. policy in Afghanistan and in the region is such that it aims to maximize its interests and win in any negotiations. Three rounds between Iran and the United States in Iraq during 2006–2007 serve as a vivid example. In the course of the negotiations, the United States wanted Iran's role mostly for solving daily matters such as establishing stability, battling terrorists and violent groups, blocking these groups' movement across the Iran–Iraq borders, etc. It did not want Iran negotiating on the future political-security trends in the Iraq government in the post-exit era. Iran fears the same story is occurring in Afghanistan. In such circumstances, the benefits Iran seeks will be less than it gives. For this reason, one may argue that only a national and strategic issue such as Iran's nuclear program, which puts Iran on an equal footing with the United States, has the potential to direct the two sides towards a grand deal.

7

# The Inter-Services Intelligence and the Afghan Taliban

## THE TALIBAN: FROM THEIR EMERGENCE TO THEIR COMING INTO POWER IN KABUL (1994-1996)

When the Taliban first arrived to Southern Afghanistan in November 1994, their ideology fell on fertile soil. More than 15 years of war had left their mark on the country. The constant interference of foreign powers proved to be particularly fatal. Specifically, the unequal treatment during the resistance against the Soviet occupation (1979-1989) had increased the mistrust among the tribes and ethnic groups. The United States and Saudi Arabia, amongst others, had given around ten billion dollars of subsidies to the mujahedeen in Afghanistan during the Soviet occupation. These funds were distributed with the help of Pakistan's Inter-Services Intelligence (ISI). The ISI preferred the Pashtun tribes around Peshawar. They were therefore systematically given preferential treatment in the distribution of weapons and money by the Americans. Conversely, Pakistan regarded the south of Afghanistan around Kandahar as backward and the Durrani Pashtuns dominating the area at the time as untrustworthy.

The clashes between various factions and warlords in late 1994 had led to the disappearance of the old and more moderate leadership, and thus left room for the Taliban extremists. The whole country was divided among various warlords, forming and dissolving alliances as they pleased. In order to finance their war, the warlords exploited the population, cut down almost all forests and sold anything that wasn't nailed down. The on-going insecurity in turn called the truck mafia into action, which was operating from the Pakistani city of Quetta and from Kandahar. The fragmentation of the southern Afghan territory by many local warlords led to a serious restriction of their activities.

Although the exact origin of the Taliban movement is controversial and shrouded in myth, we can be certain that the above-mentioned situation-lawlessness and lack of leadership-has paved the way for this radical movement. The Taliban still had to manage without the support of the ISI, which at that time was backing Hekmatyar's Hizb-i Islami. However, in 1994, the defeat and the loss of prestige of Hekmatyar was becoming apparent, and Pakistan began to look for a new deputy. Then there was the desire of the new Pakistani Prime Minister, Benazir Bhutto, to open a trade route to Central Asia as quickly as possible. Because of the fighting around the capital, the northern route via Kabul to Mazar-i-Sharif and on to Uzbekistan was impassable. Therefore, the idea to open the route via the southern part of the ring road from Quetta via Kandahar to Herat and on to Ashgabat established itself. The plan aroused the suspicions of the local princes, who feared Pakistan might be preparing a military invasion of the eastern neighbours.

The first battle between Taliban and Hekmatyar fighters began in mid-October 1994. At Spin Baldak on the Afghan-Pakistani border, the Taliban overran a garrison of Hekmatyar. With the consent of Pakistan they then conquered a vast weapons and ammunition depot, built by the ISI. Consequently, the Taliban were able to continue fighting for quite some time. In addition, the Pakistanis had the opportunity to hide their support for the Taliban. This action can still be viewed as tolerated by Pakistan, but anything that happened after November 3rd must be considered active help. On this day, Taliban marched out at the request of the Pakistani to free a convoy detained by southern Afghan warlords. Shortly thereafter, they went on to take Kandahar. Already at that time, foreign diplomats were speculating that the Taliban were operating with the covert support of Pakistan. At the same time, the Pakistani Interior Minister Babar boasted the success of "his boys". However, the Taliban continued to try to demonstrate their independence and to resist the Pakistani influence.

While to many the origins of the Taliban still appeared mysterious, by the end of year, some sources were "concerned that the GOP [Government of Pakistan] (ISI) is deeply involved in the Taliban takeover in Kandahar and Qalat." The same source also expressed concern that the influence of the unpopular Pakistanis in the south could further destabilise the country and sooner or later lead to an Afghan-Pakistani conflict. Meanwhile, the Taliban continued their conquest of Afghanistan and marched north.

Pakistan was still putting its eggs into two baskets: On the one hand there were the Taliban, who had contributed to the opening of smuggling routes in the south, and on the other hand there was Hekmatyar and his Hizb-i Islami, who were exerting pressure on the government in Kabul. Whether it was a double game of the ISI, or whether the simultaneous support of both Afghan factions rather represents a power struggle between the civilian government of Benazir Bhutto and the ISI is unclear. In the second case, the support for the Taliban came firstly from the Home Office and its director Nasrullah Babar, while the ISI and the army still supported Hekmatyar, who was, however, involved in a gruelling two-front war. In mid-February the religious students coming from the south had taken over his headquarters. They opened the roads to Kabul and made possible the supply of the city after the long siege. Thus, the Taliban gained great sympathy among the population, but also satisfied a key demand of the transport mafia.

After Hekmatyar and his Hizb-i-Islami had been the Crown Prince of the ISI for a long time and had enjoyed generous support, the relationship between Pakistan and the Taliban in early 1995 changed radically: "[a]t around this time the weight of opinion within the upper echelons of the ISI – (…) – now began to swing towards the Taliban. While in late 1994 Babar appears to have been the leading voice in the Islamabad establishment propounding the student's cause, by January the ISI was taking a growing interest." During that time, Taliban warfare also changed dramatically. This may reflect the fact that the former Afghan Defence Minister Tanai was reactivating his still existing network of connections to other officers of the communist regime. "None of this could have been done without permission, if not active encouragement, from the ISI itself."

After their rapid initial successes, in the first half of 1995 the Taliban suffered some heavy defeats. Ahmed Shah Massoud and his fighters drove them from the area in front of Kabul, and in the West, they had to desist from their attacks on Herat, after Ismael Khan had received support from Massoud, who had the Taliban bombarded for several days. However, a poorly planned offensive of Khan against the weakened Taliban ended in a disastrous defeat and the final loss of Herat. The defeat, however, seems not only to have been due to poor planning. Western intelligence services suspected "infusions of well-trained re-inforcement and new weapons-now supported by a functioning logistics machine". Following this, riots broke out in Kabul. A mob attacked the Pakistani embassy and killed an employee. Thus the relations between the two countries hit rock bottom. Afghan President Burhanuddin Rabbani accused Pakistan openly of trying to oust him with help of the Taliban. The Pakistanis were not very cautious and openly admitted to supporting the Taliban in front of the Americans. The Pakistani ambassador defended himself saying "that in the wake of last months' sacking of the Pak embassy in Kabul, GOP Afghan policy has been increasingly driven by intense domestic opposition towards Afghanistan."

In March 1996, Pashtun scholars came together for a large gathering. The discussions on the future of Afghanistan "were conducted in strictest secrecy, and all foreigners were expelled from Kandahar for this time. Pakistani officials, however, were present to monitor the Shura, including Qazi Humayun, Pakistan's ambassador in Kabul, and several ISI officials, including Colonel Imam, Pakistan's consul general in Herat." The meeting had been convened as a result of the stalemate between the Afghan factions. Rabbani's position had been consolidated and his prestige abroad increased. Consequently, Pakistan tried to forge an alliance against Rabbani with Hekmatyar, the warlord Rashid Dostum and the leaders of the Jalalabad Shura, but this was categorically rejected by the Taliban. The regional powers feared the consequences of Afghanistan dominated by the Islamist Taliban and gave massive support to Rabbani and Massoud. In return, Pakistan and Saudi Arabia increased their support for the Taliban.

True to the motto "the enemy of my enemy is my friend", Bhutto even tried to convince the U.S., which had an interest in curbing Iran, to support the Taliban. The United States declined, but also the Taliban refused to continue cooperating with other warlords. Yet the Taliban managed to convince Pakistan and Saudi Arabia to support them again. Riyadh and Islamabad had reached an agreement with them. In late September, the Taliban led a surprise attack on Jalalabad and overran it. At the same time, Pakistan let hundreds of gunmen enter unmolested across the borders into Afghanistan. The Taliban lost no time and continued their advance towards the capital from an easterly direction. A month after the attack on Jalalabad the first pickups with Taliban had already reached the streets of Kabul. The pro-government troops fled and Massoud also ordered a retreat for his troops. One of the first acts of the Taliban in Kabul was the execution of former President Najibullah, whose battered body they then put on display in the streets of Kabul.

Taking Kabul didn't mean the end of the war. The formerly warring warlords pulled together to form a new Alliance to defend Afghanistan against the Taliban. Massoud decided to make a full-scale attack on the scattered Taliban forces and advanced as far as Bagram. The success of the Taliban seemed seriously threatened. As a consequence, Pakistan again let thousands of 'volunteers' cross the border area of Pakistan into Afghanistan to fight for the Taliban. This enabled the militia of Mullah Omar to launch a new offensive and recover the lost territories.

The way was paved for the Taliban, and the prevailing lawlessness and lack of leadership since the departure of the Soviets have certainly increased their acceptance in parts of the population. However, their success is down to more than just this. In addition to these pull factors a number of push factors have played their part. This includes logistics, enabling the Taliban to carry out their operations equipped with enough weapons and ammunition. They also had enough fighters as new religious students from the Pakistani madrassas could enter the country unimpeded at all times. Furthermore, indoctrination and training played a crucial role. The Taliban broke up the deadlock with mobile warfare and relatively quickly caused large shifts in territorial ownership. Mobile warfare was made possible because the Taliban had large numbers of vehicles (mainly white Toyota pick-ups) and sufficient communication infrastructure available. This included a mobile communications network and a wireless network for the Taliban leaders, both of which had been set up by Pakistan. Moreover, Pakistan had roads, the Kandahar Airfield and fighter jets for the Taliban repaired. They could also benefit from the experience of former officers of the communist army. These had been reactivated through the network of former Defence Minister Tanai, who had found refuge in Pakistan after a failed coup against Najibullah, which had most likely been supported by Pakistan in the first place. But corruption and the effects of money are also not to be underestimated. Many field commanders quite simply let themselves be bought. In any case, the substantial backing from Pakistan has significantly promoted the rapid advance and the takeover of Kabul by the Taliban.

## THE TALIBAN IN POWER IN KABUL (1996-2001)

The support of the Taliban by the Pakistani government and the ISI continued after the gang around Mullah Omar took Kabul in September 1996 and overthrew the Tajik-dominated government of Rabbani and Massoud. Abdul Salam Saif, the Taliban ambassador in Pakistan, wrote what previously was the only detailed inside account of the movement, in which he describes in detail how he was inundated with offers from the Pakistani intelligence officials. The ISI continued pumping money, weapons and advisers into Afghanistan to help the Taliban win against the Northern Alliance. In addition, Pakistan provided diplomatic support, organised training for Taliban fighters, some of whom it had itself recruited, planned and commanded offensives, delivered ammunition and fuel and on several occasions apparently got directly involved in combat support. Undoubtedly, the Pakistani army and intelligence agencies, with the ISI at the forefront, made a vital contribution to the Taliban becoming a highly effective military force. The covert support of the Taliban by the ISI came from the corps headquarters in Peshawar. To give an example: a contact person deemed trustworthy by the U.S. consulate in Peshawar in October 1996 reported the border crossing from Pakistan into Afghanistan of an ISI convoy, consisting of 30-35 ISI trucks and 15-20 fuel trucks, at Torkham. The ISI itself in late 1996 estimated the total Pakistani aid to the Taliban to be as high as 20 million rupees. A number that may well be set too low. Two years later, a Pakistani source of the U.S. State Department put the support of the Pakistani government for the Taliban at "about a million dollars every few months".

According to a 2001 report by Human Rights Watch, the first direct military contacts between the Afghanistan office of the ISI and the Taliban after they seized power was established by sending a small team of Pakistani military advisers to the former stronghold of the Afghan army in Rishikor. The base in Rishikor, southwest of Kabul, was subsequently used as the main training centre for Pakistani volunteers, who had been carted off to fight for the Taliban in Afghanistan. No later than 1999, the accommodation of the Pakistani military and intelligence personnel were in a guarded area within the camp. According to a DIA-report, Pakistani religious students also received military training at Kandahar and Herat. There, a combination of members of Pakistan's Frontier Corps (FC), staff of the Najibullah era, as well as former supporters of the Wahhabi warlord, Abdul Rasul Sayyaf, and the long-standing ISI protégé Hekmatyar provided training. This use of Pakistan's Frontier Corps was apparently not an isolated case. In addition to the training of fighters, company-size FC elements in Afghanistan were also used for command and control tasks and, if necessary, for fighting action itself. The reason for the use of the FC was that its units, as opposed to those of the Punjabi-dominated army, were completely or at least predominantly composed of Pashtuns. This represents the Taliban and the people in the South of Afghanistan.

Also by supplying fuel and ammunition, the ISI was trying to consolidate its influence on the Taliban operations. Here, the intelligence service based its actions on the system which it had set up during the Soviet occupation to control the military operations of its Afghan deputies. According to this system, large amounts of ammunition and fuel were made available to the Taliban commanders only when an operation has been approved by the ISI and the Pakistani military. The fact that the Taliban weren't happy with this system meant that they began looking for alternative arms suppliers, which is why soon private actors began to be involved in arms trade with the Taliban, too. A private offer was available particularly because the Bhutto government in 1994 had fired dozens of ISI officers, some of which with ties to the Taliban. Some of these officers had then founded their own import-export firms or participated in existing companies that were organising large private security and import-export-led operations. Thanks to these new business relations as well as their old Taliban connections, the ex-ISI officers now acted as weapons suppliers to Afghanistan.

After General Pervez Musharraf had come to power by an army coup in 1999, he increased the Pakistani support for the Taliban. Musharraf publicly declared that Pakistan's strategic interests lie in supporting the Afghan Pashtuns, whom he associated solely with the Taliban. The new ruler then went on to say that: "This is our national interest [...] the Taliban can not be alienated by Pakistan. We have a national security interest here [...]". Apart from army chief Musharraf, the power within the military junta lay in particular with three hard-line generals who had made the decisive coup of 1999: Mahmoud Ahmad, Mohammed Aziz and Muzaffar Usmani. All three were passionate supporters of Islamic fundamentalist parties and the Taliban. Aziz, Director of Covert Operations in the ISI in the late 1990s served as the main organiser behind the military victories of the Taliban against the Northern Alliance. Ahmad-nota bene one of the most vocal supporters of the Taliban within the regime-in his function as ISI chief practically made the foreign policy of Pakistan. Thus, the U.S. State Department concluded in September 2000: "While Pakistani support for the Taliban has been long-standing, the magnitude of recent support is unprecedented." The Clinton Administration at that time also appeared increasingly concerned that the direct participation of

Pakistan in Taliban military operations had become more and more frequent in recent months, and that Pakistani military personnel had taken a more active role in the fighting. Towards the end of the year 2000, Pakistani aircraft helped Taliban forces with troop rotations during combat operations and staff of the ISI as well as of the army were involved directly in the planning of major military operations of the Taliban. In November 2000, UN General Secretary Kofi Annan Pakistan accused them at least implicitly of providing such support. Thus, the UN Security Council in January 2001 finally imposed sanctions against the regime in Kabul, which were aimed directly at getting it to stop the Pakistani weapons deliveries to the Taliban. But apparently, the sanctions missed their effect, for an intelligence dossier stating that Pakistan was circumventing the UN sanctions by continuing to deliver fuel and other goods to the Taliban was presented to the Security Council by both Russia and France. In April and May 2001, a few months before September the 11th, 30 ISI trucks were still crossing the Pakistani border into Afghanistan every day-the same number that the U.S. consulate in Peshawar in October 1996 had reported immediately after the coming into power of the Taliban. Some of these convoys were equipped with artillery shells, tank ammunition and anti-tank missiles.

The intentions and actions of Pakistan regarding the Taliban immediately after the terrorist attacks of September the 11th 2001 can not yet be conclusively assessed due to the few and contradictory sources. What is certain, however, is that the Pakistani military regime in accordance with its longstanding Taliban policy tried to persuade the U.S. to refrain from a military campaign against the Taliban, or at least limit it to air strikes, and to negotiate with the government in Kabul to find a solution. ISI director and de facto Foreign Minister Mahmoud Ahmad tried to convince U.S. Ambassador Wendy Chamberlin that the aim of the United States of eliminating Osama bin Laden and al-Qaeda could best be achieved by forcing the Taliban to do it themselves: "[…] it is better for the Afghans to do it. We could avoid the fallout. If the Taliban are eliminated […] Afghanistan will revert to warlordism." In September 2001, Ahmad not only met with many members of the Bush administration, but also twice with Mullah Omar in

Kandahar. The question of whether or not at that time he made a last-minute attempt to get the Taliban to extradite Osama bin Laden after all, whether, as the U.S. State Department believed, this was merely a delay tactic, as claimed by Ahmed Rashid, or whether, quite to the contrary, Ahmad Mullah Omar encouraged them to brave an American attack rather than turn in Bin Laden, as is claimed by leaks to the CIA, must be left unanswered due to contradictory source material. In any case, during the ensuing Operation Enduring Freedom, the attack by the US-led coalition on the Taliban government, the ISI played a great double game. On the one hand, Pakistan officially made a U-turn, presenting itself as a close U.S. ally in the "war against terrorism" and accepting the "seven points" of the U.S. government, pledging to stop supporting the Taliban and, explicitly, promising to stop all supplies of fuel as well as any other goods and to cancel the transport of weapons and fighters into Afghanistan. On the other hand, and with the consent of Musharraf the ISI continued providing the Taliban with weapons, ammunition and fuel. As before, ISI trucks were rolling into Afghanistan on a daily basis. In addition, dozens of members of the Frontier Corps and ISI officers remained in Afghanistan to assist the Taliban in their defence. CIA agent Gary Berntsen realised "from the beginning of the conflict that ISI advisers were supporting the Taliban with expertise and material [...]". This double game was to shape and Pakistan's Taliban policy after the expulsion of Mullah Omar's gang from Afghanistan and continues to do so to this day.

## THE TALIBAN INSURGENCY (2002-2010)

Although Pakistan officially became coalition partner of the United States in the Global War on Terror after the overthrow of the Taliban regime by the Northern Alliance and the American Operation Enduring Freedom in late 2001, it simultaneously continued supporting and directing the Taliban as a deputy government in Afghanistan. As opposed to how it is usually being represented in the Western media, the uprising against the US-and NATO-backed Afghan government of Hamid Karzai is not a monolithic, centrally run movement, but highly fragmented. The three main groups are the Taliban of Mullah Omar, the Hizb-i-Islami of Gulbuddin Hekmatyar and the Haqqani network. These three militant groups have all been protected by the ISI since their expulsion from Afghanistan. In Balochistan, the Taliban were left undisturbed and allowed to settle. Just as they did with the Taliban leaders, the ISI granted refuge to Hekmatyar who, after secret talks with the ISI in Dubai, moved from his exile in Iran to Peshawar in the North Western Frontier Province (NWFP), and was able to operate freely under the protection of the ISI.

Thus, the ISI let Hekmatyar set up a base in a refugee camp outside Peshawar, where many of his former combatants were living. Jalaluddin Haqqani was eventually granted refuge in North Waziristan, where he rebuilt his network on both sides of the border. Thereby, the Pakistani military and the ISI played a central and active role, which included urging the Haqqani group take up the fight again and promising them money, weapons and other kinds of support.

The ISI didn't only apply pressure to Haqqani fighters, but also warned Taliban families from returning to Afghanistan. Otherwise, the ISI would extradite them to the Americans. In order to pull off the balancing act as a U.S. ally and supporter of the Taliban, the ISI developed a dual policy.

While Pakistan was extraditing al-Qaeda fighters to the U.S., the Taliban were protected. In the first five years after their flight from Kabul not a single Taliban commander was extradited to the Americans. A year after 9/11, as Ahmed Rashid concludes, it was therefore clear that Musharraf's support for the war fought by the U.S. and its allies in Afghanistan did not mean the promised strategic U-turn (which would end the traditional support of the army for Islamic extremists) but only a short-term tactical move to appease the United States and to prevent an Indian hegemony in the region. For Pakistan, the Taliban remained a deputy, through whom it believed to be able to regain control in Afghanistan in the future. According to a prominent former commander of various militant groups, who, as a fighter, leader and trainer of insurgents in Kashmir, Bosnia, Chechnya and Afghanistan has been in the pay of the ISI since the nineties, it had been as early as the end of 2001, shortly after the fall of the Taliban government, that in the NWFP a meeting between Taliban leaders and several former ISI agents had been held, during which strategies for opposition against the U.S. military were being planned and Afghanistan was divided into individual areas of operation. Among the approximately 60 attendees were the Ambassador of the Taliban government in Pakistan, Abdul Salam Saif, Mohammed Haqqani, one of the sons of Jalaluddin Haqqani, the former ISI agent Colonel Imam, (who, in the course of his illustrious career had been officer in the Special Service Group (SSG) of the Pakistan Army, Consul General in Herat, Afghanistan, as well as trainer and mentor of militant groups like for example the Taliban), but also Major General Zahirul Islam Abbasi, also a former ISI officer, (who, as commander of the Pakistani army in Kashmir had planned and executed attacks on positions of the Indian army, and who had been convicted of involvement in an attempted coup against the government of Benazir Bhutto in 1995). Abbasi was said to have been one of the most active supporters of the insurgents in Afghanistan in the years after September the 11th.

The involvement of the ISI in the early stages of the revolt against the Karzai government and international troops (2003-2005) has been widely documented. After the Taliban attacks in Afghanistan had increased in 2003, the ISI provided support again. U.S. and NATO intelligence shows a systematic and pervasive system of ISI collusion. The ISI held training camp for Taliban recruits north of Quetta, handing out money and weapons from the Gulf states and organized shopping tours in Quetta and Karachi, where the Taliban were able to stock up on material, buying hundreds of motorcycles, pickup trucks and satellite phones. Pakistani army trucks drove Taliban fighters to the border at night in order to infiltrate Afghanistan and were there to receive them when they returned several days later. In doing so, the Pakistani artillery provided fire protection as well as medical care near the border to the Taliban. Moreover, the Pakistani army officers upheld communications from the border with Taliban commanders in Afghanistan via mobile phone. Just like in the early days of the Mullah Omar gang, the Taliban, the ISI and the madrassas of Jamiat Ulema-e-Islam (JUI) were holding in place a well-organized system. Young militants in the madrassas first underwent "religious training" for several weeks before being recruited by Taliban recruiters-who often appeared in the company of ISI officers-and sent to the front. Every month, the heads of all JUI madrasas met with an ISI officer in Quetta to discuss the operational procedures and funding.

The great double game soon proved to be an institutional difficulty for the ISI. Under the watchful eyes of Western intelligence agencies, it was almost impossible for them to help the CIA on the one hand and on the other hand to lead the Taliban. This challenge was overcome through privatisation, specifically the construction of a new secret organization that was to operate outside the military and intelligence apparatus. Former ISI-coaches of the Taliban as well as retired Pashtun officers of the army and especially the Frontier Corps were re-hired on a contractual basis. Logistics and funding no longer went directly via the ISI but the less closely observed Frontier Corps. As already described, the participation of a frontier corps had already been a feature of Pakistan's support of the Taliban Government from 1996-2001

By the end of 2005, even retentive analysts of the U.S. State Department stated in a report to Vice President Cheney: "Some Taliban leaders operate with relative impunity in some Pakistani cities, and may still enjoy support from the lower echelons of Pakistan's ISI." In 2006, the Taliban intensified their offensives in the south and east of Afghanistan. The battles in Helmand provided clear evidence to the NATO of Pakistan's support of the Taliban. A joint intelligence report of the U.S., NATO and the Afghan executive of June 2006 describes the role of Pakistan unequivocally: "ISI operatives reportedly pay a significant number of Taliban living/operating in both Pakistan and Afghanistan to fight. [...] A large number of those fighting are doing so under duress as a result of pressure from ISI [...] The insurgency cannot survive without its sanctuary in Pakistan, which provides freedom of movement, safe havens, logistic and training facilities, a base for recruitment, communications for command and control, and a secure environment for collaboration with foreign extremist groups. The sanctuary of Pakistan provides a seemingly endless supply of potential new recruits for the insurgency [...]". The interface between the ISI and the Taliban was in Quetta-the lair of the Rabari-Shura-in whose vicinity the ISI had training camps and where the Pakistani gave logistical assistance to the Taliban. There are clear indications that in the capital of Balochistan the ISI went as far as to give direct help to organise Taliban offensives. For example, according to a report published by WikiLeaks from the "Afghan War Diary", ISI agents met with the Taliban leaders in Quetta in June 2006. At this meeting they are supposed to have urged the Taliban to attack Maruf, a district of Kandahar. In fact, the Taliban soon after launched an offensive to regain control of Maruf. Apart from the two sources cited here, there is further evidence that the ISI continued putting fighters and commanders of the Taliban under pressure. An example is the case of the local commander Lal Din, who was killed in an attack of the coalition forces in January 2007. Shortly afterwards, members of a Provincial Reconstruction Team (PRT) in eastern Afghanistan gave evidence of what Lal Din's younger brother, Fakir, had told them: namely, that Lal Din had confided to Fakir that he had been urged by the ISI to continue his fight in Afghanistan. If we cast our minds back to the fact that as early as 2002 the ISI had put pressure on the Haqqani group to resume the armed fight and had threatened fugitive Taliban families with extradition to the U.S. unless they remained in the Pakistani cities to which they had fled, it becomes evident that Pakistani intelligence plays the role not only of supporting the Taliban, but rather as the driving force behind the insurgency in Afghanistan.

The drafted support of the ISI for the insurgents in Afghanistan continued over the following years and reached a bloody climax with the suicide attack on the Indian Embassy in Kabul on July 7, 2008. This attack, in which 40 people, including the Indian military attache, were killed, was most likely the act of the Haqqani network and the ISI. Five days after the attack, the Chairman of the Joint Chiefs of Staff, Admiral Mullen and the Deputy Director of the CIA, Stephen Kappes, travelled to Islamabad and showed General Kayani and the political leaders their evidence of the complicity of the ISI and the fighters of Haqqani. Musharraf and Kayani confirmed "that elements of ISI may be out of control" and the Pakistani government responded to the visit-during which Mullen and Kappes had put them under pressure by making concrete demands-by arresting several members of the Taliban Shura in Quetta. However, the Haqqani network was never addressed-although army and intelligence service would have been in a position to do so. The U.S. diplomats in Pakistan recognised: "The Army/ISI can do the job, but they cling to 'old think' [...]".

A variety of different and independent sources indicate that the extensive, comprehensive and systematic support for the Taliban and the ISI has been maintained also during the last two years. The U.S. State Department clearly stated in a secret background analysis of 30 December 2009: *"Pakistan's intermittent support to terrorist groups and militant organizations threatens to undermine regional security and endanger U.S. national security objectives in Afghanistan and Pakistan. Although Pakistani senior officials have publicly disavowed support for these groups some officials from the Pakistan's Inter-Services Intelligence Directorate (ISI) continue to maintain ties with a wide array of extremist organizations, in particular the Taliban, LeT* [Lashkar e-Taiba] *and other extremist organizations. These extremist organizations continue to find refuge in Pakistan and exploit Pakistan's extensive network of charities, NGOs, and madrassas. This network of social service institutions readily provides extremist organizations with recruits, funding and infrastructure for planning new attacks."* Even the Saudi General Intelligence Presidency (GIP), which has traditionally played an important role in the region, considers the Afghan Taliban to be largely under the control of Pakistan. Some Taliban were indeed said to be against such a strong influence of Pakistan and would have preferred to pursue their own goals without outside interference, General Massoudi, Director General of Internal Affairs of the GIP in January 2010 told Barnett R. Rubin, the Special Advisor to the Special Representative to Afghanistan and Pakistan of the U.S. government during a meeting. However, this was but a weak group. The vast majority of the Taliban, he continued, were exploited by foreign powers, and only used as "fuel for the fight". These powers, like Iran and Pakistan made the uneducated Afghans believe that the U.S. was working against the Afghan people. The Saudi intelligence service identified two reasons for Pakistan's Afghanistan policy. Firstly, Pakistan was very concerned about losing influence in Afghanistan to India and Iran. "The Pakistanis felt that they deserved to have a big part in Afghanistan [...]. They wanted to be 'the closest friend' and were offended when they thought Iran or India were taking this role." Secondly, the Pakistani-Afghan border was an important factor, "even if the Pakistanis didn't say it. This single issue was a very important factor in the 1980's when Pakistan was deciding which mujahidin groups to support. [...] Pakistan would support only those leaders who promised to recognize the Durand Line as an international border. This was why Pakistan did not support Ahmad Shah Massoud. Incidentally, at that time Masudi was working for GIP chief Prince Turki al-Faisal with Afghanistan as an area of responsibility.

Interviews with several commanders of the Taliban and the Haqqani network in Afghanistan, carried out by Matt Waldman of the Carr Centre for Human Rights Policy at Harvard, illustrate the kinds of assistance that the ISI provided the insurgents with and the considerable influence of Pakistan on the resistance in Afghanistan. Even if with a critical analysis of the source these statements have to be taken with some caution, they seem to be credible in their central points, on the one hand through the corresponding testimony of the commanders of various resistance groups and the other by the fact that they are confirmed by documents from the U.S. State Department, countless front reports of the American military in Afghanistan, testimony of former Pakistani generals as well as statements of Afghan government officials. For example, in 2010, Talat Masood, a retired Pakistani general and one of the leading experts of the Pakistani military, claimed that the ISI has maintained its traditional links to the Taliban. And according to Afghanistan's national security adviser, Rangin Spanta, Pakistani influence on Afghanistan is still huge. When for example his government wanted to talk with the Haqqani group, it was only possible to do so via the ISI, which operates as the true power factor behind the insurgency. Furthermore, the relationship with the ISI outlined by the commanders of the Taliban to Waldman essentially corresponds to the status quo since the emergence of the Taliban in the mid nineties: The Pakistani intelligence provided shelter to the Taliban and protects them with supplies, ammunition and money on a grand scale. In addition, the ISI provided the Taliban with tactical, operational and strategic intelligence. The interviews even suggest the conclusion that the ISI supported the most violent and brutal commanders and units within the movement. The ISI continues to tolerate and support military training camps for insurgents and participates in their recruitment in a large number of madrassas that encourage their students to actively fight in Afghanistan.

The interviews, however, strongly suggest that the ISI not only supports the Taliban, but also exerts a strong influence on the group around Mullah Omar-both at the strategic and the operational-tactical level. This influence appears to happen both directly-through several ISI agents in the Quetta Shura-as well as indirectly, through the arrests of unpopular commanders. More will have to be said on the subject of the arrest of Taliban commanders. The presence of several ISI agents in the Quetta Shura means that the Pakistani intelligence service is involved at the highest management levels of the Taliban. A vice minister of the former Taliban regime, which is still collaborating frequently with the Taliban, said that the ISI takes responsibility for the meetings of the Quetta Shura and exerts pressure on the participants prior to the meeting, especially when important decisions are to be taken. The testimony of another expert Taliban commander is representative of many others: "Every commander knows about the involvement of the ISI in the leadership but we do not discuss it because we do not trust each other, and they are much stronger than us. They are afraid that if they say anything against the Taliban or ISI it would be reported to the higher ranks – and they may be removed or assassinated … Everyone sees the sun in the sky but cannot say it is the sun." And the commander added: "The leadership of the Quetta Shura is in the hands of the ISI". In the face of the powerful internal forces of the movement one political leader went as far as to say, probably exaggerating a bit: "Everything is controlled by the ISI. Without the agreement of the ISI, then the insurgency would be impossible [...]". These statements by the Taliban leader are confirmed by a comprehensive study of the history and structure of the Quetta Shura, which comes to the conclusion that the ISI "maintains a hand in controlling its operations." However, in accordance with the brazen duplicity of his country, the Pakistani Brigadier Sejaad in autumn 2009 told representatives of the American and Canadian troops and Afghan border police that the existence of the Quetta Shura was pure fabrication and that the Americans had been taken in by rumours. The results of Waldman about the Haqqani network correspond largely with those about the Taliban: Even the commanders of Haqqani report that their group is funded by the ISI, which is also taking care of training and recruitment, and is represented in the group of leaders of the network.

Based on his interviews, Waldman answered three more crucial questions that are controversial among observers: Firstly, the support of the Afghan resistance is official ISI policy, secondly it is offered by both active and former ISI officers, and thirdly it is approved at the highest level of Pakistan's civilian government under President Zardari and Prime Minister Gilani. There is sufficient evidence in the source material presented here to prove that the current support of the Taliban continues to be official policy of the ISI (meaning that active ISI officers are involved in it too). The same conclusion is reached in a study by Seth Jones, who notes that the United States in mid-2008 had collected solid evidence of the complicity of the leaders of the ISI.

While it is beyond doubt that the assistance of the Taliban is sanctioned by the upper echelons of the ISI, the involvement of Pakistan's civilian government, in office since 2008, can probably not yet be conclusively evaluated. Still, the thesis of Waldman is supported by the study of Christine Fair, which also comes to the conclusion that the Army does not operate alone. In sharp contrast, the leaders of the Pakistani government presented themselves to their American colleagues as a reliable ally in the war on terror and underlined their determination to fight the Taliban. The United States seemed at first to buy into these affirmations. Thus, the embassy in Islamabad in February 2009 stated that Zardari and

Gilani had turned against the Taliban. According to them, the military and the ISI had not yet taken this step and would continue to support the insurgents in Afghanistan as an instrument of foreign policy. But apparently the U.S. changed their assessment. For, already in September 2009 an assessment of the Afghanistan/ Pakistan strategy in the State Department repeatedly stated that "the Pakistani establishment" was supporting the Taliban as a key part of its National Security Strategy, directed at India as the perceived primary threat. The somewhat vague term, "Pakistani establishment" probably includes the civilian government of Pakistan and has been coined in order to avoid having to explicitly name the latter.

The documents published on the Internet platform WikiLeaks as the "Afghan War Diary" in the summer of 2010, which portray the ISI as the main foreign supporter of the Taliban, seem to illustrate three other characteristics of the relationship between Pakistan and the insurgents in Afghanistan: The key role of the former ISI Director General Gul, conspiracies to kill Afghan leaders like Hamid Karzai as well as the orchestration of suicide bombings by the ISI. The sources are problematic, since the documents are mostly reports from the front of soldiers and employees of the intelligence services of the international forces and don't amount to intelligence service analyses, or even "finished intelligence". In addition, the sources of the reports are often connected to the Afghan secret service (who would consider Pakistan an enemy) or are paid informants. Though plausible, these characteristics therefore still need verification by independent sources. However, neither the Afghan government nor the government of a NATO state doubted the key points of the documents. Their representatives, such as U.S. President Barack Obama, emphasized on the contrary, that they contained "nothing new". In addition, numerous reports are based on sources classified as reliable by the U.S. military, and current as well as former members of the U.S. executive consider the image of the collaboration of the ISI with the Taliban to be largely consistent with classified intelligence analyses. Despite the questionable quality of the sources the main findings of the Afghan War Diary regarding Pakistan's support for the Taliban should therefore be briefly summed up.

According to numerous documents, General Hamid Gul, who had led the ISI in the final stages of the Soviet occupation of Afghanistan from 1987 to 1989, remains a driving force and organizing hand among the Taliban, as well as the groups of Hekmatyar and Haqqani, whom he had already supported as ISI director. The front reports describe Gul as a major arms supplier of the Taliban and as a mastermind of suicide bombings. Gul is also said to have urged the Taliban commanders to put their operational focus on Afghanistan, so that Pakistan in return accept their presence in Pakistan's tribal areas. These reports are given additional weight by the pressure of the U.S. on the UN to put Gul on a list of international terrorists, and by testimony from senior members of the Obama administration, who described the general as a critical link between active Pakistani officers and the insurgents.

According to the documents, ISI agents have even hatched plans to assassinate Afghan leaders. President Karzai is said to have been among the persons targeted: In a warning in August 2008, an ISI colonel is identified who is said to have told a Talib to bring about the assassination of Karzai. Finally, the Afghan War Diary also recorded the attempts by ISI agents to manage the network of suicide bombers in Afghanistan, who since 2006 have been plying their deadly trade. Various documents describe how current and former ISI agents, among whom the apparently omnipresent General Gul, recruit candidates for suicide attacks in madrassas in Peshawar, who are then trained in Pakistan. American intelligence agencies realised that the Haqqani network unleashed suicide bombers to attack the representative of the Indian government in Afghanistan, aid workers and engineers on behalf of the ISI. This evidence for the involvement of the ISI in suicide attacks corresponds to the already discussed complicity of Pakistan's secret service in the suicide attack on the Indian embassy in Kabul in July 2008 and is supported by the study of Matt Waldman.

## A SYMBOL OF PAKISTAN'S DOUBLE GAME

In Mid-February 2010, the *New York Times* reported on its front page the arrest of Mullah Abdul Ghani Baradar Akhund, the number two of the Afghan Taliban leaders, by Pakistani security forces. Baradar was arrested at an Islamic school near Karachi. In the United States, this arrest was hailed as a great success. On the one hand because this appeared to deal a serious blow to the leaders of the insurgency in Afghanistan, but on the other hand also because many experts and commentators seemed to recognise this as a long-awaited change in the strategy of the Pakistani leaders. Soon, however, critical voices were increasing, not least from Pakistan itself, which considered the operation against Baradar and other cadres of Taliban and al-Qaeda to be the pursuit of Pakistan's own interests rather than a cooperation in the "war on terror".

Baradar, probably born in 1968, is a Zirak-Durrani Pashtun and belongs to the Popalzai tribe. During the Soviet occupation, he fought with the mujahedeen against the Soviets. After the occupation, he is said to have founded and led an Islamic school in Maiwand together with Mullah Omar. In 1994 he was among the founders of the Taliban, who, according to their founding myth, created the new movement under the impression of the disgusting behaviour of some commanders. Varying information is circulating about his function during the Taliban era. He is said to have served as governor of the provinces of Herat and Nimroz, have been deputy chief of staff and held the position of deputy defence minister of the Taliban government. After the commencement of operations of the United States and its allies to topple the Taliban in October 2001 Baradar is said to have got his fellow combatant Mullah Omar to safety in the mountains with a motorcycle. He himself was imprisoned by coalition troops, but was set free after a short time following intervention by the ISI. Since then, Baradar has increasingly become the real leader of the Taliban. Mullah Omar appeared increasingly less frequently and operational decisions seem to have been increasingly made by Baradar. Meanwhile, he is considered "de-facto leader" of the Taliban.

Baradar also has connections with President Karzai. When, in late 2001 he returned to Afghanistan with the help of the Americans and tried to regain control in his home region, he got into a dangerous situation during negotiations with warlords. Baradar saved him and in return got the promise that he would not be prosecuted by the government of Hamid Karzai for his time as Taliban minister. Karzai is also said to have promised him to let the Taliban participate in a new Afghan government. This deal never materialised, and after the coalition troops attacked his home, Baradar fled to Pakistan. From there, he was involved in the development of resistance against the U.S. and NATO forces. Baradar became more and more of a leader figure, even though his name and prominence were probably familiar only to a few. His rise was also helped by the elimination of colleagues and rivals, such as the notorious Mullah Dadullah. Since 2007, Baradar also seems to have been the strong man in the highest military body of the Taliban, the Quetta Shura.

During the whole period, the contact between Baradar and the government in Kabul seems never to have been interrupted. According to a Newsweek article by Ron Moreau, who has communicated with Baradar also by e-mail, the Taliban leader actively supported entering into discussions with the central government of Karzai on at least two occasions, 2004 and early 2009. Baradar therefore had a very influential position: Firstly, as a leading member of the Quetta Shura, he had a crucial role in shaping the military strategy of the Taliban in Afghanistan. Secondly, he also had ties to Pakistan's ISI, which becomes evident, if from nothing else, from the fact that the agency released him from American captivity. And thirdly, Baradar has never let the connection to the government in Kabul be interrupted and has signalled his readiness for dialogue.

On the morning of the 8th of February 2010, Pakistani security forces stormed a madrassa in Karachi. They arrested several people. The ISI had allegedly become active following a tip-off, but had been unable to locate the leader of the Taliban themselves. Therefore, he had requested the assistance of American experts. When Baradar switched on his mobile phone, the trap snapped shut. The technicians of the CIA had located his position and guided the Pakistani security forces to it. It is unclear who knew how much about the person they targeted. The ISI was said to have asked the

Americans for help without informing them about the purpose, and the statement of the CIA "that the ISI initially wasn't aware of the fact that they had arrested Baradar either caused hilarity in Islamabad". While, after learning of the identity of the high-ranking prisoner, the arrest was celebrated as a huge blow to the Taliban in the United States, some questions arose in connection with the spectacular way in which it had been carried out. The mere fact that Baradar was arrested near the metropolis of Karachi should be cause for reflection, as the Pakistanis have been denying the fact that their country served as a refuge and abode of leaders of both the Taliban and the al-Qaeda for years. Three explanations are possible:

1. It was a fluke. The ISI really had no idea who they were arresting;
2. It was a change of strategy. Pakistan actually has made a U-turn on its Taliban policy and will deny the insurgents help in the future;
3. It was part of the double game. Pakistan is once again playing a double game and has, with Baradar, taken the most influential person who sought a dialogue and a solution through negotiation with the Government of Karzai, out of circulation, because Pakistan saw its strategic objectives endangered.

The first explanation can be excluded, because on the basis of the above-mentioned earlier contacts of ISI to Baradar it may be assumed that he was well known in Pakistan. A high NATO official confirmed this assessment: "Baradar is too high-profile for them not to have known who it was." Nor is it likely that individual elements of the ISI were acting independently. This leaves the question of whether the change in thinking that has long been desired by the U.S. has actually taken place in Pakistan or whether the leaders of the country have once more betrayed their allies in favour of their own goals.

Whatever the case may be, the United States responded to news of the arrest with pleasure. Experts and commentators spoke of a "sea change in Pakistani behavior", a "turning point in Pakistan's policy towards the Taliban" or a "strategic recalibration".

With the arrest, Pakistan seemed actually to have met a key requirement of the Americans, namely to begin cracking down on the Taliban with more energy than before. The Taliban are infiltrating Afghanistan from the Pashtun tribal areas in Pakistan and carry out attacks on NATO troops in the country. 2010 attacks on supply lines in Pakistan also became more frequent. The arrest of Baradar was neither the first nor the last. In fact, the Pakistani authorities can present us with an impressive list of arrested Taliban and al-Qaeda extremists. The names include that of the former finance minister as well as the former police chief of the Taliban. Ashley Tellis has no fewer than 17 names in his report, which could actually indicate a change in the Pakistan's attitude. Many indications, however, contradict this interpretation and once again blame the familiar double game of the Pakistani intelligence service ISI, the military and the Pakistani government.

Tellis points out that except for Baradar and Maulavi Abdul Kabir, none of those arrested belonged to the Quetta Shura and therefore none had the corresponding influence within the Taliban. Doubts are also in order about the seriousness of the arrests. On several occasions, the Pakistani authorities have arrested Taliban leaders only to set them free again. Maybe sometimes even with the express consent of the civilian leaders. In late March or early April 2010, according to Waldman, around 50 Taliban were released from captivity. This after President Zardari had personally assured them that they would be released: "reportedly, he told them they were arrested because he was under a lot of pressure from the Americans". In addition to this, there is another important aspect: In addition to pressure from the Americans, Pakistan is at risk of a negotiated peace between the government and the insurgents in Afghanistan, without its interests being adequately considered. Precisely these fears were fuelled by secret negotiations that Baradar and other Taliban leaders arrested in February 2010 had undertaken with the Karzai government. Baradar and the other high-ranking detainees like Mullah Abdul Rauf Aliza and Mullah Ahmed Jan Akhundzada belonged to the moderate forces within the Taliban who were ready to engage in peace negotiations. And Thomas Johnson and Chris Mason have come to the conclusion that the arrests were intended to withdraw any Taliban leaders who had a positive attitude towards negotiations with the Afghan government from circulation. For them, it is evident that: "This is not cooperation against the Taliban by an allied state; it is collusion with the Taliban by an enemy state." Waldman quotes a diplomat, according to whom the Pakistani Government had all high-ranking Taliban, who had signalled their readiness for peace talks arrested by February 2010. He concludes that Pakistan wanted to demonstrate that it would block negotiations until it would be fully involved into the process. That message seems to have been understood like this also by the rebels. In interviews, most of those asked interpreted the arrests as an attempt to block the peace negotiations. Voices expressing strong doubts about a change of thinking within the military and civilian government can also be heard from within Pakistan itself. Members of the Pakistani executive reveal their intention to stop the secret peace negotiations Baradar had held with the Afghan government, excluding Pakistan. A member of the security forces confirmed: "We picked up Baradar and the others because they were trying to make a deal without us. [...] We are not going to allow them to make a deal with Karzai and the Indians." Western observers in the country are sharing this view. For example, a high NATO staff admitted that: "We have been played before. That the Pakistanis picked up Baradar to control the tempo of the negotiations is absolutely plausible." A former diplomat with extensive experience in the Middle East also considers the wave of arrests to be a warning of ISI directed at the Taliban. Finally, a report of the American Congressional Research Service about the assassination of Osama bin Laden in May 2011 also noted that Washington and other Western governments have seemingly been anxious for some time that Pakistan had begun to take a more aggressive and unilateralist course in 2010 to determine the progress of peace negotiations in Afghanistan. Signs suggesting this were the arrests of certain Taliban who had pushed negotiations with the Karzai government, as well as the protection of the Haqqani Network in North Waziristan by Pakistan.

Thus, there remains little room for other explanations than the one that Pakistan has once again been playing a double game: On the one hand, it appeased the U.S. by giving them the impression that it was now seriously cracking down on the extremists on its territory. On the other hand, it influenced the strategy of the Taliban so that negotiations with the Karzai government without Pakistani permission are not an option, thus keeping the Taliban as a proxy for the enforcement of its own strategic interests in Afghanistan. At the same time it strengthened its control over the Taliban.

Since September the 11th 2001, the subsequent acceptance of the "Seven Points" by President Musharraf and the start of Operation Enduring Freedom in autumn 2001, Pakistan has been presenting itself as a reliable coalition partner of the United States and the West in the "war on terrorism"-and has been publicly acknowledged as such by NATO countries. In December 2009 President Obama reiterated characteristically: "[...] we are committed to a partnership that is built on a foundation of mutual interest, mutual respect and mutual trust". And as recently as April 2010, the U.S. Department of Defense called Pakistan an Ally and "effective partner". As a result of its apparent strategic U-turn, Pakistan has received $ 11.6 billion in Coalition Support Funding (CSF) for its security apparatus since the September the 11th, and on top of that another 6 billion dollars in economic aid, all by the United States. This means that Pakistan has received almost 90% of the total CSF worldwide. And the U.S. intend to pay $ 7.5 billion additional aid dollars over the next five years. Pakistani officers even sit in the Tripartite Joint Intelligence Operations Centre, which is located in the ISAF headquarters in Kabul.

Behind this façade of a faithful ally in the "war on terrorism," Pakistan is playing a bold double game, by means of which the outcome of the war in Afghanistan has been blown wide open: As was demonstrated unequivocally in the present study, the ISI at the forefront does give the Taliban-since the foundation of Mullah Omar's group from 1994 to today-complete, very comprehensive and systematic support. The ISI supplies the Taliban with money, weapons, ammunition and intelligence, provides for their military training, organizes the recruitment of new Islamist militants in the madrassas and helps in planning military offensives. Although the organisation, the nature and partly also the extent of assistance vary and have evolved over the 16 years, the support outlined is an iron constant in the relationship between the ISI and the Taliban-from the founding of the "religious students" and their government in Kabul to their armed uprising in 2010. Moreover, since the flight of the Taliban from Afghanistan in the winter of 2001/2002, the ISI has been harbouring Taliban leaders in Balochistan and also supports the other two major factions of the rebellion in Afghanistan, the Hizb-i-Islami of Gulbuddin Hekmatyar and especially the Haqqani network. There can be no doubt: Without the support and guidance from Pakistan, the insurgency in Afghanistan in its present extent would be impossible.

But the ISI does not only fuel the Afghan insurgency by increasing the capacity of the Taliban and its allies as by far the most important of its foreign sponsors. It also manipulated the intentions of these groups. The ISI has a significant influence on the insurgents-including at the strategic level-which is being applied both directly, through ISI agents in the Quetta Shura, as well as indirectly, through (threatened) arrests (as in the case of Mullah Baradar). Since 2002, the Pakistani intelligence service has been putting its Afghan proxy under a lot of pressure to continue the armed struggle against the Kabul government and the international forces by threatening to murder, arrest or extradite them to the U.S. The attempt of the ISI to control, or at least to influence them, can be detected already during the period of struggle of the mujahedeen against the Red Army and has been shaping the sometimes-problematic relationship between the ISI and the Taliban since the beginning.

The Pakistani military and the ISI play their big double game with almost diabolical insolence. On the one hand, a portion of the billions of dollars they receive from the U.S. for the "war on terror" ends up by reaching the Taliban-of the main enemies of the United States in this war-and their allies, who, with this money, kill American soldiers in Afghanistan. On the other hand, the ISI and the Pakistani military and intelligence agencies exploit the American troops to increase their control over the Taliban and to keep the Afghan insurgency alive. This happened during the arrest of Mullah Baradar and other senior Taliban in February 2010.

But why does Pakistan in general and the ISI in particular play this great double game? Why does the ISI still support the Taliban on a grand scale? This in spite of the carrot and stick policy of the United States, which is manifested in massive pressure, sweetened with two-digit billion sums. Despite the growing blowback caused by the Taliban in Pakistan, who, since 2007, have developed into a serious threat for Pakistan and have at times controlled large areas in the FATA (Federally Administered Tribal Areas) and the NWFP (North Western Frontier Province). Even though Pakistan's Afghanistan policy can certainly not be explained in a purely mono-causal way, there is a superior motif that since the mid-1990s has been present in all major stakeholders: The perception of India as the largest and existential threat. This perception, associated with deep fears, explains the aim of Pakistan's security strategy of a stable Government in Afghanistan, which, if not directly controlled by Islamabad, should at least be well-disposed towards it, and in any event should be free of Indian influence. For 15 years, the ISI has been linking this hope almost exclusively with the Taliban. The concept of "strategic depth" is closely connected with this strategic national interest: This means access to enough space west of the Indus for a reshaping of the Pakistani army, if they were to be pushed behind the river by an Indian invasion, and also implies a pro-Pakistan government in Afghanistan. Although the need for "strategic depth" has been convincingly refuted by Pakistan's civilian strategists, the concept will always be playing a paramount role in the thinking of military leaders. As recently as 2010, General Kayani, the Chief of Staff of the Pakistan army, has reduced the aim of his country to a simple denominator: "We want a strategic depth in Afghanistan."

In a way that is incompatible with this primary objective of Pakistan's security strategy, namely to minimise the influence and presence of India in Afghanistan, New Delhi has been taking an important role in the civilian reconstruction in Afghanistan, in which it has already invested between 0.5 und 1.3 billion dollars: India has been financing roads, bridges, canals, schools, training Afghan officials and providing even for the reconstruction of the Afghan Parliament. India's reconstruction strategy, one of the best and most comprehensive ever in the Hindu Kush, was designed to gain ground in every sector of Afghan society, to give India a good reputation in the Afghan population, to derive the maximum political advantage and of course to prevent Pakistani influence. In addition to increased development assistance, India has, encouraged by the U.S. government, increased its investments in and its trade with Afghanistan. India also maintains close relations with the Karzai administration. It has established a network of four consulates in Afghanistan, including by reopening of consulates in Kandahar and Jalalabad, which had been closed since 1979, and the country's Foreign Intelligence Service, *Research and Analysis Wing (RAW)* has also expanded its presence and increased its activities. In addition to the civil commitment, India would also like to take an important role in training the Afghan security forces. " will not leave Afghanistan because we have strategic interests there", YK Sinha, secretary for Afghanistan, Pakistan and Iran in the Indian Foreign Ministry, told a representative of the U.S. government at a meeting in February 2010. In short, India has been trying to profit from the lack of Pakistani influence over the Afghan government in an increasingly offensive way. The ISI in turn tries to counter India's-perceived or actual-influence by supporting the insurgents in Afghanistan as a deputy.

A secondary theme for the Pakistani support for the Taliban is the question of Pashtunistan and the controversial border demarcation with Afghanistan. During the second Anglo-Afghan war, Afghanistan had had to cede parts of Western Balochistan, Quetta and the bulk of the FATA to Britain in the Treaty of Gandamak in 1879. In 1893, Sir Mortimer Durand in accordance with this contract determined Afghanistan's present borders with Pakistan (then British India) thereby permanently dividing the Pashtun tribal areas. The "Durand Line" has since then not been accepted by any Afghan government and has always been rejected by a large number of Pashtuns on either side of the border. Pakistan has therefore traditionally tried to gain influence among the Pashtun, to prevent the emergence of a Pashtunistan and to silence Afghan demands for territory in northwest Pakistan. This objective provides a second important explanation as to why the ISI has been continuously supporting the Taliban since the mid-nineties. For unlike the Ghilzai-Pashtuns, who dominate in the upper echelons of the Taliban, their historical rivals, the Durrani Pashtuns, who, in turn, have most government posts in Kabul are known to support of the idea of a "Pashtunistan" decidedly and make claims to Pakistani territory. For Islamabad, Taliban depending on Pakistan therefore take on the meaning of a kind of universal advantage: Their support ensures continued influence in Afghanistan without the Taliban-dominated government in Kabul, although Pashtun, bringing up the question of "Pashtunistan" and the Durand Line. Pakistan's Afghanistan policy is thereby strongly justified by a historical perspective. On the one hand by the fateful legacy of the colonial boundary between Pakistan and Afghanistan, but above all by the by profound anxieties putting a strain on the relationship between Pakistan and India, which began with the emergence of the two States in the wake of the decolonization of British India in 1947. Since then, the rivalry has been cemented by four wars.

## EPILOGUE: THE LONG SHADOW OF ABBOTTABAD

The targeted killing of Al-Qaeda leader Osama bin Laden in the North Western Frontier Province (NWFP) village by U.S. Special Forces on 2 May 2011 in Abbottabad, only fifty kilometres north of Islamabad as the crow flies, catapulted the relations between the Pakistani army and Islamist extremists in the headlines of world press. Experts were rubbing their eyes in amazement. How was it possible that the most wanted man in the world could settle in the immediate vicinity of a military garrison and remain undisturbed for almost five years? Some people, like the former MI6 agent Nigel Inkster of the International Institute for Strategic Studies (IISS) expressed their surprise that the ISI, "by far the most competent and professional intelligence service in South Asia, should have failed to notice or investigate the location where bin Laden was found, given its unusual character and proximity to important military facilities, the security of which would have been a constant preoccupation." Furthermore, the analysis of a mobile phone belonging to the courier of Osama bin Laden that was seized during the commando action revealed close ties between the Qaeda leaders in hiding and Islamist Harkat-ul-Mujahideen (HUM). The Pakistani HUM, which has originally operated primarily in Kashmir has traditionally had close ties to both the ISI and Al Qaeda and is likely to have played an important role in the logistical support of Osama bin Laden in Abbottabad. Not only the site, but also the timing of the assassination raised questions about the role of the ISI. Finally, the relations between the United States and Pakistan had been increasingly strained since the beginning of the year, and between the CIA and the ISI a downright intelligence war had broken out behind the scenes, in which the affair of the CIA Contractor Raymond Davis represents an important milestone in a spiral of escalation. At the time, some analysts therefore rightly pointed out that Pakistan had already several times plotted successes in combating high-level terrorists in particularly favourable moments as a kind of liberating act, "and perhaps played the 'Osama card' just as U.S.-Pakistan relations were at an acutely low ebb."

As early as late April, the Chairman of the Joint Chiefs of Staff, Admiral Michael Mullen, had publicly accused the ISI on one of his many visits to Islamabad in an unusually undiplomatic note of directly supporting the Haqqani network and of fomenting the fight against international troops in Afghanistan. After the killing of Bin Laden these opinions were increasingly being voiced. Hanif Atmar, former Afghan Interior Minister identified the ISI as one of the sources of funding insurgents in Afghanistan-in addition to Al Qaeda and the "war economy". The former U.S. ambassador in Afghanistan, Zalmay Khalilzad, accused Pakistan of playing a double game in a column in The National Interest. As was the case of the Bush Administration, Obama and his Government hadn't succeeded in causing a change of direction of Pakistani politics either: "Islamabad wants to keep the pipeline of American assistance flowing while limiting U.S. anti-terror operations in Pakistan, Particularly the drone attacks. It is also escalating pressure on U.S. forces in Afghanistan by, among other things, allowing factories to operate in places like Chaman that are producing improvised explosive devices [IEDs] designed to maim the legs and genital areas of soldiers. Its overall design seeks to turn its neighbor into a Pakistani satrapy."

In the weeks after the killing of Bin Laden, IED factories continued to be a defining feature of American-Pakistani relations. In mid-May, Marc Grossman, (the special envoy for Afghanistan and Pakistan of the Obama administration) and CIA Deputy Director Michael J. Morell gave General Kayani and ISI Chief Ahmed Shuja Pasha one IMINT video with the exact locations of two factories in which Afghan insurgents produced IEDs as part of a confidence building measure. One of the factories was in a girls' school in Miram Shah, the hometown of the headquarters of the Haqqani Network in North Waziristan, and the other one was in South Waziristan. When on June 4th units of the Pakistani military finally stormed the two facilities, they found them both deserted. It seems likely that the ISI had warned the extremists. A high-ranking officer of the Pakistan military also claimed that the United States had shared information about other locations of facilities of the insurgents like arsenals, which had subsequently also been found empty. Even the Pakistani officer expressed the suspicion "that perhaps there was a tip-off." However, the Pakistani leaks were not limited to weapons factories and weapons caches: A senior representative of the Obama administration admitted that due to lack of confidence the Pakistani military would be often not be privy to details of the drone attacks since in the past, target people had been able to escape them after specific warnings: "That would presumably be by the Pakistani side, which still favors a strategy of choosing between 'good' Taliban, those who do Pakistan's bidding in Afghanistan and 'bad', those who do not."

In early July, a prominent former commander of various militant groups, who had been in the pay of the ISI as a fighter, leader and trainer of insurgents in Kashmir, Bosnia, Chechnya and Afghanistan since the nineties, went public. In an interview with the *New York Times*, he said that the Pakistani military and ISI leaders continue to support the Afghan Taliban as a deputy in their fight against the Afghan government and international troops. "There are two bodies running these affairs: mullahs and retired generals," added the former commander, and specifically named former ISI directors. "These people have a very big role still."

The Afghan government has also begun to realise that success in peace efforts with the Taliban can only go via Pakistan as a vital force behind the insurgency. As a consequence, President Hamid Karzai travelled to Islamabad in June, where during a meeting with the civilian and military leadership he sought to win the support of Pakistan for the peace talks. Finally, by means of threats and arrests the ISI continues to thwart the efforts of individual commanders to enter into negotiations with the government in Kabul without Islamabad's consent. As late as the beginning of this year, for example, Mullah Agha Muhammad, a brother of Mullah Baradar, was briefly detained by Pakistani security forces to prevent him from opening discussions with the Afghan Government; the same warning that had previously been addressed to his brother a year before. In this sense, former UN special envoy for Iraq and Afghanistan, Lakhdar Brahimi and former U.S. UN Ambassador Thomas Pickering who together lead an international task force on Afghanistan, recently concluded that the Pakistani military wants to influence any future agreement between the Taliban and Kabul, and therefore seeks to control the insurgents. But yet another factor has recently been added to the efforts of Pakistan: Islamabad tries to use to its advantage the fact that for the peace process Kabul is dependent on its eastern neighbours, insofar as that Afghanistan is supposed to be moved into a new strategic direction and to be removed from its alliance with the U.S. and India and into the Pakistan-China axis.

# 8

# Taliban-style and Pakistan

The war between India and Pakistan over the fate of Kashmir is as old as both states. When Pakistan was formally created in 1947, the rulers of Muslim-majority states that had existed within British India were given the option of joining India or Pakistan. The Hindu monarch of the predominantly Muslim state of Jammu and Kashmir chose India, prompted partly by a tribal rebellion in the state. Pakistan responded by sending in troops. The resultant fighting ended with a 1949 cease-fire, but the Pakistani government continued covertly to support volunteer guerrilla fighters in Kashmir. Islamabad argued then, as it does now, that it could not control the volunteers, who as individuals were not bound by the cease-fire agreement. (On the other hand, Maulana Abul A'la Maududi, the late founder of the Islamist party Jamaat-e-Islami, argued that as individuals, these "mujahideen" could not legitimately declare Jihad, either.)

Pakistani officials admit to having tried repeatedly to foment separatism in Kashmir in the decades following the 1948 cease-fire. These attempts were largely unsuccessful; when separatist violence broke out in the late 1980s, the movement was largely indigenous. For their part, Indian officials admit their own culpability in creating an intolerable situation in the region. They ignored Kashmir's significant economic troubles, rampant corruption, and rigged elections, and they intervened in Kashmiri politics in ways that contradicted India's own constitution. As American scholar Sumit Ganguly explains, the rigged 1987 state-assembly elections were the final straw in a series of insults, igniting, by 1989, widespread violent opposition. By 1992, Pakistani nationals and other graduates of the Afghan war were joining the fight in Kashmir.

What began as an indigenous, secular movement for independence has become an increasingly Islamist crusade to bring all of Kashmir under Pakistani control. Pakistan-based Islamist groups (along with Hizb-ul-Mujahideen, a Kashmir-based group created by Jamaat-e-Islami and partly funded by Pakistan) are now significantly more important than the secular Kashmir-based ones. The Indian government estimates that about 40 percent of the militants in Kashmir today are Pakistani or Afghan, and some 80 percent are teenagers. Although the exact size of the movement is unknown, the Indian government estimates that 3,000 to 4,000 "mujahideen" are in Kashmir at any given time.

Whatever their exact numbers, these Pakistani militant groups — among them, Lashkar-i-Taiba and Harkat-ul-Mujahideen — pose a long-term danger to international security, regional stability, and especially Pakistan itself. Although their current agenda is limited to "liberating" Kashmir, which they believe was annexed by India illegally, their next objective is to turn Pakistan into a truly Islamic state. Islamabad supports these volunteers as a cheap way to keep India off balance. In the process, however, it is creating a monster that threatens to devour Pakistani society.

### *Schools of Hate*

In Pakistan, as in many developing countries, education is not mandatory. The World Bank estimates that only 40 percent of Pakistanis are literate, and many rural areas lack public schools. Islamic religious schools — madrasahs — on the other hand, are located all over the country and provide not only free education, but also free food, housing, and clothing. In the poor areas of southern Punjab, madrasahs funded by the Sunni sectarian political party Sipah-e-Sahaba Pakistan (SSP) reportedly even pay parents for sending them their children.

In the 1980s, Pakistani dictator General Mohammad Zia-ul-Haq promoted the madrasahs as a way to garner the religious parties' support for his rule and to recruit troops for the anti-

Soviet war in Afghanistan. At the time, many madrasahs were financed by the zakat (the Islamic tithe collected by the state), giving the government at least a modicum of control. But now, more and more religious schools are funded privately — by wealthy Pakistani industrialists at home or abroad, by private and government-funded nongovernmental organizations in the Persian Gulf states and Saudi Arabia, and by Iran. Without state supervision, these madrasahs are free to preach a narrow and violent version of Islam.

Most madrasahs offer only religious instruction, ignoring math, science, and other secular subjects important for functioning in modern society. As Maududi warned in his 1960 book, First Principles of the Islamic State, "those who choose the theological branch of learning generally keep themselves utterly ignorant of [secular subjects, thereby remaining] incapable of giving any lead to the people regarding modern political problems."

Even worse, some extremist madrasahs preach Jihad without understanding the concept: They equate Jihad — which most Islamic scholars interpret as the striving for justice (and principally an inner striving to purify the self) — with guerrilla warfare. These schools encourage their graduates, who often cannot find work because of their lack of practical education, to fulfill their "spiritual obligations" by fighting against Hindus in Kashmir or against Muslims of other sects in Pakistan. Pakistani officials estimate that 10 to 15 percent of the country's tens of thousands of madrasahs espouse such extremist ideologies.

Pakistan's interior minister Moinuddin Haider, for one, recognizes these problems. "The brand of Islam they are teaching is not good for Pakistan," he says. "Some, in the garb of religious training, are busy fanning sectarian violence, poisoning people's minds." In June, Haider announced a reform plan that would require all madrasahs to register with the government, expand their curricula, disclose their financial resources, seek permission for admitting foreign students, and stop sending students to militant training camps.

This is not the first time the Pakistani government has announced such plans. And Haider's reforms so far seem to have failed, whether because of the regime's negligence or the madrasahs' refusal to be regulated, or both. Only about 4,350 of the estimated 40,000 to 50,000 madrasahs in Pakistan have registered with the government. Some are still sending students to training camps despite parents' instructions not to do so. Moreover, some chancellors are unwilling to expand their curricula, arguing that madrasahs are older than Pakistan itself — having been "designed 1,200 years ago in Iraq," according to the chancellor of the Khudamudeen madrasah. The chancellor of Darul Uloom Haqqania objects to what he calls the government's attempt to "destroy the spirit of the madrasahs under the cover of broadening their curriculum."

Mujibur Rehman Inqalabi, the SSP's second in command, told me that Haider's reform plan is "against Islam" and complains that where states have taken control of madrasahs, such as in Jordan and Egypt, "the engine of Jihad is extinguished." America is right, he said: "Madrasahs are the supply line for Jihad."

## *Jihad International, Inc.*

If madrasahs supply the labour for "Jihad," then wealthy Pakistanis and Arabs around the world supply the capital. On Eid-ul-Azha, the second most important Muslim holiday of the year, anyone who can afford to sacrifices an animal and gives the hide to charity. Pakistani militant groups solicit such hide donations, which they describe as a significant source of funding for their activities in Kashmir.

Most of the militant groups' funding, however, comes in the form of anonymous donations sent directly to their bank accounts. Lashkar-i-Taiba ("Army of the Pure"), a rapidly growing Ahle Hadith (Wahhabi) group, raises funds on the Internet. Lashkar and its parent organization, Markaz ad-Da'wa Wal Irshad (Centre for Islamic Invitation and Guidance), have raised so much money, mostly from sympathetic Wahhabis in Saudi Arabia, that they are reportedly planning to open their own bank.

Individual "mujahideen" also benefit financially from this generous funding. They are in this for the loot, explains Ahmed Rashid, a prominent Pakistani journalist. One mid-level manager of Lashkar told me he earns 15,000 rupees a month — more than seven times what the average Pakistani makes, according to the World Bank. Top leaders of militant groups earn much more; one leader took me to see his mansion, which was staffed by servants and filled with expensive furniture. Operatives receive smaller salaries but win bonuses for successful missions. Such earnings are particularly attractive in a country with a 40 percent official poverty rate, according to Pakistani government statistics.

The United States and Saudi Arabia funneled some $3.5 billion into Afghanistan and Pakistan during the Afghan war, according to Milt Bearden, CIA station chief in Pakistan from 1986 to 1989. "Jihad," along with guns and drugs, became the most important business in the region. The business of "Jihad" — what the late scholar Eqbal Ahmad dubbed "Jihad International, Inc." — continues to attract foreign investors, mostly wealthy Arabs in the Persian Gulf region and members of the Pakistani diaspora. (As World Bank economist Paul Collier observes, diaspora populations often prolong ethnic and religious conflicts by contributing not only capital but also extremist rhetoric, since the fervor of the locals is undoubtedly held in check by the prospect of losing their own sons.)

As the so-called Jihad movement continues to acquire its own financial momentum, it will become increasingly difficult for Pakistan to shut down, if and when it tries. As long as "Jihad International, Inc." is profitable, those with financial interests in the war will work to prolong it. And the longer the war in Kashmir lasts, the more entrenched these interests will become.

## ADDICTED TO JIHAD

As some irregulars are financially dependent on what they consider Jihad, others are spiritually and psychologically so. Many irregulars who fought in Afghanistan are now fighting in Kashmir and are likely to continue looking for new "jihads" to fight — even against Pakistan itself. Khalil, who has been a "mujahid" for 19 years and can no longer imagine another life, told me, "A person addicted to heroin can get off it if he really tries, but a mujahid cannot leave the Jihad. I am spiritually addicted to Jihad." Another Harkat operative told me,

We won't stop — even if India gave us Kashmir.... We'll [also] bring Jihad here. There is already a movement here to make Pakistan a pure Islamic state. Many preach Islam, but most of them don't know what it means. We want to see a Taliban-style regime here.

Aspirations like these are common among the irregulars I have interviewed over the last couple of years. The "Jihad" movement is also developing a spiritual momentum linked to its financial one. Madrasahs often teach their students that Jihad — or, in the extremist schools, terrorism under the guise of Jihad — is a spiritual duty. Whereas wealthy Pakistanis would rather donate their money than their sons to the cause, families in poor, rural areas are likely to send their sons to "Jihad" under the belief that doing so is the only way to fulfill this spiritual duty. One mother whose son recently died fighting in Kashmir told me she would be happy if her six remaining sons were martyred. "They will help me in the next life, which is the real life," she said.

When a boy becomes a martyr, thousands of people attend his funeral. Poor families become celebrities. Everyone treats them with more respect after they lose a son, a martyr's father said. "And when there is a martyr in the village, it encourages more children to join the Jihad. It raises the spirit of the entire village," he continued. In poor families with large numbers of children, a mother can assume that some of her children will die of disease if not in war. This apparently makes it easier to donate a son to what she feels is a just and holy cause.

Many of these families receive financial assistance from the militant groups. The Shuhda-e-Islam Foundation, founded in 1995 by Jamaat-e-Islami, claims to have dispensed 13 million rupees to the families of martyrs. It also claims to provide financial support to some 364 families by paying off loans, setting them up in businesses, or helping them with housing. Moreover, the foundation provides emotional and spiritual support by constantly reminding the families that they did the right thing by donating their children to assist their Muslim brethren in Kashmir. Both Lashkar-i-Taiba and Harkat have also established charitable organizations that reward the families of martyrs — a practice common to gangs in inner-city Los Angeles and terrorist groups such as al Qaeda and Hamas. Although these foundations provide a service to families in need, they also perpetuate a culture of violence.

### *Bad Boys*

The comparison to gangs and terrorist groups is particularly apt because the irregulars often hire criminals to do their dirty work — and sometimes turn to petty or organized crime themselves. Criminals are typically hired to "drop" weapons and explosives or to carry out extreme acts of violence that a typical irregular is reluctant or unable to perform. For example, members of the Dubai-based crime ring that bombed the Bombay stock exchange in March 1993 later confessed that they had been in Islamabad the previous month, where Pakistani irregulars had allegedly trained them to throw hand grenades and fire Kalashnikov assault rifles. Law-enforcement authorities noted that the operatives' passports contained no Pakistani stamps, suggesting the complicity of the Pakistani government.

Criminals joining supposed Jihad movements tend to be less committed to the group's purported goals and more committed to violence for its own sake — or for the money. When criminals join private armies, therefore, the political and moral constraints that often inhibit mass-casualty, random attacks are likely to break down. Criminal involvement in the movement also worsens the principal-agent problem for Pakistan: pure mercenaries are even harder to control than individuals whose goals are at least partly aligned with those of the state.

## EXPORTING HOLY WAR

Exacerbating the principal-agent problem, Pakistani militant groups are now exporting their version of Jihad all over the world. The Khudamudeen madrasah, according to its chancellor, is training students from Burma, Nepal, Chechnya, Bangladesh, Afghanistan, Yemen, Mongolia, and Kuwait. Out of the 700 students at the madrasah, 127 are foreigners. Nearly half the student body at Darul Uloom Haqqania, the madrasah that created the Taliban, is from Afghanistan. It also trains students from Uzbekistan,

Tajikistan, Russia, and Turkey, and is currently expanding its capacity to house foreign students from 100 to 500, its chancellor said. A Chechen student at the school told me his goal when he returned home was to fight Russians. And according to the U.S. State Department, Pakistani groups and individuals also help finance and train the Islamic Movement of Uzbekistan, a terrorist organization that aims to overthrow secular governments in Central Asia.

Many of the militant groups associated with radical madrasahs regularly proclaim their plans to bring "Jihad" to India proper as well as to the West, which they believe is run by Jews. Lashkar-i-Taiba has announced its plans to "plant Islamic flags in Delhi, Tel Aviv, and Washington."

One of Lashkar's Web sites includes a list of purported Jews working for the Clinton administration, including director of presidential personnel Robert Nash (an African American from Arkansas) and CIA director George Tenet (a Greek American).

The group also accuses Israel of assisting India in Kashmir. Asked for a list of his favorite books, a leader of Harkat recommended the history of Hitler, who he said understood that "Jews and peace are incompatible." Several militant groups boast pictures of burning American flags on their calendars and posters.

## INTERNAL JIHAD

The "Jihad" against the West may be rhetorical (at least for now), but the ten-year-old sectarian war between Pakistan's Shi'a and Sunni is real and deadly. The Tehrik-e-Jafariya-e-Pakistan (TJP) was formed to protect the interests of Pakistan's Shi'a Muslims, who felt discriminated against by Zia's implementation of Sunni laws governing the inheritance and collection of zakat.

Iran helped fund the TJP, probably in hopes of using it as a vehicle for an Iranian-style revolution in Pakistan. Five years later, Haq Nawaz Jhangvi, a Jamaat-ul-Ulema-e-Islam (JUI) cleric, established the SSP to offset the TJP and to promote the interests of Sunni Muslims. The SSP was funded by both Saudi Arabia and Iraq. Since then, violent gangs have formed on both sides.

After Lashkar-e-Jhangvi, a Sunni sectarian gang, attempted to assassinate then Prime Minister Muhammad Nawaz Sharif in early 1999, Sharif proposed to expand the special military courts that try terrorist crimes from Karachi to the rest of the country. Pakistan's Supreme Court later deemed the special courts unconstitutional. Musharraf has continued Sharif's attempt to rein in the terrorist groups by implementing, among other things, a "deweaponization" plan to reduce the availability of guns to sectarian gangs and criminals.

The problem for Musharraf is that it is difficult to promote the "Jihad" in Kashmir and the Taliban in Afghanistan without inadvertently promoting sectarianism in Pakistan. The movements share madrasahs, camps, bureaucracies, and operatives. The JUI, the SSP's founding party, also helped create both the Taliban and Harkat. Deobandi madrasahs issue anti-Shi'a fatwas (edicts), and boys trained to fight in Kashmir are also trained to call Shi'a kafirs (infidels). Jaesh-e-Mohammad, an offshoot of Harkat and the newest Pakistani militant group in Kashmir, reportedly used SSP personnel during a fundraising drive in early 2000. And the SSP's Inqalabi, who was recently released after four years in jail for his alleged involvement in sectarian killings, told me that whenever "one of our youngsters wants to do Jihad," they join up with the Taliban, Harkat, or Jaesh-e-Mohammad — all Deobandi groups that he claims are "close" to the SSP.

Sectarian clashes have killed or injured thousands of Pakistanis since 1990. As the American scholar Vali Nasr explains, the largely theological differences between Shi'a and Sunni Muslims have been transformed into full-fledged political conflict, with broad ramifications for law and order, social cohesion, and government authority. The impotent Pakistani government has essentially allowed Sunni Saudi Arabia and Shi'a Iran to fight a proxy war on Pakistani soil, with devastating consequences for the Pakistani people.

### Whither Pakistan?

Pakistan is a weak state, and government policies are making it weaker still. Its disastrous economy, exacerbated by a series of corrupt leaders, is at the root of many of its problems. Yet despite its poverty, Pakistan is spending hundreds of millions of dollars on weapons instead of schools and public health. Ironically, the government's "cost-saving" measures are even more troubling. In trying to save money in the short run by using irregulars in Kashmir and relying on madrasahs to educate its youth, Pakistan is pursuing a path that is likely to be disastrous in the long run, allowing a culture of violence to take root.

The United States has asked Pakistan to crack down on the militant groups and to close certain madrasahs, but America must do more than just scold. After all, the United States, along with Saudi Arabia, helped create the first international "Jihad" to fight the Soviet Union during the Afghan war. "Does America expect us to send in the troops and shut the madrasahs down?" one official asks. "Jihad is a mindset. It developed over many years during the Afghan war. You can't change a mindset in 24 hours."

The most important contribution the United States can make, then, is to help strengthen Pakistan's secular education system. Because so much international aid to Pakistan has been diverted through corruption, both public and private assistance should come in the form of relatively nonfungible goods and services: books, buildings, teachers, and training, rather than money. Urdu-speaking teachers from around the world should be sent to Pakistan to help. And educational exchanges among students, scholars, journalists, and military officials should be encouraged and facilitated. Helping Pakistan educate its youth will not only cut off the culture of violence by reducing ignorance and poverty, it will also promote long-term economic development.

Moreover, assisting Pakistan will make the world a safer place. As observers frequently note, conflict between India and Pakistan over Kashmir is one of the most likely routes to nuclear war in the world today. The Pakistani militants' continued incursions into Indian-held Kashmir escalate the conflict, greatly increasing the risk of nuclear war between the two countries.

Although the United States can help, Pakistan must make its own changes. It must stamp out corruption, strengthen democratic institutions, and make education a much higher priority. But none of this can happen if Pakistan continues to devote an estimated 30 percent of its national budget to defense.

## THE PAKISTANI TALIBAN

Supporters of the Afghan Taliban who sought refuge in Pakistan's tribal areas morphed into a distinct entity following the Pakistani army's initial incursion into the semiautonomous region in 2002. In December 2007, about thirteen disparate militant groups coalesced under the umbrella of Tehrik-i-Taliban Pakistan (TTP), also known as the Pakistani Taliban, led by Baitullah Mehsud of South Waziristan. Pakistani authorities accused him of orchestrating the assassination of former prime minister Benazir Bhutto in December 2007. Short-lived ceasefires signed with Islamabad in 2008 and 2009 provided opportunities for the Pakistani Taliban to regroup and make territorial gains, analysts say.

After a U.S. drone strike killed Baitullah in August 2009, his cousin and deputy Hakimullah Mehsud assumed leadership of the TTP. Hakimullah was reportedly prepared to take part in imminent peace talks with Islamabad when he was killed in a U.S. drone strike along with a top deputy in November 2013. But analysts say the prospects for peace talks were dim. Hakimullah declared war against the state, saying in October 2013: "Pakistan's system is un-Islamic, and we want it replaced with an Islamic system. This demand and this desire will continue even after the American withdrawal [from Afghanistan]." Stephen Tankel, scholar at the Carnegie Endowment for International Peace, notes that if talks had been allowed to fail, Pakistani public opinion would have turned more decisively against the Taliban rather than the United States, which many blame for the insurgency's resilience.

A shura council chose hard-liner Mullah Fazlullah as Hakimullah's successor shortly after his death. Fazlullah, who gained infamy for ordering the assassination attempt on Pakistani schoolgirl and activist Malala Yousafzai, rejected talks with the government. Analysts question whether Fazlullah can maintain TTP cohesion as the first emir from outside the Mehsud tribe.

The predominantly Pashtun group draws membership from all of FATA's seven agencies as well as several settled districts of

Khyber Pakhtunkhawa in the northwest. The TTP has declared jihad against the Pakistani state, seeks to control territory, enforces sharia, and fights NATO forces in Afghanistan. "We will target security forces, government installations, political leaders, and police," Asmatullah Shaheen, head of the shura council that selected Mullah Fazlullah, told Reuters, adding, "We will not target civilians, bazaars, or public places. People do not need to be afraid."

It's difficult to assess the size of the Pakistani Taliban. "There are not reliable estimates of how large the TTP is, largely due to challenges associated with even defining the borders of the group and the loose-knit nature of how it is organized along either subtribal or subregional lines," CTC's Rassler says.

The Pakistani Taliban has targeted security forces and civilians alike; among its most audacious attacks have been bombings of Islamabad's Marriott Hotel in September 2008, which killed at least sixty people, and Peshawar's Pearl Continental Hotel in June 2009, in which seventeen were killed. TTP expressed transnational ambitions when it claimed responsibility for a failed bombing in New York's Times Square in May 2010.

The Punjabi Taliban, a loose conglomeration of militant groups of Punjabi origin, gained prominence after major 2008 and 2009 attacks in the cities of Lahore, Islamabad, and Rawalpindi. The network has both sectarian and Kashmir-oriented aims. It has chafed at the Pakistani Taliban's central leadership, *Jane's Intelligence Review* reported in late August 2013, but is uniquely capable of "mount[ing] complex operations in urban environments," particularly in Punjab, Pakistan's most populous and politically significant province.

The Haqqani Network, whose operations straddle the porous Afghan-Pakistani border known as the Durand Line, has proven a valuable ally to the Pakistani Taliban in some of these pursuits. The Haqqanis have not only fought alongside the TTP and Afghan Taliban in Afghanistan, but have also served as influential mediators between the TTP and Islamabad. Pakistan has long been a supporter and beneficiary of the Haqqanis, according to CTC. The network has helped Islamabad manage militant groups in FATA, and provided leverage against India in the struggle over Kashmir.

Pakistan sees the Pashtun group, which has been among the most lethal to NATO forces in Afghanistan, as a potential source of leverage after the scheduled withdrawal of coalition troops at the end of 2014.

## THE CHANGING FACE OF TERRORISM

Violence in Pakistan has been on the rise, particularly since 2007, as terrorist groups have targeted political leaders, the military and police, tribal leaders, minority Shia, and schools. Though virtually unheard of a decade ago, suicide bombings have become ubiquitous in recent years—a reflection of al-Qaeda's influence, experts say. Three such attacks were documented in 2002 and 2003 combined; at the trend's peak in 2009 there were seventy-six attacks, and there were thirty-seven in the first ten months of 2013, according to the New Delhi–based South Asia Terrorism Portal (SATP).

Besides providing militant groups in Pakistan with technical expertise and capabilities, al-Qaeda also promotes cooperation among them. CTC's Rassler wrote in 2009 that al-Qaeda "assumed a role as mediator and coalition builder among various Pakistani militant group factions by promoting the unification of entities that have opposed one another or had conflicting ideas about whether to target the Pakistani state."

The Taliban, meanwhile, has become ever more entrenched in Pakistan, building a nationwide network by finding common cause with terrorist groups that target the Shia and the Pakistani state while establishing roots—and a lucrative criminal enterprise—in Karachi. Pakistani paramilitary Rangers launched a campaign in September 2013 to address the city's criminal and terrorist groups, reportedly arresting over 1,500 suspectsin a month. Meanwhile, Pakistan's political parties advocated negotiations with the Taliban in part to stave off even higher levels of violence in Punjab and other populated areas, Tankel writes. SATP reported 2,745 civilians and 601 security forces killed in terrorist violence in the first ten months of 2013—roughly on pace with the prior two years.

"Ample evidence exists of tacit Pakistani consent and active cooperation with the drone program." —International Crisis Group

### *Counterterrorism Challenges*

Pakistani security forces have at times struggled to muster the capacity and will to confront domestic militants, even though the army and police are increasingly targeted by militant groups. Some experts say that since the bloody encounter between Pakistan's security forces and militant Islamic students in Islamabad's Red Mosque in 2007, some groups previously under state patronage broke away. In October 2009, militants attacked army headquarters in Rawalpindi and held around forty people hostage for over twenty hours. Such attacks heralded a new period in army and ISI relations with many of these militant groups, analysts say.

Even though the Pakistani army and the ISI have been more willing to go after militants, analysts say they continue to form alliances with groups such as the Haqqanis that they can use as a strategic hedge against India and Afghanistan. In a September 2011congressional testimony, then chairman of the Joint Chiefs of Staff Admiral Mike Mullen referred to the Haqqani network as a "strategic arm of Pakistan's Inter-Services Intelligence agency." Pakistan's security establishment has denied these charges.

The revelation in May 2011 that Osama bin Laden had been hiding in a compound around the corner from the Pakistan military academy at Kakul raised new questions about the ISI's commitment to counterterrorism. CIA director Leon Panetta said the agency ruled out partnering with Pakistan on the bin Laden mission out of concern that it would be compromised. President Asif Ali Zardari, writing in the immediate aftermath of the operation, said allegations that Pakistan harboured terrorists amounted to "baseless speculation."

The CIA has conducted an extensive targeted killing campaign to supplement Pakistani counterterrorism efforts, particularly in the rugged, remote terrain of North and South Waziristan. U.S. drones are currently launched from Afghan soil, but it's unclear whetherthis arrangement will continue after the scheduled U.S. withdrawal in 2014. If the targeted killing program is called off, veteran intelligence analyst Bruce Riedel argues, "Al-Qaeda will regenerate rapidly in Pakistan. Its allies like the Taliban and Lashkar-e-Taiba will help it to rebuild. The ISI will either turn a blind eye or, worse, a helping hand." The program's detractors have questioned the United States' ability to distinguish between militants and civilians, and argue that strikes may contribute to radicalization in the frontier provinces.

Prime Minister Nawaz Sharif, who began an unprecedented third term in June 2013, has railed against U.S. drone strikes as an affront to Pakistani sovereignty while advocating for talks with the TTP. Yet, the International Crisis Group notes, "Ample evidence exists of tacit Pakistani consent and active cooperation with the drone program." Pakistan's leadership seeks greater say over targeting, the ICG says, "often to punish enemies, but sometimes, allegedly, to protect militants" with whom the security services have cooperative relations—including elements of the Haqqani Network and Taliban.

Meanwhile, Pakistan's own counterterrorism efforts have come under the scrutiny of human rights observers. Amnesty International and Human Rights Watch charged security forces with torture, extrajudicial killings, arbitrary detention of tribal-area residents, and the enforced disappearance of "journalists, human rights activists, and alleged members of separatist and nationalist groups." A new legal framework awaiting Parliament's approval would relieve an overwhelmed criminal justice system by establishing new federal courts equipped to handle terrorism cases, advocates say. But critics caution that the law would codify prolonged, warrantless detentions by the state.

## ISI AND ITS CHICANERY IN EXPORTING TERRORISM

Spying is the second oldest profession and nowhere else has it flourished more in a short span of time, that too, with professional élan, than in Pakistan. Known by an innocuous sounding Inter Services Intelligence, abbreviated ISI, it is a wellspring of power and one of the most virile intelligence agencies in the Third World. Its forte lies in intrigue, hatching conspiracies, brokering terrorism and paddling misinformation.

In recent months, the ISI has been in the limelight, its skulduggery having received a new thrust; - and notoriety, fresh showing. A report has been submitted to the House of

Representatives by a US task force on terrorism and unconventional warfare. The report, titled, *"The New Islamic International"* is significant in revealing the exploits of the ISI. That the original document is dated 1 Feb, 1993 and that it has some inaccuracies, does not make the findings any less weighty.

A chilling account" of the role of the ISI's involvement with Sikh militants, bombing of *Kanishka* and American, indifference, even complicity, has been chronicled in a TV documentary of the "Fifth Estate" of the Canadian Broadcasting Corporation (CBC). The documentary deplores the stark incertitude of the US administration, although it had all the evidence at its command. What is worse, by overplaying India's human rights record, Washington has rewarded and encouraged ISI in its evil pursuits. Another TV feature produced by CNN, traces the ISI connection to Afghan *Mujahideen* and their involvement with the bomb explosion at the World Trade Centre. The two documentaries together, and the Canadian one by itself constitute the most damning indictment of the ISI Involvement in terrorism in India.

There is no let-up in ISI's activities in Kashmir, which include recruitment, training, arming and induction of terrorist bands, besides guidance in planning and conduct of operations. ISI has a strong connection with Sheikh Mubarak Shah Jiiani and his fundamentalist outfit AI Fuqra. The group was responsible for "a decade long string of assassinations and bombings in the name of Islamic purity."' Lately, the ISI has ventured in the heartland through promotion of narco- terrorism chauvinism. That the organisation has a collaborator in the Nepalese Parliament, is sinister enough, but far more portentous is the patron-age bestowed by the Bangladesh Government to the organisation for promoting insurgency in the North East. Recently, a diabolic plot has been unravelled, which suggests that ISI, with a view to destabilising the country and creating mayhem, had planned to repeat the Bombay blasts and ignite communal riots all over India to coincide with the Republic Day celebrations. With the arrest of four Pakistanis, one Bangladeshi and one Indian in the capital by the Delhi police, a major breakthrough in exposing diabolic designs of the ISI has been achieved. "Though intelligence agencies are still trying to fully comprehend the ramifications of the latest ring unearthed by them, the case is perhaps the most brazen attempt of Pakistan-trained nationals being sent to create terror countrywide; the low intensity proxy war transcending to practically open hostilities."

## MISSION, BUDGET AND ORGANISATION

The ISI was founded in 1948 by a British army officer, Maj Gen R Cawthome, then Deputy Chief of Staff in Pakistan Army. He conceived it as part of the military establishment, intended to combine and co-ordinate intelligence set-ups of the Services. Over the years, it gathered influence and when Zia seized power, it acquired real muscle. Today, the ISI has achieved the dubious distinction of being the most dreaded outfit, within; and a master-hand in dispensing terrorism, without.

ISI charter incorporates gathering of external and internal intelligence; co-ordination of intelligence functions of the three Services; surveillance over its cadre, foreigners, media men, politically conscious segments of Pak society, diplomats of other countries accredited to Pakistan and Pak diplomats serving outside the country; interception and monitoring of communications; and conduct of covert offensive operations.

Unlike intelligence agencies of other countries, the top and middle rung officers of the ISI are exclusively drawn from the military establishment. Its chief is designated as director general and appointed from amongst the serving lieutenant generals; although there has been one exception when a retired officer was assigned to the post. During Yahya Khan's rule, the DG also headed the newly created National Security Council and that added to his stature and influence. Under the DG there are three deputy director generals (DDGs), one each from the army, the navy and the air force. The ISI mans a Military Liaison Section (MLS) in the Ministry of Interior. ISI is a major beneficiary of Pakistan's national budget, with a large unaccountable chunk coming from the defence outlay. In Pakistan, no one knows, not even the Prime Minister, as to how much ISI costs to run or precisely how many people it employs. But today, the ISI enjoys total support of the Prime Minister.

The fact that, both, she and her father had suffered at the hands of ISI has been forgotten and treated as a closed chapter. She has learnt the bitter lesson from her previous tenure as the Prime Minister, when she confronted the organisation and tried to clip its wings. In the battle of wits, the ISI won and retained its clout; she lost and was sent packing. ISI continues to call the shots, the inspired views of its devaluation notwithstanding.

During the late 80s the most powerful component of the organisation was Joint Intelligence Bureau (JIB), which handled political intelligence. In her earlier incarnation as the PM, Benazir ordered transfer of the functions of JIB to the Interior Ministry, but the rumour has it that the sensitive files and dossiers were, instead, moved to the GHQ. Later, they found their way back to the very drawers and cabinets from which they were taken out. And now the ISI has become a law unto itself.

An equally powerful component of the ISI is the Joint Counter Intelligence Bureau (JCIB), it continues to wear authority and influence on its sleeves. It has a director for field surveillance, who keeps a watch on Pak diplomats accredited to other countries. The bureau conducts intelligence operations in Asia and the Middle East. Its special spheres of interest are. the countries of South Asia, a common knowledge; and China, a fact not so well known. ISI's operations in China were started in collaboration with the CIA and perhaps continue to be so; this activity is passionately disguised and denied for obvious reasons. Lately, Afghanistan and Muslim republics of the former Soviet Union too, are being handled by JCIB and these countries have become a favourite haunt of ISI agents." The wing also keeps IS Directorate under surveillance through a section referred to as ISSS and prepares reports for the chief executive; for the latter purpose, there is a director attached to the PM's Secretariat.

Joint Intelligence Miscellaneous (JIM) deals with espionage in foreign countries and offensive intelligence operations. J&K affairs, including infiltration, exfilteration, propaganda and shady operations, is the mission assigned to JIN (an abbreviation standing for Joint Intelligence : North) under DDG External II, a post generally held by a major general. While the IN is staffed by military technocrats, who could be described in modern parlance as system analysts, the cloak and dagger stuff is the preserve of operational cells and forces, dedicated to the mission. Those exclusively set up for J&K have been periodically wound up and then re-created with the aim of causing confusion. During Zia's time, a special cell was established for Afghanistan which had under it deputy directors responsible for political affairs, training, arms distribution and refugees. This was disbanded after the Jallalabad fiasco. Although no precise information is available, it is believed that a similar cell was created for imparting training and distribution of arms to the Sikh extremists and it continues to be active.

Another field in which the ISI has been highly successful, is gathering of signal Intelligence. This mission is assigned to JSIB (Joint Signal Intelligence Bureau) which has DDs (Deputy Directors) Wireless, Monitoring and Photos on its establishment. The organisation runs a chain of intercept stations along the entire Indo-Pak border, besides providing communication support to the militants operating in the Valley. In the spring of 1992, it was estimated that there were about 200 clandestine radio stations operating on the Indian soil.

JIX is the largest wing, which serves as the secretariat. It co-ordinates the functions of other wings and field organisations, prepares intelligence estimates and threat perceptions, besides giving administrative support to the organisation.

# Bibliography

Ahmad, Ilyas : *Sovereignty, Islamic and Modern*, Allies Book Corporation, Karachi, 1965.

Ahmad, Khurshid : *Islam : its Meaning and Message*, Islamic Council of Europe, London, 1976.

Bahedur, Kalim : *The Jamaat-i-Islami of Pakistan*, Progressive Books, Lahore, 1978.

Debray, Regis. *Revolution in the Revolution*. New York: Grove Press, Inc., 1993.

Evelyn Goh, *Meeting the Afghanistan Challenge: The U.S. in Southeast Asian Regional Security Strategies*, DC: East-West Center, 2005.

Fletcher, Arnold: *Afghanistan, Highway of Conquest*, Ithaca, New York, Cornell University, 1965.

Habberton, William: *Anglo-Russian Relations Concerning Afghanistan 1837-1907*, Urbana, University of Illinois, 1937.

Hoffman, Bruce, *Inside Terrorism in Afghanistan*, New York: Columbia University Press, 1998.

James, Piscarton : *Islam in the World of National States*, Macmillan, New York, 1982.

Janowitz, M.: *The Professional Soldier: A Social and Political Portrait*, N.Y., The Free Press, 1960.

Martin H. Greenberg: *Studies in Nuclear Terrorism*, Boston: G.K. Hall & Co., 1979.

Norris, James A.: *The First Afghan War 1838-1842*, Cambridge, University Press, 1967.

Puryear, V. J.: *International Economics and Diplomacy in the Near East*, London, Oxford University, 1935.

Singhal, D. P.: *India and Afghanistan: 1876-1907. A Study in Diplomatic Relations*, St. Lucia, University of Queensland, 1963.

Walker, Benjamin : *Foundation of Islam : the Making of World Faith*, Rupa & Co., New Delhi, 2001.

# Index

## L



## M



## O



## P



## R



## S



## T



❑❑❑